DESIGNING SPATIAL CULTURE

Designing Spatial Culture investigates a powerful experiential dialogue formed between the habitation of space and a diversified cultural realm. This creative proposition binds and positions human activity and experience framing its histories, currency and future. Whilst the book distinguishes between the conditions of the existing urban/ architecture/ interior canon, it embraces a new agency of space, showcasing the encounters, assemblies and designs that shape human behaviours and the cultural forms of the built environment.

Using authoritative case studies, the book examines many locations and spaces, ranging from new urban landscapes, historical domestic spaces and contemporary architecture. It embraces the most lavish and flamboyant to the most simplistic and minimal, establishing a connected cultural narrative. The book shifts the focus in the spatial realm from an object-based experience (where space is filled with things) to a more complete immersive experience (combining physical and digital).

A key part of this exploration is the relationship between the architecture and the interior which is often the most predominant spatial experience and fundamental to the understanding of spatial experience and existing cultures. Without the architectural enclosure, the interior would lose its site context and structure for its existence. Without an interior, architecture would not fully develop an engaging spatial experience for the user. The book rationalises this through extended use of a spatial probe which documents and summarises an evidence-based research project capturing spatial culture data from a predominantly domestic setting. The book is essential reading for students and researchers in architecture, interior design and urban design.

Roderick Adams is Deputy Head of Design, researcher and senior academic at the School of Design, University of Northumbria. His work develops new interdisciplinary research that connects education and the international professional practices of design. His current research projects explore spatial and interior cultures, workplace design, productivity, design anthropology and sustainable design futures.

DESIGNING SPATIAL CULTURE

Roderick Adams

LONDON AND NEW YORK

Designed Front Cover: Image of intersecting spaces of the Bauhaus Design School hallway, Dessau Germany. 2023. Credit Author.

First published 2024
by Routledge
4 Park Square, Milton Park, Abingdon, Oxon OX14 4RN

and by Routledge
605 Third Avenue, New York, NY 10158

Routledge is an imprint of the Taylor & Francis Group, an informa business

© 2024 Roderick Adams

The right of Roderick Adams to be identified as author of this work has been asserted in accordance with sections 77 and 78 of the Copyright, Designs and Patents Act 1988.

All rights reserved. No part of this book may be reprinted or reproduced or utilised in any form or by any electronic, mechanical, or other means, now known or hereafter invented, including photocopying and recording, or in any information storage or retrieval system, without permission in writing from the publishers.

Trademark notice: Product or corporate names may be trademarks or registered trademarks, and are used only for identification and explanation without intent to infringe.

British Library Cataloguing-in-Publication Data
A catalogue record for this book is available from the British Library

Library of Congress Cataloging-in-Publication Data
A catalog record has been requested for this book

ISBN: 978-1-032-21876-2 (hbk)
ISBN: 978-1-032-21875-5 (pbk)
ISBN: 978-1-003-27039-3 (ebk)

DOI: 10.4324/9781003270393

Typeset in Optima
by Taylor & Francis Books

Katya, a huge thanks for your help, patience and continued love.

Theo, Eden and Mabel please read in plain sight ... D.R.G.

CONTENTS

List of figures	*ix*
List of tables	*xi*
Acknowledgements	*xii*

Introduction: Spatial culture – a human condition	1
1 Spatial cultures – a critical introduction: Defining spatial culture	14
2 Cultures, conundrums and encounters: Cultural (land) scapes	34
3 A spatial probe – investigation into space: Spatial narrative investigations	50
4 Ethnography and the human perspective: Ethnography and anthropology	67
5 Determining spatial culture: Atmosphere, Character, Enclosure, Space	81
6 Explaining spatial culture: Comfort, Object, Surface, Experience	100
7 Understanding spatial culture: Colour, Light, Taste and Place	117
8 Cultural placement mapping: Physical/digital cultures	134

viii Contents

9 Summary – a cultural analysis   153
   Image credits   163

Bibliography   *167*
Index   *174*

FIGURES

0.1	Beamish Living Museum – General Store	3
1.1	Durham Cathedral (2022)	19
1.2	Cultural dynamics of space-located culture – Levels 0–4	21
1.3	A regenerative cultural circle illustration	26
1.4	George Gilbert Scott – Grand Midland Hotel, St Pancras, London 1873	28
1.5	IKEA furniture store. Kouhoku, Japan, 2006	29
1.6	Prada store, Tokyo. Herzog and de Meuron 2000	30
2.1	Ancient chalk drawing, Uffington, England	35
2.2	City of New York (1850). Library of Congress geography map division, Washington	37
2.3	Houses of Bournville, Birmingham, UK	41
3.1	Contents of the (physical) cultural probe pilot – Japanese	52
3.2	Domestic apartment (Japanese participant 2020)	63
4.1	Spatial Culture Ecosystem	68
4.2	Bio-realism – Richard Neutra Design Philosophy that blended spatial atmospheres	73
4.3	Spatial cultural territories	75
4.4	Theme Vals Spa by Peter Zumthor (1996), setting a powerful cultural indicator of space using atmosphere	76
4.5	Spatial proximities	79
5.1	The Eames House. Case Study House No. 8, Los Angeles	82
5.2	The Rabbit Hole Restaurant, Durham	84
5.3	Tobermory Harbour, Isle of Mull, Scotland – an example of spatial character "of place"	86

5.4	Glastonbury Festival – character of place	87
5.5	Pierre Cardin's Bubble Palace, in Theoule sur Mer, France (1975)	89
5.6	Brutalist Architecture – Newcastle City Hall 1968	93
5.7	Science Museum, London	96
6.1	Farnsworth House. Mies van der Rohe 1951	103
6.2	Object collections from a domestic dwelling	107
6.3	Surface patternation, The Broad, Los Angeles. Diller Scofidio + Renfro	110
6.4	Citizen M Hotel, Victoria London	113
7.1	TV Studio – Eurovision song contest Stockholm 2016	119
7.2	Amsterdam Light Festival 2015	122
7.3	Hill House – Charles and Margaret Macdonald Mackintosh 1902. Drawing Room Detail	125
7.4	Spatial interpretation. Venice Biennale 2019	129
7.5	Place – traditional Funfair environment	131
8.1	Residential floor space[1] per capita in m^2	136
8.2	Floor plan of French town/city centre house (Constructed 1920). Rennes City Centre. Hallway	145
8.3	Floor plan of suburban Terrance House. Eikenbosch, Cape Town.(Constructed c.1999). Lounge space	145
8.4	Plan of flat in the town centre, Stourbridge, West Midlands, UK (c. 1901). Lounge space	146
9.1	Analysis of the Cultural Probe Data	155

TABLES

3.1	Exemplar pilot probe data	53
8.1	Cultural mapping objects (detail from Table 3.1)	138

ACKNOWLEDGEMENTS

The author would like to thank the people, design professionals and agencies for their insight and articulation in developing the key themes and positions suggested within the text and the team at Routledge for having patience and foresight during the development of the book.

Various academic teams from across the UK and specifically the Interior Design Team, Northumbria University – Lucy Marlor, Seton Wakenshaw, Dr Julie Trueman, Scott Ryalls, Dr Oliver Hemstock, Sophie Chrisp, Natalie Straker and Dr Marco Zilvetti.

All students and graduate Interior Designers from Northumbria and other UK Institutions.

School of Design led by Dr Heather Robson and supported by the university.

INTRODUCTION

Spatial culture – a human condition

The book explores and locates how located human cultures are influenced and shaped by the design of inhabited space. The book reveals both the bold and intricate associations that form between various spaces and cultural contexts with the inhabited environment. Whilst, this is a broad remit, the book collates and centralises the spatial design disciplines (referencing interior design, architecture, urban and landscape design) but deliberately uses a more trans-disciplinary design approach that actively draws upon other design disciplines (graphic, fashion, interaction and product design) to give alternate approaches to the creative cultural context. This fuels a more rounded approach to the development of the creative process and outcome of the spaces discussed. Whilst the book does not intend to suggest new or altered design proposals through the influence of cultural ideology, it does examine closely the existing spatial design continuum establishing changing design processes and the altering of cultural form through the use of space. The work is supported by context and references from the social sciences (psychology, sociology, anthropology, geography) that investigate the human condition (behaviours, relationships, communities etc.). It transports the reader on a weaving narrative that underpins, positions and locates culture within a combination of the human, design and spatial realms. The book contributes to the definition of spatial culture as an expansive and agile terminology that embraces an overall sense of place, connected landscape and what it means to be human.

> I started out trying to create buildings that would sparkle like isolated jewels now I want them to connect to form a new kind of landscape to flow together with contemporary cities in the lives of their peoples.
>
> *(Zaha Hadid, Architect in Glancey 2006)*

DOI: 10.4324/9781003270393-1

2 Introduction

This book undertakes several detailed investigations into a diversified range of postmodernist and emergent meta-modernistic spatial positions. These include the established typologies, like architecture, cityscapes, urban and interior design, but explores new imaginary and digital spatial aspects affected by memory and emotion (Danilova 2021).

The investigations and case studies are selected from direct human experience which radiates out, embracing the changing agencies of space, showcasing the encounters, assemblies and designs that shape and support the cultural forms within and of the built environment. Whilst the title of the book designates the word "Designing" as part of the title, this is part of the nomenclature of the discipline and refers to Adams's (2020, 6–7) descriptions of the three forms of environment that can be applied directly in a cultural setting. The first one is the *designed* space where the shape and form are pre-planned from a predetermined set of requirements, forming a brief. The second is *emergent* space where it begins as one entity and gradually changes into something else through changing activity and re-habitation. The final spatial form is *agile* space, where the spatial form is predetermined but can flex (or be mobile) to accommodate other designated lifespans. All three forms of space can have dedicated cultural reference (where cultural norms can be applied) and are often designed as part of larger schemes both inside and outside the architectural shell.

By a broad application of "designed" spaces, the work specifically examines the constructions of cultures through various built environment scenarios[1] which focuses on a new interwoven dialogic spatial position between the habitation, socialisation, traditional and temporal presentations of culture (Figure 0.1). The chapters include a decolonised proposition that binds and positions human activity and experience, framing its stories, histories, currency and future. The book narrative distinguishes between the conditions of the existing urban/architecture/interior canon and by doing so examines the identity of culture within space and how this underpins spatial arrangement and organisation of habitation for the future.

Definitions and identities

Space in its truest sense is an area, gap, or expanse which is free, available, or unoccupied. Technically, space is ubiquitous, located to and within the human realm, both on and off the planet, often undiscovered and undeterminable. Perec (1997, 5–39) suggests that space can be seen as banal, obvious and an ordinary part of the weave of daily life. It is often not truly recognised as significant until identified or removed. The Earth's relative position has enabled the evolution of life and can be calculated and plotted to the other solar bodies (Cox 2014, 2–24). Whilst understanding our place in the solar landscape is important, the primacy of cultural reference is magnified through its proximity on or near Earth. However, the relationship

FIGURE 0.1 Beamish Living Museum – General Store
Author

between humans and the Earth is fundamental to our existence, primed by the natural world and evolved through the development of human civilisation. Our understanding of our planet in many ways is limited and still evolving. The primacy of the human–earth relationships stems from how we inhabit, create and occupy space, which in turn determines how we live and shape our lives. As humans develop and evolve, the cultures that surround, locate and resonate with our presence on the planet help establish our spatial presence either of or through the spaces we occupy, emboldened by our evolving traditions, ideas and ideals.

Culture is an overarching term that describes a set of human-orientated customs, beliefs, knowledge arts and habits. It embodies language and specifically different types of human behaviours, particularly in a socialised group function. Specific cultures often originate and are aligned to a specific group of people, regions or locations and often demonstrate the value and motif of the community. In the context of this writing, spatial cultures are specifically focused on how space supports the presentation of culture or acts as a cultural talisman itself. As the writing unfolds many case-study examples highlight a new interwoven knowledge between the spatial and cultural context that is supported and broadened. The work documents a propensity to ignore the role of space as a critical part of the cultural continuum and highlights how it forms a backbone for cultural reference and enhancement. The text is underpinned by specialist areas including work on the production of social space (Low 2017, 34–67; Lefebvre 1991, 68–168), mobility and place (Cresswell 2015, 115–160), cultural modelling for space (Mallgrave 2018, 43–56), cultural storytelling (Austin 2020, 87–107) and the cultural domesticities of spaces (Bachelard 2014; Perec 1997). This diverse platform serves to demonstrate both the porosities between space and culture and the alignment of the social sciences within designed space.

Human cultures are located in assembled spatial situations of differing scales and intensities. Cities, their identities, exterior and interior assemblies and cultural meaning are often determined by thier people (Sudjic 2016, 3–33)[2] by their contextual design (Adams 2020, 91–124)[3] and cultural production (Low 2017, 34–67). This is primarily shaped by human motif, habitation and the occupation of space and the development of place as a valued concept of dwelling. Dwelling is defined by Norberg-Schulz (1985, 7) as a "means to meet others for the exchange of products, ideas and feelings, that is, to experience life as a multitude of possibilities". He suggests that it strengthens an acceptance of human values and highlights the importance of creating and enclosing spaces for privacy (something that has been challenged through the digital "lenses" of the pandemic). Through several genealogies (Cresswell 2015, 23–61, Low 2017, 11–33) there is a recognition differentiation between space (however well-defined) and place. The chapters include several differentiators and descriptions of space and place outlining the importance of their relationship and the impact on constructing spatial cultures. Low (2017, 11–14) describes the breadth (and uncertainties of this) of the term genealogy as an "assemblage of ideas" describing several overlaps, embedding and the coterminous positions of space and place. Cresswell (2015, 52–54) outlines contemporary philosophical languages for space and place. He specifically explores the construction of place and the processes of "gathering" (things, emotions, people, memories, etc.) and how this differentiates between a gather (inside) and the origins of the gathering (outside). His discussion particularly highlights both assembly and the transient nature of culture within space.

Exterior cultures

Determining spatial culture must include discussions of the outside. Transferring from the inside to the outside. Being outside. However, the relationship between the two realms and an understanding of human culture and space usually begins with an enclosed environment. This is the elemental trait of how space and culture connect and is often driven by the placement of humans in the world or as Heidegger (1962, 138–145) proposed "Being-in-the-world". He explores the relativity of humans in space and their closeness, remoteness and distance within the world. This develops a process where spatial cultures are affected and valued through scales of space relative to the human body. However, the externality of spatial culture is a deeply powerful position. Ancient civilisations and indigenous communities used their position on land as a cultural statement about their relationship to the Earth. Whether this is through huge earthbound markings or a deep "connected" understanding of the way mother earth behaves, cultural histories have been defined by the relationship of human communities on the planet. Ancient Egyptian, Aboriginal and Mayan communities used landscapes, forests and deserts to define and build their cultural identity. The expanse and scale of the landscape helped bond communities to the land. This was much more than just about establishing a dwelling or colonisation through crop cultivation and boundaries. This was about building a deeper empathetic and symbiotic relationship with the planet allowing human civilisation to grow and flourish. Civilisation grew much of its knowledge about the earth by forming cultural landmarks and signposts for the next generation to inherit. But as civilisations progressed, the development of architecture (and the forming of built communities) forced a better understanding of how things are connected, mapped and scaled from an exterior world. Mercantile activities slowly moved from the land to a built environment, changing the permanency and scale of space which altered the placement and situating of cultures within human civilisation and society.

Peter Sloterdijk, through his opus trilogy (*Bubbles* 2011, *Globes* 2014, *Foams* 2016) proposes a complex and detailed examination of the scale of humans by suggesting that the relationship we have with ourselves, our body and our skin is like the enclosure of an interior and the relationships we form with society and the external world. Sloterdijk's descriptions within his introduction to his foam theory (2016, 71–76) are similar to building human relationships with space and the world. He promotes the cohesions between space and scale and how this regulates understanding and adhesions of a

6 Introduction

community, socialisation and human cultures. His spherological constructs (and concepts for space) challenge the nature of human adjacency and proximity, but by using an eclectic range of examples he develops an understanding of spatial story-telling and connectedness. He uses scale as an experiential metaphor in the examination of human consciousness, probing the nature of the "insideness" and "outsideness" of human environments. Further visual experiments of human scale include the *Cosmic Voyage* (Silleck 1996) which portrays the magnification of spatial situations and promotes the value of scale when examining the relationships between humans and their environment. Other notable experiments include the conceptual pre-Google-Earth film by the Eames Studio for IBM, *Power of Ten* (Eames and Eames 1977). Both use human scale to explain spatial and positional understanding of the Earth.

Exterior cultures are often defined by a continual change and motions of the population, creating an urban "blur" where villages, towns, conurbations, suburbia and cities grow and extend. But at this stage, it is important to recognise where and how the differences between a rural and urban environment affect the ideas of culture. As a herding species, human beings are naturally drawn to population hubs and human "activity". Cities are considered a place for new visual and spatial experiences. Cities draw people towards them for employment and careers. Usually, it is a place of contrasts where a modern and forward-thinking environment can make way for poverty and ill health. The Victorian city was seen as a place of diseases, pestilence and crime. But the modern city is the place where new human developments happen first, continually changing and affecting how cultures reveal themselves. The city environment oozes movement and pace, suggesting that the architecture, buildings and spaces form a continual cycle of regeneration. However, while the city is important for the development of human culture, so is the rural environment. Only 6% of the UK land mass is classified as urban fabric (Rae 2017, continuous or discontinuous). The rest is divided up into areas of parkland, arable, pasture and forest. This suggests that the urban areas of the UK could disproportionally create a cultural bias (based on land use, not population). The rural environment is less densely populated (17%[4]) and instinctively connected with the Earth, offering a more sustained cultural heritage and definition. This produces altered and ingrained manifestations of culture which separates these spaces from the more agile urban cultural realms.

Significantly the in-between landscapes that are formed between the rural and city communities are often where the most significant cultures germinate. In this hinterland between the high-rise city forms and the cultivation of the land, these (sub)urban realms provide a rich broth of societal origins that can frame many types of culture that form the basis of societal norms. Spatially, this transmogrifies the urban "cityscape" drawing from many aspects of regional communities providing space for culture to grow. Many cities are defined by their cultural roots which help develop cultural significance and large diverse communities. It is also defined through a patterning (and language) of space (Alexander et al. 1977) both horizontally and vertically, with housing, businesses and leisure. These make up significant inhabitation of the outlying towns and areas forming the extended cityscape. Spatial areas of the city are diversifying. Early cities were formed through trade and were located on trade routes and transport arteries. Architecture helped shape the city spaces mostly with vistas, squares and avenues and many cities have recognisable "Old Town" areas often surrounded by newer modern annexed areas. Cities were often shaped by their activities and populations (e.g., industrial, finance, arts or residential). But plans and dreams often went sour, and populations retreated out of the central city areas (often due to lack of employment, crime or living costs) out to the suburbs. However, as many cities altered and grew, the populations shifted (either natural or forced) moving and diversifying the cultural focus of the city.

Regenerated industrial sites have given great impetus for sustainability to our cityscapes. These old sites of industry and manufacture present many new opportunities to alter and skew the cultural directions of the cityscape through the reimagining and revaluing of a new city-centric domestic, business and leisure space. Old port sites and industrial complexes become arts venues or business centres that can stimulate the regeneration of cityscapes (Smith 2019). The insertion of a cultural centre or museum into a city can generate a "ripple effect" that impacts the economic and cultural dynamics of the city. (Moore 2017). Cities are also re-designated and carved up into different "quarters" or along arterial routes like roads, waterways or railways allowing them to define their own forms of cultural reference and flavour. Cycle paths reactivate old railway lines (above and below street level), adding new motions and connectivity to the cityscape. Coffee shops, cafes and bakeries appear on every corner encouraging fast-moving urbanites to pause and grab a refreshment, which in turn ensures the cities remain populated and active. Cities promote cultural attachment allowing different forms of culture to locate and relocate within the city space. This is often through a changing diversity of the populations, allowing culture to emerge and grow. Global communities bring new experiences and richness to the external urban environment and this often manifests itself through annual festivals and celebrations of cultural independence and diversity. This porosity and acceptability enable the city to grow and become more transparent through the "attitude" of its territories and surfaces.

Interior cultures

The origins of a spatial culture are rooted in the different experiences of the urban and built environment, which flex between the physical (space) and imagined (place) experience. Whilst many spatial cultures can be described

8 Introduction

as individual, in most situations and societies, humans positively copy or emulate others' beliefs, actions and ideas as part of a definition of cultural *norms* and choices of aesthetics and taste, many as a way of societal acceptance, but also to fit in and conform. In most societies, culture is conditioned through a series of core cultural beliefs (set out as a framework in Lewis 2006, 17–25) from birth with many following this through their lives, generally conforming (or rejecting) this society-led approach. This action establishes the basis of their cultural origins and a sense of belonging and encourages an individual interpretation and approach to lifestyle.

This kind of approach can be applied to the way interior space is formed. Interior culture becomes more interactive and personalised, developing immersive spaces that attract, react, and perform. Spaces are increasingly personalised, both in the way they respond to the human user, and the way they represent culture. These internal cultures are diverse and have many functions. Some are commercial where the interior space responds to a specific need or function. Others are domestic spaces that provide comfort and solace from the external environment. There are also hybrid spaces that are located as an in-between space using an internalised richness and comfort as an external open experience. Internal spaces shape and touch our lives and are positioned to be places of desire. This desire can be created through the pages of glossy design magazines, glimpses through a window or looking at social media posts. Social media influencers often attempt to shift societal views and cultures by influencing the right way to behave through visual suggestion, influencing taste, choice and attitude. This includes the activities, selections and alternatives within the interior space. Colours, fabrics, lighting, furniture and objects are all part of this complex mix. There are of course people that like to move outside the norms and create spaces that are unusual and different. These are often the designers who bring new forms of materiality, juxtaposition and coordination to the development of space. Typically, this develops from the use of space and place which forms new contexts for human location and habitation. Both are intrinsically different but are connected manifestations housed within architecture and the constructed interior. Added to this are the differences between personal and public environments. These are positions specifically in different human realms. Personal space is usually private, independent and shielded from view. It is an environment that often directly reflects the inhabitants but helps form behaviours for space that align with how public space is used. Public and civic environments are different in that they are designed for service applications (libraries, schools, town halls etc.) or commercial applications (bars, restaurants, retail shops etc.). This involves organising space that can be used for civic activity, promotion, communication, selling and merchanting and involve arranging spaces for groups and communities of people to come together.

Specifically, the culture of the interior uses a philosophical ethos that develops between spaces and forms a located culture. This promotes the use and organization of physical aspects of the building, architecture, furniture and objects. In turn, these locate the non-physical ideas of location like memory, sound, atmosphere and ambience. The interior propagates this binary attraction and encourages the deconstruction of experience through the development of an interior system of culture allowing the user to pause, engage and remember the different elements of the experience. Geertz (2017, 89) uses a system to explain how the elements of culture interrelate and form constructed meaning. This can be interpreted using spatial systems and metaphors to consider how people dwell, occupy, move, stop, pause and transition through space and how this constructs meaning and builds a memorable experience. The interior aims to be distinctive and purposeful mixing of the experiences of space and place binds all the actions into a cohesive environmental and cultural narrative.

A new cultural perspective

Cultures of space are wonderfully diverse and often reflect the colour, content and the *lived* nature of human lives. These cultures are assembled over time and are universal to the human condition; they are present in every city, town, home, dwelling and habitation from across the globe. Histories of migration, emigration and immigration have helped move human populations around the planet. This movement of people has both consolidated, constructed and relocated human cultural form. As different forms of culture move, there is change and alteration to this form, but fundamentally cultures move with people. New spaces are constructed and allow these cultures to reconstruct themselves and flourish in a new place. The globalised cultural structure has been developed largely through the establishment of population, economy, the urbanisation of cities and ongoing industrialisation. Cultures are largely formed around a blend of human civilisation, history and religion, but mostly reveal themselves through the constructions of society and the development of a community. Human civilisations are founded on the way humans have changed and evolved and culture is a reflection of this. The squares, piazzas and streets of Rome developed by the Italians and the Papacy in the 15th and 16th centuries are only marginally different to the establishment of Brazilla from the Brazilian Jungle in the mid-20th century by the urban planning of Lúcio Costa, architectural spaces and building by Oscar Niemeyer and the avant-garde landscape design by Roberto Marx. The cultural practices of early cave-dwelling and loft-style modern living could not be more different, but in many fundamental ways, they have changed very little; location, shelter, protection, space and aesthetics. These simple conditions demonstrate the fundamental principles of spatial culture and help shape the spaces we have today. Our spatial ideologies drive a need and focus on spaces that function well, support human work and socialisation, and drive the advancement of a diversified and democratic

10 Introduction

community. But, this also highlights a confluence of the relationships between human activity, our dwelling on the planet, landscape, city, architecture and interior spaces. In one position it reveals a singular ordinariness to this relationship (How do we live?), but it also exposes an extraordinary position where human culture is or needs to be continually modified by its relationship to space and place. This signals some of the key points in human civilisation and forms the basis for considerations of future humanisation both on and off-world.

The narrative within this book is connected through three central chapters which are focused around three specific realms (Figurative, Sensory and Textual) which helped shape a series of themes which describe the relationships between space and culture. This is supported by a *Cultural Trail* which draws key parts of the narrative together and is positioned strategically within each of the chapters (and summarised at the end). This trail constructs a narrative of spatial cultures which critiques the central elements of the spatial disciplines. There is an overview of the origins of the discipline(s) demonstrating the way that they respond to human needs, function, values, ideals, aesthetics and taste. This includes using essential historical references of all the main spatial disciples highlighting their impact on human civilisation, the emergence of the city and the establishment of recognisable human cultural forms.

The book examines the construction and placement of culture(s) through the built environment and focuses on a new dialogic spatial position formed between the habitations and socialisations of space using a diversified cultural realm. Whilst the book distinguishes between the conditions of the existing urban/architecture/interior canon, it also examines the identity of culture within space and how socialisation underpins spatial arrangement and organisation. The writing examines how culture is located and displayed in different urbanised settings, placing the human context at the heart of the discussion. It positions spatial culture as an inherent part of everyday life, but also as a hidden regulator and driver of community where social justice and the advancement of civilisation are celebrated. Using an inclusive perspective, the book collates archival and contemporary spatial contexts which helps to validate a new warranty for society and the earth, actively contributing to the development of new and sustainable ecological habitats.

Assembling culture

The book chapters aim to connect a series of positions that assemble the relationships between spaces, define the human experience of space and suggest a structure for spatial culture to be qualified and documented. These assemblies build towards a new cultural framework that connects the design and formulation of cultures that bind geographies, cities, architecture and interior *inscapes* (Casson 1968), forming a new definition for *space* and *place*.

Chapter 1 sets out the context of spatial culture and its relationship to design. It breaks down the ideas and concepts of spatial culture by investigating the identities and experiences, comparing the elements and how spaces (interior/exterior) are organised and assembled (in cultural themes) and linking them to the range of locations and dynamics of space. Architecture and design processes are used to establish the ground rules of spatial practice and how the professional practices (and the clients) shape space and place to satisfy human needs, function, aesthetics and value. Spatial culture is deconstructed and applied to the *emergent, agile and designed* approaches to space and how these harbour, regulate and drive community leading to a wider and more inclusive global society. This helps to define spatial culture using active and passive contexts. Chapter 2 uses case studies to explain the experiential *narratives* of space which create a distributed journey initially from the arrival into the urban context. This then moves through the urban environment, city and architecture into the interior space examining the inclusivity and diversity of place-making that occurs and how spaces are imagined, designed and used, both inside and outside the building (through historical case studies). The chapter explores the idea of spatial corridors and urban threads that connect different spatial encounters and objects anchored in the use of space by individuals and groups. Chapter 3 is anchored by a spatial probe that was developed and distributed to examine how spatial cultures manifest themselves within habitational spaces across the world. It alters the polarity of space by using the interior as a starting point radiating out beyond the immediate interior to include architectural space, exterior forms and the city relevant to the culture of the built environment. The probe aims to document space and the locations of the selected cultural markers and preferences in different spatial settings in a global context. Ethnography and the *placement* of culture within space are discussed in Chapter 4. The chapter outlines the *Spatial Culture Ecosystem* framework which sets out a process of cultural recognition within planned and organised (architectural and interior) space. The ecosystem documents the spatial habitat specifically exploring its organisation, architecture, interior and connected cultural relationships. Chapters 5, 6 and 7 are thematic chapters grouped around three typographical realms. This is supported by the use of case studies to describe (through new interpretations) each theme and its relation and influence on spatial culture. Each chapter is driven through the use of four grouped themes based around different types of relationships (Chapter 5 – Figurative realm, Chapter 6 – Sensorial realm and Chapter 7 – Textual realm). The case studies are used to show tangible examples of spatialised cultures in action. Chapter 8 investigates the counterculture of the conflict and compatibility between the cultures of physical space and digital space. It identifies new forms of spatial culture (post-Covid) and examines the change of emphasis between proximity, enclosure, protection and hygiene, and the altered cultural fluidity that this creates. The chapter also explains new locations in space, using animation, projection and how digital applications reveal the intimacy and personalisation of space through the presentation of urban, architectural and interior forms. The philosophical narrative for the chapters and the book centre on the diversity of the human experience and the cultural terrain formed by different types of space. The book unpicks the duality of spatial cultures through an examination of the physical and digital aspects of space (cities, buildings and interiors). Further ethereal cultures (atmosphere, character, light, sound etc.) are woven through the investigation strengthening spatial constructivism and demonstrating how subtle creative cultures flourish. Primarily utilising architectural and interior realms, the book explores the origins of the spatial environment, forming a dialogue that explains the transmission of cultural reference within space. It harnesses and rationalises the relationship between people and their environments redefining knowledge for a new era of creative and cultural exchange.

Using exemplar and case studies reference, the book examines many locations and spaces, ranging from new urban landscapes, historical domestic spaces and contemporary architecture. It embraces the most lavish and flamboyant to the most simplistic and minimal, establishing a connected cultural narrative. It seeks out the critical components that help ignite and locate human spatial culture by focusing on the use and organisation of space, allowing the spatial elements and the proximity of experience to orientate new cultural encounters. The book shifts the focus in the spatial realm from an object-based experience (where space is filled with things) to a more complete immersive and meta-modernistic meaning for the spatial experience. It documents the lived urban environment, highlighting the proxemic and tactile experiences moving across trans-scalar constructed terrains which harness the cultural diversity that completes the spatialised experience. By exploring the position and content of the human cultural realm, the following chapters explore how space and culture mingle and help inform each other using different descriptions in case studies. The descriptions focus on a cultural democracy of space, exploring the rich process of space enabling cultural liberalism and creative lives. Suzanne McLeod (2021, 6–7) develops the notion of creative lives through the application of museum and exhibition spaces. By using the works of Lefebvre, she crafts a dedicated argument around equal cultural representation and the meaning of space.

> Arts and culture are understood as mechanisms of building meaning and experiencing value in everyday lives and the social purpose of museums, galleries and heritage sites simply becomes one of enabling (or constraining) equitable nurturing of these opportunities.
>
> *(McLeod 2021, 7)*

Within the book, the chapters are connected by a story-telling device that links each of the themes (in each chapter) and forms a ***Cultural Trail*** which accompanies the chapters identifying key anthropological aspects that connect the grouped spatial realms and topics aligned to the different spatial typologies. This linking of the different book elements will help to contextually map and layer the urban environment, ensuring the cultural narrative directly reflects the habitations of space. Each of the chapters will focus on human sociology and the patterns of behaviour that occur within space and the cultures that surround everyday life. The book uses the *Trail* to polarise each chapter and build up cultural knowledge and theoretical content of space and place.

Notes

1 The book includes many spatial examples, case studies and cultural imagery that demonstrate a diverse and democratic approach to the examples presented. The book includes a range of examples from the built environment scenarios predominately from the UK and Europe and this is balanced by using the international cultural probe (Chapter 3) that explores the typologies and positioning of international cultures both within and of space. The aim is to highlight a cultural democracy (Macleod 2021, 6–7) and the richness between the different forms of human culture and spaces of occupation.

2 Sudjic (2016) focuses on the description of the people of the city showcasing how the meaning, qualities, values and culture of the city evolve. Chapter 2 helps to frame how cities are established through existing cultural references and knowledge. Chapter 3 outlines that cities are continually altering through technological advancement and repurposing. This is also enhanced through migratory behaviours driving the movement of cultures.

3 Adams (2020) includes a comparative perspective of five global cities, their design context, spatial legacy and culture. The descriptions are descriptive and allow for an understanding of cultural reference, historical context, their locations, their industrialisation and the way the cities evolved through time.

4 https://assets.publishing.service.gov.uk/government/uploads/system/uploads/atta chment_data/file/1028819/Rural_population__Oct_2021.pdf

1

SPATIAL CULTURES – A CRITICAL INTRODUCTION

Defining spatial culture

Active and *passive* spatial cultures: How and why are they different? This chapter breaks down the ideas and concepts of spatial culture by investigating global spatial practices by comparing the elements and how spaces (interior/exterior) are organised and assembled (in relation to cultural themes), linking to the range and methodologies of the professional practice. The chapter introduces the use of statement architecture in cities to a more secretive and concealed urban environment, the covert and enclosed spaces of the city. This leads to the blurring of the boundaries between spaces and reveals how the *hidden* space emerges out from the urban environment, diversifying the way a city expresses itself. Architecture and design processes are used to establish the ground rules of spatial practice and how the professional practices (and the clients) shape space to satisfy human need, function, aesthetics and value. Spatial culture is deconstructed and applied to the *emergent, agile and designed* approaches to space and how these harbour, regulate and drive community leading to a wider and more inclusive global society (Adams 2020, 6–7).

Spatial cultures can express both our individuality and our solidarity with others. Space can signal our values and lifestyles, allegiances, and aesthetic sentiment in both an active and passive way. We can use it to help generate feelings of excitement or calm, we can communicate our willingness or otherwise to be approached, interrupted, greeted and engaged as part of social intercourse. Space can control the proximity of others. It can demonstrate our dominance or submission and, significantly, our status in society. We can use it to bring people together or keep them apart. We can use it to convey the rules of acceptable behaviour. These are created through a bricolage of human characteristics like social traits, behaviours and ideas, particularly as these can be learned from other individuals. Critically, when considering a spatio-cultural

DOI: 10.4324/9781003270393-2

Spatial cultures – a critical introduction   **15**

context, an understanding of how behaviours are located (in a figurative or spatial context) is a key requisite to how culture is understood. Defining the placement of culture through human behaviour encourages cultural mobility, and the transference between individuals and groups underpins how cultural behaviours are implanted and embedded as developed cultural traits. These traits are often complex and intertwined and are usually transmitted between humans in communities and social groups. Human culture has a powerful evolutionary complex moving in different patterns and speeds transmitted by society, geography, race, age, mobility and spatial type. Within the cultural range, space is an important platform and vessel, shaping and containing cultural activity and reference. Increasingly, space is being positioned as a critical lever to explain how culture is positioned in society.

> Anthropologists have begun to shift their perspective to foregrounding spatial dimensions of culture rather than treating this as background so that the notions that all behaviour is located in and constructed of space has taken on a new meaning.
>
> *(Low and Lawrence-Zuniga 2003, 1)*

Cultures are synchronous and form part of the constructs of human existence; they develop and embolden the spaces and subsequent actions that humans undertake, reflecting the ideals, customs and social behaviours. However, Ingold (2018, 88–90) offers an alternative view through cultural ecology, which explores the role that culture has in helping humans adapt to their environment. But this theoretical view is conflicted as some use culture as a set of beliefs and practices that go beyond the normal maintenance of social systems to an entire ecosystem comprising of human relations to the land, sea, plants and animals. Ingold highlights the instability in the human–environmental relationship but repositions it as the "very engine of history" reinforcing the critical and fundamental bond between human activity and cultural materialism.

In a primary setting, Bourdieu (1977, 72–87, 159–171) uses the term *Habitus* to suggest the way ordinary life (or culture) is naturally formed through the human mind, body and emotions. He makes ordinary the normality of life and the family, positioning the socialisation of people as the basis for the cultural landscape. Often these human landscapes are represented by the display (human) or curation (object) and are underpinned by physical and intellectual beings. Harman (2018, 246–252) introduces us to a sense of being that circulates around the object (in its broadest application). He commentates and draws in a range of disciplines including architecture. He uses shifts in practice (from Starchitects to sustainability and social responsibility) to demonstrate the power of architecture when seen as an object which purifies and simplifies the understanding of form and space. He particularly cites Wiscombe (2014, 34–43) and the need for a *flat*

16 Spatial cultures – a critical introduction

architectural ontology and the "wish to treat all objects as equal objects, whether small, large, human, non-human, natural or artificial". Whilst Harman focuses on equality, he also promotes a level of unity in the built environment, preserving and promoting cohesion within the cultures of space.

Cultural origins

Understanding how cultures are represented and form part of the global landscape is an important part of being human. Early civilisations like the Egyptians, Inca and Aztecs fought to define and build architecture and space to represent their civilisations and their beliefs. These spaces and structures were often vast, decorated and mapped out messages to the gods. In a contemporary setting, these spaces are often regarded as mythical in their complexity and holding a spirituality of past cultures. There is clear evidence of planning and the direct relationships to the communities, civilisations and in many cases their otherworldliness. This can be seen in other settings like the stone circles at Stonehenge or Avebury, UK. Large European cities like Rome, Lisbon and Athens all share the status of spaces that were planned early, providing spaces for the populations and civilisations to gather and develop. The early cities were formed by the relationship with the sea which provided an entry point for trade and the movement of people, forming a backdrop for their societies to develop. These complex amalgams of people developed their beliefs and religious settings, initialising financial, mercantile and trading cultures that were used to build economic empires stimulating the rise of geopolitical and cultural wealth. The expansion of mineral and manufacturing economies started to establish national economies and the growth of import and export trading. The trading wealth allowed for the development of more elaborate and permanent architecture, avenues and cityscapes and most modern cities have remnants of their origins implanted into their modern topography. These urban developments helped other spaces be transformed outside of the city. The countryside was beginning to be changed by designers like Lancelot "Capability" Brown (1716–1783) (Phibbs 2017, 121–145), a renowned landscape architect who crafted much of the English *landscape garden style*. He shaped huge country estates, rolling vistas, lakes and signature trees and monuments. He incorporated the design of "place-making" of the architecture in the landscape.

Planning of the urban fabric has continued to be a critical part of the city and cultural development of civilisation. The biologist Edward O. Wilson (1984) describes the cityscape as the "greatest of machines", suggesting that cities have become a natural human ecosystem designed and shaped in our own image, by humans for humans requiring service and maintenance to survive. Lynch (1964) suggests the most important part of the City and its planning is in its legibility and the mental image that the citizens hold of where they live. He also introduced the idea of the patternation of the city, where districts, areas, roads and landmarks are easily identifiable.

> Although clarity or legibility is by no means the only important property of a beautiful city, it is of special importance when considering the environments at the urban scale of size, time and complexity. To understand this we must consider not just the city as a thing itself, but the city being perceived by its inhabitants.
>
> *(Lynch 1964, 3)*

Other city designers like Jan Gehl and Jane Jacobs advocate clear planning of the city for pedestrians and communities focusing the design on how the communities and neighbourhoods provide service to the people. Conscious urban planning impacts thousands of lives and is usually a large-scale commitment of time and money and there are many examples where urban planning decisions have either been short-sighted or have had to be reversed due to a lack of understanding of human behaviours and culture.[1]

As the cultures of the city alter and move, an improved level of stability and permanence is forged, outwardly reflecting the nature and power of the diverse communities within the city. As Gideon (1959, 41–42) muses "a city is the expression of the diversity of social relationships which have become fused into a single organism" and "in cities that have been developed by the united efforts of their citizens, everything – even to the last detail – is permeated with a wonderful strength". Weinthal (2007, 113–121) reminds us of the power of zooming into the city to see both the details and the larger scaled items. She suggests that cities rely on scale to define a level of intimacy in the larger spaces, suggesting that the "details of the streetscape such as the width of the streets, the heights of the buildings, landscape and the overall scale and detail are what make the exterior similar to interiors". She goes on to align the city and its (night-time) presentation as a form of extended stage set. By attempting to reduce the perception of the city to a series of squares, streetscapes, regions and territories, the city becomes more regionalised and local, blending different kinds of space with different kinds of experiences. This begins to modulate the city encounter zooming between large, constructed vistas of the city surrounded by buildings and different heights, levels and sightlines, down to the proximal and intricate experiences, smells and tactility of buying a sandwich and a coffee. While both scaled experiences are critical parts of moving through and experiencing the city, they do challenge and define knowledge of the urban regions, allowing inhabitants to become more embedded within the fabric of the city.

To blend architectural thinking and ideology into building enclosure, Casson (1968, 15–21) considers the movement of the interiority of the city from an "imaginative handling of space" to a more inventive "Inscape", which separates the internal environment from the architecture condition by

18 Spatial cultures – a critical introduction

creating two spatial phases that define the design of space. The first is a "personalised bubble" around the user, extending the human senses and wrapping a close environmental setting around the body. The second is "the larger environment of "architecture", the dimensions of which are determined by social hierarchy, emotional state, and background culture". As Casson separates the design and architecture disciplines, he simplifies the connections between mood and objects as part of the interior canon, deliberately situating interior character as both "*integrated*" and "*superimposed*" within the architecture. Highmore (2009, 7) develops a notion of a "sensescape" for the designed environment, examining the connection between people, objects and space.

> To see design in terms of sensescapes is, I think, a crucial way of understanding the interconnectedness of the design environment, and the way in which bodies and objects are entangled. To think of design in this way is to take a more microbiological approach to design, to treat design as a series of relays, where the 'object' of study isn't the thing, but the relationships between a network of things and subjects.

Identities and experience

Ingold (2000, 224) cultivates a deeper awareness and orientation of dwelling by magnifying the significance and experience of the cultural identities of space through mapping (mental or artefactual) and the embodiment of the whole environment. Experiencing space is a complex idea that most humans don't readily think about. It is a background consideration, highly ubiquitous and universally accepted to be part of the occupied experience of the built environment. But, when you deconstruct and mediate the relationships and social coding(s) (Griffiths and von Lunen 2016, 45, 160) the interior directly influences human behaviour, consciousness and capability. It moves from a simple aesthetic consideration to an essential and often complex environmental component supporting and contouring our values, identities, behaviours and cultural identities of space (Figure 1.1). Whilst Mulholland (2008, 36) suggests that culture is "ordinary and ubiquitous" and without an obvious "centre", Rowntree (1964, 11) steers this narrative, suggesting that a spatial designer's primary function is to "create a place with an identity of its own, rather than to assemble a fascinating collection of materials and objects". This deepens the hominid connections to located space using anthropology, design ethnography and participatory design. Identity is also deeply connected to location and site. The *Genius Loci* or spirit of the place (Exner and Pressel 2009, 18–19; Norberg-Schulz 1980, 3–18) contributes to the phenomenon of identity and experience and helps determine the mood of how cultures impact and develop space. This "spirit" is an important consideration in determining how human cultures impact and develop space and

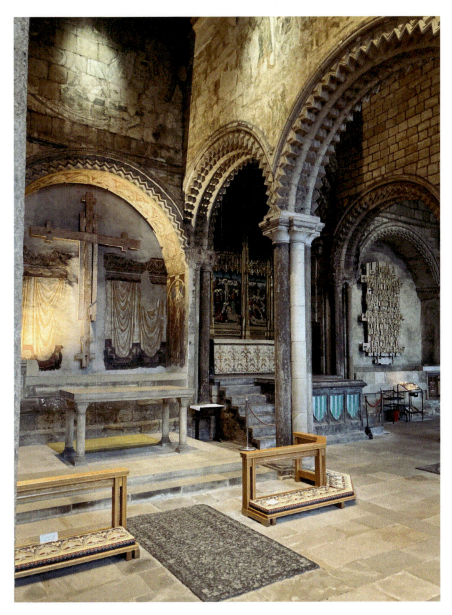

FIGURE 1.1 Durham Cathedral (2022)
Author

helps reinforce a "structure of feeling" developed as part of the Meta-modernist movement (Vermeulen and van den Akker 2010).

Human experiences are created by "being immersed, surrounded and enclosed" (Benedikt 2002 1–8) within the physical and digital environments of the interior. These experiences are intertwined with the contextual ideas

20 Spatial cultures – a critical introduction

of *space* and *place* which position between location, movement and activity. The pandemic restrictions have placed the practices of dwelling and habitation in domestic spaces under scrutiny. Anthes (2020, 209) reminds us that

> Scientists have demonstrated the impact that our buildings can have on our health, behaviour, and happiness. They shape our sleep patterns and stress levels; our diets and moods; and our physical fitness, job performance, immune responses and social interactions.

This positions a rethink of space as a possible medicine (Rice 2020) or as a form of immunisation (Schinkel and Noordegraaf-Eelens 2011, 8). Individual domestic cultures are often adapted and represented as enclosed private spaces that protect and isolate the inhabitants. These spaces can be likened to protective bubbles or spheres which separate and internalise the relationship between the home and domestic dwelling. Sloterdijk's (2011, 61) work on *spherology* advocates culture as a series of affiliated spheres constructed as an imaginary foam which drapes and envelops the built environment and interior spaces. His descriptions help to contextualise the ubiquity and the specificity of cultural aspects within manmade spaces, including the introduction of a boundary principle (Sloterdijk 2011, 327) where an egg is used as a metaphor to examine the fragile identities and boundaries associated with the internal/external aspects of existence.

Cultural dynamics of space

The cultural dynamics of space (see Figure 1.2) are usually defined by its location, content or use. The built environment can be categorised into five specific levels (and scales) of description. The first is driven by the geographical location and urban configuration of the populated landscape. This is usually impacted by large-scale natural features such as rivers, seas, coasts, forests, mountains and valleys. Human settlement and the built environment (city, town, villages, suburbia, parishes, wards) emerge from this landscape and are populated with buildings, avenues, streets, parks and urban spaces. These are the first-level cultural layers that affect and impact the shape of human society and the formulation of communities. These large-scale layers are critical to the development of human civilisation and develop cultural impact; they have been constructed to be permanent and long-lasting, helping to anchor regional identity and cultural sustainability. Their permanence can enhance and restrict cultural development in equal measure by having significant regional cultural influence, but also are difficult to flex in line with the natural changes in human lives. The second level begins to be a little more intimate and understandable and concerns the regions or districts of a city or town. Most large-scale urban developments are actively subdivided, creating districts with their own identity and cultural

Cultural Dynamics of Space – Located Culture

Level Zero –
The natural environment - The Earth
- Rivers
- Sea and Coasts
- Forests and Valleys
- Mountains Uplands
- Deserts and Plains

Level One –
Human Settlement -
- Cities
- Urban environments
- Towns and Surburbs
- Villiages and Parishes
- Hamlets and Wards

Level Two –
Borderless territories -
- Urban regions
- Districts and quarters
- Zonal areas
- Paths, Nodes and Landmarks
- Slums and Ghettos

 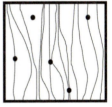

Level Three –
Domestic Residential -
- House
- Flat
- Bungalow
- Apartment
- Cottage
- Coverted Industrial
- Container dwelling/
- Lodge/ Gatehouse
- Cabin/ Rural
- Caravan/ Canalboat /Mobile

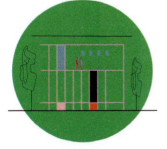

Level Four –
Pubic/ Civic/ Commercial -
Governmental spaces
- Institutional
- Commercial
- Leisure
- Religious
- Industrial
- Specialist
- Hotel
- Restaurant
- Office
- Retail
- Bar/ Pub
- Health/ Spa

FIGURE 1.2 Cultural dynamics of space-located culture – Levels 0–4
Author

22 Spatial cultures – a critical introduction

mix. These are usually anchored geographically to roads, rivers and urban boundaries. They are often territories defined by activity but described as "cultural zones" (E.g., arts, creative economy, business, civic) which act quite differently, depending on the cultural profile of the city. When the zones relate to domestic living, they begin to actively shape the way culture forms within a city. This is where cultural communities are formed around spaces in the built environment. This is where a range of different types (and ranges) of buildings and their activities begin to cohere around certain cultural identities. A range of spatial typologies begins to form (e.g. retail, office, museum, exhibitions, galleries) or are located to trigger cultural regeneration or reflect and support the local society and community. The final level of cultural dynamic examines the relationship between the interior and the actions of the human occupants and how the interior supports cultural experience by modifying and adapting through use. Whilst architecture often creates a static volumetric experience, the interior encounter is assembled as an agile and moving encounter of cultures continually being changed and replaced. It is an aesthetic, tactile, tasteful and stylistic experience. Sorrells (2015, 82) supports geographic and temporal cultural agility by suggesting that

> culture is not simply floating out there in some unidentified space; rather, culture is constantly and continually replaced in new environments and new places, however temporary, cyclical or fleeting.

This roving placement of culture in spaces is represented through the design of the interior and constructed room space(s) including transitional and connecting spaces. These spaces do create pauses, separations and gaps in the spatial continuum and help to blend different forms of exteriority and interiority, culturally linking space to space, interior to interior, and activity to activity. They are important as they present a blur in boundaries where elements from different spaces connect, promoting the translation and transmission of tastes and cultures. Increasingly, interior typographies and related cultures are transmogrifying beyond the confines of the building into the urban environment. No longer hidden from view, the interior is more visible than ever, contributing to the cityscape, peeping out from within the architecture. Sennett (2016) outlines in his lecture a rich collection of references to the interiorities of space and its evolving relationship to the outside and the exteriorities of the city.

Figure 1.2 outlines the five levels of the spatial environment that are the locations for culture to exist. It begins with the Earth and a range of natural and external locations that traditionally have located and developed human cultures for millennia. As it moves through levels 0–2, the scales and typology of the urban environment are documented. Each one of these locations harbour and promote different forms of located cultural reference. They vary in scale and type, locating activity and behaviour within the urban environment moving from the natural environment to structured forms of human settlement and architecture into more borderless urban zones and regions. The architectural topology of the city is both unique and ubiquitous and all cities can be defined by their skyline. Architecture presents a language that can determine how close people live and work together. The architecture helps form the layouts and vistas that are provided within the cityscape. These viewpoints help the inhabitants to orientate and understand their city. The nodes, pathways and landmarks set out the city context, making it understandable and navigable. The sightlines help provide cultural context and understanding of the process of boundary and level. But urban planning and architectural context take time to arrange and construct, often contradicting the natural pace of cultural development. City planners suggest that the (re)organisation of a city leads to culture emerging more naturally because of considerate urban planning schemes. But there are many examples of urban schemes that have not been completed due to changing moods, sentiments and cultural diversity. Beanland (2020, introduction) suggests "architecture has sought to improve the world" but highlights that urban development (and architecture) is very slow and the contexts and cultures of the future. He suggests that architecture has an important legacy and cultural future:

> We must not lose faith in architecture as a symbol of what our short time on this planet represents, we cannot let ourselves become an epoch which leaves nothing to be discovered by future generations seeking information about the second dark age of the 2020s. Architecture's ideas are its power, architecture's buildings are the promise writ large.

Level 3 moves from external to internal and a more intimate and individual presentation of cultures within the human domestic dwelling. This is where a more detailed expose of human culture presents itself (the main rationale for the cultural probe in Chapter 3), encouraging recognition of personal cultural reference and the development of social communities. This magnifies the balance and cultural overlaps between the architecture and interior realms. Increasingly, the boundaries between the exterior and interior have become unclear. Level 4 presents commercial spaces that are designed for a specific purpose. These cultural dens provide settings that detail and specify different spatial canons. Many provide specific cultural references, either mirroring domestic spaces or destination venues. Recent examples of architecture and interior schemes have become fuzzy and hybrid as exterior garden "rooms" and cultivated interior gardens abound. Whilst this is not a modern phenomenon (occurring in ancient Rome), it collates the separations between the levels when discussing the identity and boundaries of cultural influence. Stone (2020, 15) argues that some early Modernist interior spaces

24 Spatial cultures – a critical introduction

were often indistinguishable, suggesting "the division between the inside and the outside of the build all but disappeared". She cites the increasing "transparency" of contemporary architecture and the lack of definable boundaries as interruptions to the integrity of the enclosed interior, coercing the interior to "escape".

Each architecture and interior typology has its own set of cultural considerations and conditions, (e.g., townhall, shopping centre, workplace, retail, leisure, domestic etc.) and these usually overlap and increasingly affect and influence one another. Whilst each specific interior type is usually created from a brief, there is also an active bleed and synchronicity between these forms of interior. A good example is where offices have become socialization and community spaces and retail environments become reassigned to be more like leisure spaces, designed to attract customers with time and money helping to define a *"place destination"* (Mesher 2010, 83). Hotels behave more like covered streets with vast atria and concourses. Shopping malls, sports venues, airports or workplace showpieces showcase huge covered internal spaces, encouraging people to herd and act together, forming new interior identities and activities.

The interior experience is increasingly becoming drawn out through the building into external spaces, balconies and gardens, transforming the cultural identity of place and extending its complexity and hybridity. Traditionally, the design of the interior was orientated around a single brief, usually dedicated to a single typology (domestic, retail, workplace, leisure etc.). Recently, spaces have become more tangential, integrated and adaptable. Agility and flexibility (Grove 2017, 9 describes it as ambiguous and shifting) are the watchwords for new forms of new multi-use and hybrid interiors (both domestic and commercial) and the ubiquity of digital technologies means unrelated activities (like work or leisure) can be brought into any interior, altering the nature of the spatial capital. This has been highlighted by the recent pandemic lockdown where digitalisation has effectively blurred or merged any gap between personal and professional lives (recognised in pre-pandemic writing by Gillian 2019, 58–59).

Significantly this spatial blur is often reflected in the dynamics of human cultures where different societies and civilisations merge and overlap, creating fuzzy edges as cultures become interwoven, dissolve and change. It is recognised that some human civilisations have patterns of behaviour that are inherent in their origins, cultural identity and location. An example of this is monochronic and polychronic work cultures (Adams 2020, 153–154), where these opposing professional work styles are deeply embedded into nationalistic traits, societal behaviours, and cultural attitudes. Whilst these two styles of working cultures are opposite and readily identifiable, they often overlap and mix in high-density urban environments, as diverse populations cohere, creating new styles of working cultures which impact society, merging communities and diversifying spatial cultures further.

Cultural ecology

Cultural ecology is part of environmental social science that examines the way people interact and adapt to their environment through biological and cultural means. This was defined by Stewart (1972, 3) to explain the multilinear process of cultural evolution and process. He explores the conceptual positioning and challenges of cultural change suggesting, "Descriptive ethnography has produced a vast body of data concerning the customs of different groups of mankind, and archaeology together with history has reconstituted the temporal as well as the *spatial* occurrences of these customs" (ibid.). He also explores the need to explain what culture is and its evolution by proposing three positions for cultural development. Firstly, there is unilinear evolution which suggests all societies similarly develop a culture, but at different speeds. In contrast, the second position sees cultural development as completely divergent, meaning each society develops in completely different ways that are unconnected and unrelated to anything else. The third position is multilinear evolution which constitutes a more specific methodological position that basic types of culture may develop in similar ways under similar circumstances, however a few aspects of culture develop either irregularly or at different speeds relative to everything else. He concludes, examining the cultural patterns and causal interrelations in different parts of the world, constituting cross-cultural relationships. In a more general sense, the production and consumption of culture are often defined as a series of "looped" structures and diagrams where the foundations of cultural analysis are formed and repeated cyclically. These have had various incarnations, including "the domains of design culture" identified in Julier (2013, 15). The original approach was to use five separate representations/models that were interconnected and could be applied to different objects, spaces and environmental contexts. This is set out in an interpretive illustration in Figure 1.3.

Cultural ecology involves human perceptions of the environment as well as the impacts on humans from the environment and the environment on us. Cultural ecology is all about humans, what we are and what we do, in the context of being on the planet. It is primarily focused on the natural environment but includes a clear reference to all environments that surround us. Human civilisations are founded on the way humans have evolved their communities and their relationships to the environment. Attenborough (2020, 18–19) suggests that "To an evolutionary biologist the term 'culture' describes the information that can be passed from one individual to another by teaching or imitation" Whether this is early cave-dwelling or modern high-rise living, the domesticated living environment has been central to the formulation, protection of domesticity, family and society. Rybczynski (1986, 61–65) frames this through descriptions of the "Home" where the various

26 Spatial cultures – a critical introduction

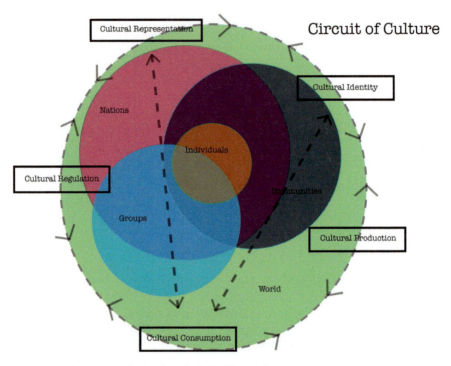

FIGURE 1.3 A regenerative cultural circle illustration
Based on Circuits of Culture Image, Du Gay 1998. Author

meaning shaped the understanding "of dwelling, of refuge, of ownership and of affection" He summarises the *home* as "the house, but also everything that was in it and around it, as well as the people, and the sense of satisfaction and contentment that all these conveyed. You could walk out of the house, but you always returned home". Starting with a simple description of how living spaces have progressed, De Wolfe (2020, 1–9) describes the importance of dwelling in desirable spaces and how improving these spaces through changing functions and attitudes allows *"interior expression"* to emerge as a cultural signal. Whilst the domestic interior is not usually seen as a public showcase (although this was significantly altered during lockdown), it is the origin of (personalised) spatial choice and determines what is wanted in a surrounding environment. These judgements are individualistic (and help demonstrate personal flair and expression) and are often guided by random stimuli. More usually, these internal decisions have been influenced by some form of specific cultural reference (functional, aesthetic, stylistic or trend) shaping the mode(s) in which we live. De Wolf (2020, 1–9) highlights the importance of personal preference and (wonderfully) cautions against accepting too much advice from overbearing professionals.

Cultural individualism

The notion that culture is defined through collective ideas and group beliefs is often driven by an individual approach and independent selection of life. Individualism, formed through a social theory which favours freedom of thought and action for individuals over collective control, helps to form a rich diversity of thinking. As cultural dynamics are continually evolving, new forms arrive and replace outmoded ideologies, identities and activities and individualism helps form this. This is often driven and reflected by the mobilisation of personal taste and perspective. This was always considered as something personal and often highly subjective and in some contexts confrontational. Plunkett (2020, Prologue) suggests that personal taste can be "visceral" and only understood through dedicated teachings, often being introduced as a "stubbornly sceptical" application. He highlights the power of individual choices and selections when creating personal spatial designs. He also laments the change in styling and the way interiors are formed, highlighting the collections and curations of the individual, "accumulation is a temptation few humans can resist" (Plunkett 2020, 197). Hicks (1979, 76) supports this viewpoint: "taste is not something you are born with, nor it is anything to do with your social background… Good taste is something you can acquire: you can teach yourself, but you must be deeply interested". Taste is part of the assembly of the cultural phenomenon of all spaces and significantly contributes to positioning the importance of space as part of the wider discussions regarding a cultural framework (of design). The cultures of design have been established through creativity, materialism, social construction, and technological advancement. The last 100 years have honed the differing creative discipline from a craft-based service, producing one-off hand-made items into a global industry, capable of branding products that are sold around the world and enabling emerging nations to become global leaders. The cultures of design can innovate, cohere and originate knowledge and are labelled as a discipline that can help *save the world*. The design disciplines (including, fashion, product, graphics, interiors and architecture) have enabled the human race to advance in many creative and technological ways and contexts. They have moved from a "multidisciplinary to interdisciplinary activity" (Julier 2013, 5) and "a cross-disciplinary tool responsive to the needs of men" (Papanek 2019, 10) and the current democratisation of design practice means that design agencies now employ designers from many disciplines (product, graphic, interior, product, fashion, anthropologists and ergonomists) to work on combined briefs and project outcomes all under one roof.

However, the domestic environment remains an individual form of space, a place where people (usually) form an emergent space for their personal situation and circumstance. A private place where space is altered and crafted to suit individual tastes and quality. This is often highlighted by the human desire to collect, select and curate objects that surround us. This often begins in childhood and develops through adulthood to form

28 Spatial cultures – a critical introduction

individual deletions of space. These determinations of personal space form new manifestations of culture and mainstream, setting new standards and examples of taste and culture. Influential examples of this move between more formal set pieces of the glamourised spaces by decadent railway architecture (Figure 1.4) to the plastic and pastoral retail environments for

FIGURE 1.4 George Gilbert Scott – Grand Midland Hotel, St Pancras, London 1873
Author

FIGURE 1.5 IKEA furniture store. Kouhoku, Japan, 2006.*

IKEA (Figure 1.5) that impact most domestic space across the world to the refined luxury of a Prada store (Figure 1.6) in Tokyo. All represent diverse timeline interior spaces that drive cultural impact and reference.

More modern approaches have been focused on mobility and agility, meaning that domestic interiors have been increasingly influenced by spatial design "make-over" programmes which help fuel a fluidity and disposable spatial culture by encouraging people to alter and manipulate their domestic spaces more freely, which in turn strengthens associations with aligned disciplines like fashion. This started with "Changing Rooms" in the mid-1990s and has been regularly in television schedules over the last 30 years. These programmes transform interior (mostly domestic) space and do offer the general public an opportunity to simplify the culture, styling and the processes of spatial design, encouraging a process of DIY and self-determined spaces where there are limited rules to break. They often galvanise and transform popular opinion, stylistic values and social trends. Whilst they have altered the public view of domestic spaces, they also bring a better understanding of trends in spatial dwelling and occupation. These interior shows encourage individuals to develop their own spaces according to their

---

* Photo by midorisyu on flickr. [Generic (CC by 2.0)]. https://flickr.com/photos/midorisyu/2767203904/in/photolist-5dwDj9-nm9Wu-5dwDcW-5dwCY1-5dsiwB-5dsiqr-5dwCVY-nm9VMnm9Vo-nm9Uy-4L6ZYQ-KpKgh-pKeWnH-pK1Krm-qpsAz9-KpPua-rTHWqs-2yTGz8-2yY5UW-nm9V1-77cvry-a9mr2ca9mpiv-a9pbHw-a9pcESa9mqfa zgiv3-8BTU8t-8BTU4P-8BWYC3-qcEur-9MWLbPqcC8d-9zBcou-idtfgi-idtvVd-9zycz P-9zBcML-qcDud-HWUEG-9zyd1v-qcDqr-HWYmX-5Esxwf-qcErsqcEgr-9zycGD-qc E9E-qcEe3-9zBct7

FIGURE 1.6 Prada store, Tokyo. Herzog and de Meuron 2000.*

own tastes and aesthetic choices, selecting objects, furniture and colour palettes to suit personal use and mood. These are largely influenced by external sources, where people look at fashions and the latest trends when deciding on the types of space they want to create. But this can also work in reverse where personalised choices and spatial styling can influence others and the surrounding communities. These personal assemblies of space highlight interior spaces as adaptable and form a type of *"spatial bricolage"* (when describing spatial anthropology research methodology; Roberts 2020, 52–60), which promotes an approach that is moving and individually agile. *"Space is a reservoir of energy; a force field that senses, and responds to, the presence of those who dwell within it; those who live it"* (Roberts 2020, 1).

Space and place

An important consideration in the special disciplines is the powerful relationship between *space* and *place* (also see sections in Chapters 5, and 7, and Cultural narrative in Chapter 8). This has become a more significant

* Photo by midorisyu on flickr. [Generic (CC by 2.0)]. https://flickr.com/photos/midorisyu/2767203904/in/photolist-5dwDj9-nm9Wu-5dwDcW-5dwCY1-5dsiwB-5dsiqr-5dwCVY-nm9VMnm9Vo-nm9Uy-4L6ZYQ-KpKgh-pKeWnH-pK1Krm-qpsAz9-KpPua-rTHWqs-2yTGz8-2yY5UW-nm9V1-77cvry-a9mr2ca9mpiv-a9pbHw-a9pcESa9mqfa zgiv3-8BTU8t-8BTU4P-8BWYC3-qcEur-9MWLbPqcC8d-9zBcou-idtfgi-idtvVd-9zycz P-9zBcML-qcDud-HWUEG-9zyd1v-qcDqr-HWYmX-5Esxwf-qcErsqcEgr-9zycGD-qc E9E-qcEe3-9zBct7

relationship as the ethnographical foundations of culture and sociological engineering provide an integral part of the social and human context. Bachelard (2014), De Botton (2014) and Papenek (2019) offer different perspectives on space and its relationship to human culture. They provide unbridled (and incomplete) descriptions of space and place that form an understanding and perception which shapes cultural reference. Whether this is romantic and detailed (Bachelard), technical and sustainable (Papenek) or revelling in beauty and wellness (De Botton), they all use the relationship between space and place as an anchor to explore the culture of human-orientated spaces. One area of this that is contradictory is the area of containment and how architecture envelops dwelling and occupation. Space and places are seen as spatially opposing, providing different forms of environment where humans dwell. Spatial culture is a dialogic process that links the social production of space and place with the social development of the built environment (Lefebvre 1991; Low and Lawrence-Zuniga 2003; Cresswell 2015) bringing together the social, economic, ideological and symbolic experience as mediated by social processes of exchange, conflict and control.

Space is the static environment that is generally formed through the development of the built environment. However, space varies massively and has various interpretations, depending on which discipline and group you listen to. By referencing scholarship in social theory (Lefebvre 1991; Foucault 2001; or de Certeau 1988) space appears as a socialised construction formed by the behaviours and relationships of human movement and contact. Geographers and urban planners considered the primacy of space geographical topology and the city (Tuan 2001; Canter 1975). This leads to the work of environmental psychologists who explore the relationship between people in the material world through the realm of experience and emotion. This begins to harbour a more humanistic aspect of space and how it is developed. As Canter (1975, 130) positions, spatial relationships are primarily concerned with "people in relation to physical artefacts, people in relation to other people, groups in relation to the physical artefacts and groups in relation to other groups". The main fields for spatial development are architecture and design. There have been many positions related to architecture developing space over the last 400 years. Recently architecture has been using form as a description of architecture rather than the concept of space. Heatherwick (2015), Hadid (2009) and Zevi (1993) describe architecture "as" space and, whilst all frame architecture through form, there is a hybridity to the way space is understood. Libeskind (2001, 17) suggests "the magic of architecture cannot be appropriated by any singular operation because it is always already floating, progressing, rising, flying, breathing."

In a spatial continuum, the understanding and perceptions of a *space* change into *place* (please see further definitions in Chapters 5 and 7). A key aspect of all space is how it changes as we pass through it. As we register it

32 Spatial cultures – a critical introduction

in our minds and our memories, space takes on a different form of complexity. As we move from the static to the more kinetic, we find that space becomes more like a place, often described as placemaking. This gives a sense of "kinetics" or "non-static" existence, often defined as "a place". As the user stands still within an environment, the movement of vision (focusing and refocusing on objects or space) will create changing relationships, both physical and psychological. So, space is not always static, although the structure forming it or the fixed viewpoint of the observer appears to be. Place has a location (sometimes many) but is less defined than space and more of an abstract concept. It is more reflective and draws in other conditions like memory and often relies more on the human aspects and is frequently defined by its people, its history and its use and significance. Cresswell (2015, 55–56) describes three "levels" of place characterised by their "depth" and located connections to the surface of the world (space) through to a deeper understanding of what place means to humanity (summarised below):

1.   Description of place. This is a "common-sense approach" to the idea that the world is a series of places, each one can be studied separately and is unique in form, style and experience and is experienced uniquely by each individual.
2.   The next is using places that are socially constructed where each identified place is transient and is arranged by an underlying social process. There are likely to be collections of attributes that can be applied to specific spaces and this introduces the idea that social construction forms places that humans occupy.
3.   The final context of place is more phenomenological and this is not interested in the unique attributes of a particular place or concerned with the kind of social forces that are involved with the construction of place, but rather seeks to define the essence of human existence and experience about being "in-place".

Much day-to-day life takes place within a space, whether it is a landscape, a city, a house, or a room. People naturally trust that their built or natural environment has permanency, even though earthquakes or war can suddenly destroy what seems so certain. People perceive space with their senses directly, individually, and always in a new and fresh way. The subject of spatial cultures is complex, diverse and entirely human-centred. The discipline is defined by both individual and collective understanding and interpretation of space. The landscape for spatial cultures to emerge is vast and they are driven through the cultural exchanges and patterns (Alexander et al. 1977) within the key spatial disciplines of architecture, interior, urban planning and landscape design which embrace the shaping of space.

Cultural Trail

The descriptions of spatial culture are rooted through observation and narrative, the philosophical position is that of experiencing the space and the place of the predominantly built environment encompassing urban design, architectural and interior forms. Phenomenology (Zahavi 2018) explores the way we share similar understandings of the world and the way we construct a sphere of intersubjectivity, an implicit agreement about how the world looks, sometimes referred to as the *life-world* (first developed by Husserl 1970). Whilst a phenomenological approach is often only interested in the subjectivity of the individual, the descriptions of spatial culture are extended to consider the anthropological collective experience. Cultural phenomenology would attempt to grasp, synthesise, transform and be itself seized by the processes of explanation of experiences and objects.

This chapter develops this experiential explanation and journey with the initial identification of the phenomenon of space and place (this continues in Chapters 5 and 7). The *Genius Loci* (spirit of the place) is an important staging point (and first layer) to begin a process of revealing spatial culture in all its forms. This spirit is often the core of human experience of space and can be intrinsically personal. This ethereal form of phenomena has alternative meanings and interpretations around how the cultures of space and place are recognised. In western cultures, the spirit is often described as the distinctive feature or *atmosphere* that a space portrays. This is detected as an emotional sense that tunes our ability to find satisfaction and pleasure from the surrounding environment. In Asian cultures, it is much more symbolic and aligned with religion and the other entities and spirits that inhabit parts of spaces and places, guiding and influencing the user. Inevitably, this kind of thinking of architecture and space leads to discussions around atmosphere (which is described in further chapters) and how spaces are formed using different perspectives and understanding. The elements of both the architecture and the objects of space form the different intensities of the assembled "layers" that further position and enrich culture. The cultural layers of and within space are in continual flux and are represented and applied differently, depending on the setting and scale of space (as highlighted in Figure 1.2). The next chapter examines the diversity of the landscapes where culture exists.

Note

1 Some good examples of urban planning are presented in the film *Urbanised* (2011) by Gary Hustwit. This documentary outlines some of the design strategies behind urban design thinking and includes some excellent case studies of global urban planning projects.

2

CULTURES, CONUNDRUMS AND ENCOUNTERS

Cultural (land)scapes

The designed world is a complex mix of built environments, objects, human activity, curated material and culture that are often unwieldy and difficult to define. Whilst culture is often used as a blanket syntax or vague term, it is often misunderstood and over-used. Adding "culture" to a description somehow develops its meaning and can add a level of sophistication, deepening its connections and human history. Something that lacks culture is often described as being poor, simplistic or lacking intellectuality. To unravel some of the conundrums of culture it is useful to reference its origins and backstory. The English word for "culture" originates from the Latin word *cultura* which means growing, tending or cultivating the land. This grew into an additional meaning of cultivating the mind and human manners and behaviours. This emerged as signifying the customs, ideas, beliefs, built landscapes and the ways of life of a society, developing a sense of collective achievement, group intelligence and sharing experience. This is boosted in various trajectories through the ideas of localism and that cultures survive and are formed through local knowledge, climate, language, traditions and the human spirit. Culture develops a more sophisticated experience of the world enriching human contact and social constructivism. However, tracking and documenting culture is hampered by its complexity and diversity across the human population.

Whilst there are many attempts to capture and define the cultures of space, there is no obvious methodology to process. The cultural landscape is formed by references to individualised and collective human activity and the understanding of the cultural structure, position and meaning. In the broader view, cultural science research (sociology, micro-sociology, cultural studies, art and design history, cultural and social geography etc.) is often clustered around various topics and themes including the body, the city, the senses, everyday life, science and technology, globalisation, perception, attention, affect and

DOI: 10.4324/9781003270393-3

emotions. This work often helps to define how culture is understood and recognised. Critically, cultural structures help to capture the way culture evolves and are identified within a humanised and built environment context.[1]

However, whilst recognising the significance of how human cultures evolve, it is important to understand how cultures are located and recognised within this environment. Our bodies recognise the cultural landscape through our biological and psychological senses, collating spatial, environmental, social and aesthetic information that surrounds us. Asking ourselves some simple questions helps us understand the context of the space around us *and* what we can learn from it. Is it safe? Do I belong? Do I fit into this *cultural* environment? Do we associate ourselves with the behaviours and patterns of our surroundings? In this way, we can gauge what the cultural context is and our place in it. One of the early markers used to help locate and define human culture was the land and the natural world. Natural landscapes were presented as vistas, often with height and viewing points, not usually arranged (unless part of managed estates), possibly dotted with architecture, natural landmarks and carved and arranged drawings, demarking signs, symbols and effigies. There are vast examples of ancient markings (or geoglyphs) in the South American deserts or carved into the chalk hills in England (Figure 2.1) that represent cultural markings that help "dress" the

FIGURE 2.1 Ancient chalk drawing, Uffington, England
By USGS – World Wind (go), Public Domain https://commons.wikimedia.org/w/index.php?curid=4302322

36 Cultures, conundrums and encounters

landscape. Often representing natural organic forms or religious symbols, they stamp a visual identity on the spatial landscape.

One of the most determined landscapes to define human location is the city and its located sprawl of inhabited space across the earth. Whilst cities and urban development are increasing substantially every day, the total urban development (all cities and towns) across the world stands at 3.5 million square kilometres. To place this in context, if this was placed all together would be half of the Australian land mass.[2] Whilst this is a vast area, it is comparatively modest compared to the impact of human occupation. There are many highly populated dense areas of human occupation including Hong Kong which boast one of the highest densities of human beings with over 17,000 people per square mile[3] with more people living above the 15th Floor than anywhere in the world. This form of spatial density has only been possible due to vertical living and small units of accommodation. Hong Kong as a city is often used as a case study to explain how cities have altered through the population and urban growth, using the restricted landscape and vertical living as a model of expanded spatial morphology. It is often described that cities are made by the people[4], created by need and formed by location, often much more than just a collection of spaces and buildings. Architects like Richard Neutra (1954, 5–10) warn of the organised disorder and sensory overload created within the city and the propositions that "Design is the cardinal means by which human beings have long tried to modify their natural environment, piecemeal and wholesale. The physical surroundings had to be made more habitable and more in keeping with rising aspirations." Neutra (1954, 12–19) speaks of the opportunities in the post-war environment for re-imagining of the city by abstracting a singular *environment* and human *organism* as one. This modernistic ideology gave rise to the notion of *tabular rasa* (Sudjic, 27), which suggested a "clean slate" approach to demarking new city space. Often the Cityscape is governed and managed in a specific way, responding to its heritage and its relationship with business, trading or manufacturing. Cities that have large transient populations that migrate seeking new opportunities, employment or to start a new life. These populations evolve often helping to form unique and distinctive urban 'attitudes', drawing from historical contexts and redevelopment initiatives, enhancing the look and ambitions of the population. Most cities are developed from the cultural roots of their populations, most are entirely transitory, multi-national and highly diverse. A good example of this is the evolution and development of New York City. This city developed its city plan and areas through migratory populations looking for new opportunities in the "New World". This can be clearly seen in the map in Figure 2.2, where Manhattan Island is populated (and inhabited) first at the tip moving up through the island, becoming more formal and grid-like (and regimented) as the city grew and become more populated and industrial. The early formed streets (at the tip) were much more jumbled becoming more aligned

Cultures, conundrums and encounters 37

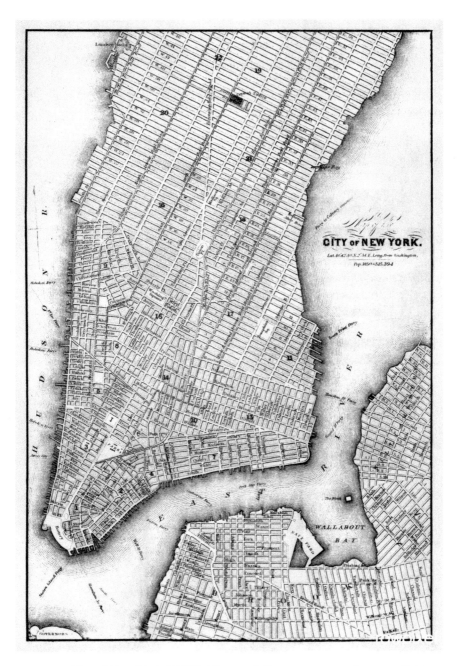

FIGURE 2.2 City of New York (1850). Library of Congress geography map division, Washington
Original from Library of Congress. Digitally enhanced by rawpixel. [Generic (CC by 2.0)] https://flickr.com/photos/vintage_illustration/50622870888/in/photolist-5u4ow D-5u4pbp-5u8Nod-2k8nrQL-2iskFXy-efT5Ds-2k8rLpa-d997Zw-d8rFhY-7gf3Vp-28 dvWVT-2k8rLqh-a95Di3-f9w3R-2k8reLR-2TVQhH-5m9UfM-a92RgP-5mebs7- 7CMH7r-5m9Ucr

38 Cultures, conundrums and encounters

to the port quays as trade grew. The areas of the city are quite well defined as the city became more established. New York is known as a place that has attitude mainly from its migratory population and its diverse cultural history. The city was formed by its location at the head of the Hudson River and its geographical topology and the use of the bedrock to form its high-rise spatial profile.

Beyond the city lies a more localised profile for the "scapes" within a spatial context. This is both within the cityscape and the wider urbanised locations. The city offer several other spatial contexts where spatialised cultures exist. Two of the most interesting are the city or central business districts (CBD) and the suburb. The business districts are areas of the city that are occupied with Businesses and commercial spaces where people often travel to work. They are also associated with the financial aspects of the city and form its global relationships. Many cities have a CBD as part of their core, like New York and Hong Kong, but also placed outside the central parts of the city in separate districts away from the tourist and cultural quarters like London and Paris. However, these places are economic drivers for the city and provide employment and service to local economies. They play a vital role in the landscape of the city and its cultural contexts. Other spatial cultures are formed through the places for living determined by the way workers are placed in relation to their domestic needs. Before strengthened transportation, workers were only able to undertake work when closely associated with the places of work. British Victorian textile mill owners in the 19th century recognised this conundrum of economics by building housing directly next to the mills where the workers were needed. This developed social housing concepts that drove the need for worker welfare and the maintenance of the workforce. These new mixed conurbations provided spatial platforms for the development of industrial towns where work and domestic life were intrinsically linked. As many large cities expanded, the area around the cities were filled with housing and social provision, creating large "sprawling" suburban areas filled with mixed-use local housing, small business and schools. This provided a clear contrast to the emergence of central and inner-city areas and were serviced through train and commuter networks bringing the worker from the outlying districts into the city. Modern cities are often represented through many different styles creating cultural themes and diverse landscapes. Finding a balance between civic quarters, business districts, commercial regions and social housing often influences the aesthetics of the city. Cities harness architectural mega-styling (like Modernism,[5] brutalism or classical) with often cultural aesthetics driving planning and skyline. Many cities also include a *cultural* quarter which helps to anchor and focus a cultural reference within the spaces of the city and beyond.

There are diverse forms of spatial practice across the globe that explore a narratological landscape. A spatial narrative is often concerned with the abstraction of an aesthetic ideal or as a functional construct of the spaces for occupation or habitation (urban, spaces and architecture). Urban planning is often determined through a differentiation of private and public space and the level of public accessibility (Exner and Pressel 2009, 20–21). This helps cohere and integrate all the aspects of the city together. This is often by the way it determines space and area but also by the way it constructs its arterial routes, roads pathways and boulevards alongside the natural features of land, rivers, coast and mountain topology. Many cities are determined by their climate and how different urban threads form the urban landscape. Urban and public spaces are connected to enable passage through the city quickly and easily. These threads form complex urban systems that include spatial corridors, rivers, canals, pathways, cycle routes and integrated public transport systems[6]. Most cities include sections of skyline and keynote architecture, often competitively (see Sudjic 2016, 114–115). This usually includes a range of monuments, squares and celebratory buildings housing religious and sporting venues. These specific city cultural *nodes* add to the diversity of the city space, framing its identity. Rossi (1984) describes the architecture of the city in two ways. Firstly, as a gigantic man-made object, growing over time. Secondly, as urban artifacts, characterised by their own history and form. Cities include huge internal spaces that are used as way of introduction, usually at train stations, airports and international hotel venues. These narratives rely on empowering internal space and the user experience of the building. This helps to refine the encounter within the space providing both a "process" in which the space can be experienced, but also encouraging the "reading of space", promoting ideas of spatial discovery and exploration. This encourages an interpretation and understanding of all the spaces of the city supporting its cultural origins, identity and reputation.

Cultural origins – garden "cities"

The garden city movement is a method of urban planning where self-contained communities (with proportionate levels of housing, employment, school, community, and leisure facilities) are surrounded by greenbelt area. The idea was initiated in 1898 by Englishman Ebenezer Howard and was structured to intertwine all the primary benefits of a countryside environment and a city environment, while avoiding the disadvantages presented by both. He outlined his thinking in his manifesto *To-morrow: A Peaceful Path to Real Reform* (2010 [1898]). Howard's plan for garden cities was a response to the need for improvement in the quality of urban life, which had become marred by overcrowding and congestion due to uncontrolled growth during the Industrial Revolution. Howard's solution to the related problems of rural depopulation and the runaway growth of great towns and cities was the creation of a series of small, planned cities that would combine the

40 Cultures, conundrums and encounters

amenities of urban life with the ready access to nature typical of rural environments. The main features of Howard's scheme were:

1. the purchase of a large area of agricultural land within a ring fence;
2. the planning of a compact town surrounded by a wide rural belt;
3. the accommodation of residents, industry, and agriculture within the town;
4. the limitation of the extent of the town and prevention of encroachment upon the rural belt;
5. the natural rise in land values to be used for the town's general welfare.

Howard's ideal garden city would be located on a 6,000-acre tract of land currently used for agricultural purposes only. It would be privately owned by a small group of individuals; this company, in retaining ownership, would retain control of land use. Revenue, to pay off the mortgage and to fund city services, would be raised solely by rents. Private industry would be encouraged to rent and use space in the town. Only a fraction of the tract's land would be built upon by the town's 30,000 inhabitants; the rest would be used for agricultural and recreational purposes. At the centre of the city would lay a garden ringed with the civic and cultural complex including the city hall, a concert hall, a museum, a theatre, a library, and a hospital. Six broad main avenues would radiate from this centre. Concentric to this urban core would be a park, a combination shopping centre and conservatory, a residential area, and then, at the outer edge, industry. Traffic would move along avenues extending along the radii and concentric boulevards. Howard stressed that the actual placement and planning of such a town would be governed by its site. In 1903 he had the pleasure of seeing his plan realised. A garden city called Letchworth was developed about 30 miles north of London in Hertfordshire. His concept of interrelating country and city in a planned city of predetermined size has enjoyed wide popularity in the planning of subsequent new towns. His emphasis on greenbelt areas and controlled population densities has become an integral part of suburban and city planning (Henderson et al. 2019, 15–23).

The Cadbury chocolate business had been successfully established in Birmingham in 1824. Through rapid expansion, they needed new premises and in 1878 the Cadbury brothers founded a new home in a 14-acre greenfield site between the village of Stirchley, Kings Norton and Selly Oak about 4 miles southwest of central Birmingham. The site comprised of meadow with a cottage and a trout stream known as the Bourn. The factory was initially going to be called Bournbrook after the cottage and the Bournbrook hall which stood nearby, but instead, Bournville was chosen combining the name of the stream with Ville (the French word for town), Bournville. Workers lived in far better conditions than they had experienced in the crowded slums of the city. The brothers wanted to explore the spatial relationships between the city and rural life and looked to the newly formed Garden City movement for inspiration for their new factory and surrounding location. The new site had a canal, train and road links and a good water supply (important for health in the mid 1800s). There was lots of room to expand as the future plans for the site were ambitious, building a new form of working and living environment full of green spaces where industrial workers could thrive away from the city pollution. "No man ought to be condemned to live in a place where roses can't grow" said George Cadbury (2011, 1–28, 181).

The village was sited perfectly for access to trains and road networks, allowing the importation of coca from the ports of Southampton and London, and the distribution of products across the UK. The suburb contained many civic and recreational buildings including a range of purpose-built semi-detached houses[7] (Figure 2.3) which were architecturally enhanced by their

FIGURE 2.3 Houses of Bournville, Birmingham, UK
Photo by Elliot Brown. [Generic (CC by 2.0)] https://flickr.com/photos/ell-r-brown/7781336944/in/photolist-cRBonN-6x7fxJ-7SmN7L-6x7kbb-9y5BKF-erZAaC-5Rj2JL-6x7eAN-6x33eT-HTjN92-9y8ANY-6x7gzo-9y5CXe-6x39FX-7Sm62j-eubEAT-bnbtRW-6x7nqC-D7BaTX-6x3bcn-6x7mEf-2nmWdXi-xQuDB3-CMLKth-kqH8Ag-kqGohn-7SiwDH-6x365z-asjg2m-6x33Ln-euaWVn-eueQCh-asjgXN-eubDfn-9y8Cid-eueUqo-9y5Dsn-9y5FZR-asgPBM-9y5EsX-7Sm6k1-eubyEr-9y5EXn-asjtiL-6x3dgV-7Sm76w-6x3dL2-f938rS-eubJit-hpoCSU

42 Cultures, conundrums and encounters

setting and rural outlook. When workers arrived they found facilities that was simply unknown in Victorian times where the factory and the chocolate production lines were a great place to work, including kitchens where workers could heat their meals and get changed in warm worker locker rooms. The nature of the founders being Quakers meant that there were daily bible readings, and a no alcohol policy reinforced and preserved a strong family atmosphere. Eventually, the factory grew to such a large capacity that many workers needed to travel to the factory from their homes in Birmingham. Bournville became famous not just for its prosperity but also for the advances and conditions of social benefits of its workforce, allowing space for the business to grow and for people to feel as though they were living in spaces large enough for them to grow too. This created a new form of spatial culture recognising that the relationship between the countryside and the city could be blended whilst the economy grew. The buildings and houses were designed in an arts and craft style and were seen as spacious, luxurious, and advanced for the time. There is a strong sense of light and space circulating through the buildings, binding the relationship between the outside and the inside.

Embodying culture

The work of the garden cities and the development of Bournville were set out as visions of space. These spatial manifestos were experimental and used the cultural nexus between living and working to lever the shape and conditions of space. By experimenting, the cultures created around and between living and working were used to create better living spaces and improve the lives of working people. Their ideals could quite easily have gone unrealised, but both these experimental environments helped define and improve the conditions for living and working, influencing both the economy and other processes of working and manufacturing. This helped deepen and embody new forms of cultural reference and start developing new ways of behaving and humanistic ideals. But, to enable them to succeed, there were many rules, structures, and expectations of living in these new forms of utopia. These spatial experiments paved the way for many other forms of experimental living creating other forms of cultural identities.

The creative work of the urban designer helps to define cultural boundaries and the spatial experiences and wellness of the human occupants. There are many blurred physical and psychological boundaries that are highlighted as humans embody and move between external and internal spatial situations. The kinetic and free-flowing movement of people creates the embodiment of culture.

The design of interiors was not generally recognised as a discrete discipline before the twentieth century. Whilst interior "designs" certainly existed before then, the formal organisation and the dressing of the architecture were cursory and lacked meaning. The developing urban environment and architecture led to the development of a culture *connected* with space. The ideas of being *inside* and not being *outside* were a human culture in itself, defining the hierarchy of the land where land owners would build statement architecture and castles to protect lands and boundaries. Geography, land masses and natural territories shaped much of the way people decided to live. Human civilisation and established cultures were still rudimentary and based on survival rather than beauty and aesthetics. However, the development of more established cultures was forming in major cities, stimulated through religion and faith, mixed languages and the fine arts of painting, sculpture, architecture, poetry, theatre and dance. Nations and regions of the world have historically gone through their own independent sequences of *cultural* change. Some of these have been forced through political and ideological circumstances, but most have been a natural evolution. Architecture and urban planning have been used to re-envisage the cityscapes and form new patterns and statements within the built environment. These newly realised utopian spaces help form strong cultural ideology and aesthetics like the design of newly formed cities like Brazilla (1960) by Oscar Niemeyer (Jodidio 2022, 49–56) or the post-independence Indian city of Chandigarh (1966) by Le Corbusier. But, there were also many unbuilt civic plans and innovative urban developments that never became realised (Beanland 2020). These developments have impacted human behaviours, driving spatial change and styling. Architecture and interior spaces were created for and through these cultural changes and have cultivated their own interpretation, translating their impact through designs. Richard Neutra (1954, 242) goes further by suggesting that the architect and designer are an "active conditioner" of humans and must take clear responsibility for both the design of a humanised landscape and its survival. He suggests a more organic approach that promotes a "dynamic life" rather than "t-squaring" which enhances the growth and pattern of the city and its cultures.

As the early interiors were formed, different forms of interiors emerged and the discipline formed, the associations to the human form became more important, critical and implicit. In his book, Casson (1968) uses the "Inscape" to explore the senses and the moods created within an interior space. He positions the cultural importance of the interior within an architectural landscape shaping the culture of the interior to reflect society and urban city life. He suggests that the interior is a "mirror of the soul" correcting himself to "reinforcement of the soul" suggesting the interior is a supporting mechanism or condition for being human. The development of experience and the process of *mood assessment* (Casson 1968, 22–153) suggests a gradual move to use the senses to shape the interior and its culture. This book highlights the humanity of the space within an interior and the way the interior both forms culture and contains it. It specifically outlines the processes for designing space and how the design of space needs to tap

44 Cultures, conundrums and encounters

directly into human sensibilities, emotions and psychologies. Experimental spaces have been used in many guises to test the human senses inside performative environments. Anthes (2020, 81–90) describes a Well-Living Lab that tests the work of office employees in an experimental situation where the environmental controls and all aspects of interior design are changed and tested to see how the "guinea pigs" react and perform to the cognitive tests building psychological resistance to the changing experience. Low (2018, IX–XIII) identifies (internal) space as having a "relational arrangement of living beings and social goods" systematically exploring phenomenological concepts and network formations that investigate the arrangements of social order, space, objects and people. She also documents a "spatial turn" which removes a historical reliance on territory as the basis for the spaces of culture, moving to a more globalised and reconfigured spatial platform which opened up more "cultural" transference and widening of the "information age".

Distance

Distance is a relative term when connected to space. It is the extent or amount of space between two entities. It is the state of being apart in space, as one thing from another. In a spatial context, distance could mean the distance between continents and cities, the gap between buildings, the space around the table, or the expansion gap between materials, and could be very small down to atomic level (Eames and Eames 1977). Distance can be measured simply by the time it took to travel between two points. It is a linear dimension. However, currently, through time-based media and digital communication, distance has altered its meaning and its use. It gets reframed when applied through the lens of spatial culture and has an important part to play when examining house space. Generally, humans like to have their own space and, even though the planet is becoming more populated, the number of people living on their own or in solo conditions is increasing; human beings are classed as a non-contact species. Certainly, westernised countries are seeing a gradual increase in the number of people living alone. Culturally this might be through selfishness or self orientation, but does suggest that living together in large groups is becoming less popular in some cultural settings. Of course, this doesn't apply in other parts of the world that are expanding. Many cities are both growing their footprint on the planet and also the number of people that are contained within the city. Distance is relative and has been almost removed as an idea through digital communications but it is still an important special consideration when examining culture. Contextually, humans will usually apologise to each other if strangers bump into each other in public, seemingly because we have not recognised personal space or distance, but this is usually down to an error, not a purposeful act. Humans are usually taught to respect people's space and understand the concept of distance. However, for most of the time in nearly all our relationships we feel uncomfortable if bodily contact is made and usually apologise if we accidentally bump into each other. Likewise, we have difficulty in understanding cultural distance. We can grasp much more clearly what is around us rather than what is in the next room, next city, next continent. Distance encourages ignorance and a misunderstanding of true contexts (Sommer 2008, 41–89).

Proximity

Human beings differ in their response to space. At one level they seek out as much space as they can, actively working hard to find the biggest spaces, the largest houses and the most remote spaces on the planet to holiday and relax. Larger spaces usually tend to have higher authority or prestige. The bigger the house, the bigger the car, and the larger the plane seat usually indicates more cost and higher luxury. On another level small spaces are more intimate and respond to human instincts of nesting, enclosure and safety, tempered by a feeling of being constricted (claustrophobia). Humans generally like to herd together with others in highly dense and crowded spaces. This is often through need or as a possible reassurance of acceptance. Some become distressed if they have too much space (agoraphobia), where the sense of distance and isolation can become overwhelming. Crowded spaces can cause claustrophobia, where the closeness of others in space can trigger the need for a flight response when others trap and confine you within space. Different cultures view spatial proximity and privacy differently. Some humans are placed (not always through their own decision) into highly dense situations, both horizontal and vertical spaces. Some cultures actively pursue more intimate/close contact living environments than others. There are some revealing results when the average house sizes are compared across the globe. They become more distilled when the average house size (occupants) shows the individual domestic densities that different countries demonstrate. (Examples are shown in Figure 8.1.)

Edward Hall[8] (1990, 1–6) outlines his experiments in personalised distance and proximity, defining the (cultural) differences in human behaviour where cultures are being established in different cultural settings. The way humans use and understand space is not a simple measurement of distance related to the activity. Humans use bodily gestures in space as a language to communicate, but the occupation of space is powerful, subtle and complex. Julius Fast (2002, 19–53) first outlined the power of body language through the examination of human communication and specifically the use of non-verbal communication. Whilst this form of human transmission does not directly affect the way space is used, the diversities around how humans occupy space and the methods in which the body is located within space alter perception and are an integrated part of the spatial culture. Spatial

46 Cultures, conundrums and encounters

proximities (see Chapter 4, Figure 4.5) are not defined by body language, but the reverse is true from the work of Hall, where space influences the way that the body reacts to a spatial situation and context. They are intrinsically linked and place the body's non-verbal communication as part of the relationship between humans and space.

Personal space

The ideas of personal spaces are understood and often governed by an innate human response to the surrounding environment and the sensing of others. The spatial cultures that determine the distances between people are seldom accidental or arbitrary. We have a common understanding of those distances that are appropriate and those that are not for all the normal settings in which we find ourselves, at least within our cultures. But this is often determined by personal preference as well as cultural dynamics. "Personal space" is commonly used in everyday language, often understood as a series of invisible "spheres" that surround the body, flexing and altering as the person moves in space and interacts with the elements of the environment (as seen in Figure 2.4). But this varies hugely across the different locations of the world. The spatial cultures associated with physical proximity are both directly impacted by the physical location (urban/rural living conditions) and the inherent patterns of behaviour. Much of this difference is created through family structures and cultural origins developing acceptable levels of personal space. Travel on any metro or underground network across the globe and you will gain a sense of how people (locally) behave with personal space. Whilst accepting that all travel on metro trains is often crowded, what you can determine are the levels of acceptability of the fellow travellers to personalised space, and therefore how culturally important it is.

Sommer (2008, 7–16) sets out an axiology of space which questions the consideration of personalised space in the design process. He suggests much more consideration of personal space by shifting a temporal perspective and culture towards user behaviour. He reinforces the critical nature of enclosing space and its functionality concerning people and their cohesiveness with space. The building and interior must develop more integrated analytical thinking where the individual approach to space must use design and behavioural science attributes more closely as part of the fluid and sequential process of design.

Personal proximal spaces radiate out from the body notionally determined by radius through physical detection (skin sensors, arms-length, sight, smell etc.). Much of the personal space is determined by knowledge and familiarity with others. The intimate rings of personal space only come into play when we are very familiar with others. Only humans that play a significant part in our lives are invited into this intimate space allowing close-order senses like smell and taste to become part of the cultures of proximity. As the rings move out from the body, contact decreases, and other senses start to determine our tolerance to humans that we are unfamiliar with. We all have certain tolerances to people invading our spaces, however "too close for comfort" they are. Small spaces like crowded trains or elevators, force us to be close to others we don't know. We accept this on the basis that these encounters are usually brief and often promoting the internalisation of behaviours, drawing in our bodies, fixing a gaze with the aim of ignoring any invaders, providing it is not too prolonged.

However, recent behaviours during the pandemic have altered this and cast a blanket of suspicion over the cultures of proximity and use of space. Globally, the lockdowns were designed to stop close contact and restrict the spread of infection. This was not culturally exclusive. Communities and regions with high population densities were (in theory) at higher and extended risk of infection. This created many stringent lockdown rules where high population densities, cities and urban areas were forced into prolonged and tight rules to prevent infections. This created localised pressure on personal spaces, impacting and developing new strands of isolation and containment. The pandemic forced new forms of spatial culture and domestic activities (e. g. home-working and home as a gym) that changed the nature of the home environment and altered the way we think and use our domestic spaces.

Cultural encounters and socialised distance

Cultural encounters are a critical part of the development of the human race. Much of human life is actively planned and structured, a cultural encounter is different, happening unevenly and unexpectedly, often without warning. It is determined through an interpretation of a variety of factors (age, experience, cultural background, time, space and the people). These situations are often located in a diverse range of settings, having a theme or focus (e.g. language, society, education, display, religion, celebration, festival etc.) that encourages social and spatial constructions and interactions which reinforce the position and diversity of the cultural experience. Low (2017, 119) narrates that a new language is created *through* space and forms an embodiment within space forming a meaning-based framework, suggesting "the unstable semi-logical relationship of language to ideas thoughts and objects that underlie a social constructivist approach to spatial analysis". This begins to bind the relationships of space and communication, using language as an agent that helps structure spatial analysis through discourse and spatial cognition. Low documents the complex conceptualisation of space acknowledging how language transforms and layers the socialisation of space.

A cultural encounter can be structured, accidental or circumstantial and forms the pieces of everyday life. The varieties of space help to sculpt the encounter, where architect Daniel Libeskind (2001, 17–25) exposes the spaces of encounter as "unpredictable" and "uncertain", suggesting that

48 Cultures, conundrums and encounters

architecture is fluid and it "wanders where it will"[9]. This unstructured narrative activates all the senses, triggering alarm, satisfaction and happiness, often simultaneously. Encounter in a spatial cultural setting is a positive thing, developing experience and the unknown. A good example of this is the city where its perspective and culture are defined by the geography and its people. But the encounter is generally unstructured but influenced by its "climate, topology and architecture" (Sudjic 2016, 1–5) and forms the identities and encounters of the space. Often the key encounters of the city are the people, which mix and define different cultural aspects, bringing life and experience to the cityscape. A humanistic cultural encounter is dualistic in the sense that humans experience the cultures around them, absorbing and contributing to the way cultures are seen, formed and communicated. But, cultures are also formed from within, allowing personal experience to help influence and form new cultural forms. This is particularly relevant through culture and space that are formed by migratory people and their backgrounds. This often creates a cultural hierarchy, where one set of cultures dominates another, or has historically relocated objects as part of museum collections. Sadly, this has led to much global conflict, persecution and oppression of indigenous and minority cultures. The last 20 years have seen a distinct recognition of this imbalance and imperfection of cultural hierarchy with the deaccession and return of cultural objects currently underway. Whilst this is still uneven, there is a better understanding and respect for the range and diversity of cultural objects, landscapes, practices and spaces.

Cultural Trail

This chapter uses landscape to frame the context for a shifting reference of cultures between the rural and urban realms and between the community and individual locations of culture. By understanding the origins and historical cultural contexts, a richer understanding of the movement and placement of culture in space can be explained through cultural frameworks and systems (see Chapter 4). Setting out the locations where culture is created and exists (Table 1.1) and developing some themes that impact human cultures (proximity, distance personal space), it is possible to see how culture and the histories of spaces are crucial to the development of human society. Exploring the whole spatial environment (like Bournville and the garden cities) develops a stronger reference to the totality of how cultures are transmitted and the importance of personal space in designed societal structures. This encourages an understanding of how cultures are recorded, documented, and transferred between generations, building resonance between culture and space across all forms of human existence. The descriptions of "inscaping" (Casson 1968) help define cultural boundaries, and the experiences of the human occupants locate the threshold within a spatial context.

This deliberately blurs the physical and psychological boundaries of the spatial environment and location, allowing for a much broader perspective of the connecting relationships between culture and spatial environment. Of particular relevance, is the "spatial turn" described by Low (2018, X) where the changes to the locality, territoriality and globalisation of culture reveal how a culturalisation of space has become mainstream and more widely "integrated" as a part of spatial practice (see spatial probe information in Chapters 3, 8 and 9) and beings to explain a merging of cultural patterns and symbols forming new forms of spatial placement. This also enriches the notion of cultural *encounters* and an understanding of spatial discovery either found or developed as part of the human context.

The following chapter is a unique research exercise anchored by a spatial probe that was developed and distributed to examine how spatial cultures manifest themselves within habitational spaces across the world. It alters the polarity of space by using the interior as a starting point, radiating out beyond the immediate interior to include architectural space, exterior forms and the city, relevant to the culture of the built environment. (Please note that the results and data in the following chapter were collated over the period of the pandemic, 2019–21.)

Notes

1 There are many texts outlining how culture is changed by the identities and evolution of the human race. Two good texts covering these topics are Ingelhart (2018, 8–14) and Hall and du Gay (1996, 1–18).
2 Land mass statistics available from: https://www.newgeography.com/content/001689-how-much-world-covered-cities
3 Statistics taken from the https://worldpopulationreview.com/countries/hong-kong-population.
4 Descriptions and the making of cities can be found in Sudjic (2016, 1–85).
5 Modernism is a twentieth century aesthetic movement trend that captured the arts, architecture, design, culture and society. A good review of the architecture of Modernism can be found in Rossi (1984).
6 A rich analysis of the public spaces of Copenhagen is presented in Gemzoe and Gehl (1996). The work includes written analysis, illustrations and diagrams of the city and movement through public spaces.
7 A good reference point for the design of the houses in Bournville is Harvey Alexander's architectural review in 1906.
8 Edward, Hall was a cultural anthropologist who established the basis for experimental human proxemics. These have been used extensively in the development of spatial culture and are outlined in many texts including Lawson (2001, 128–163) and Sommer (2008, 51, 94–95).
9 A case study example is the Vanke Pavilion, Milan Italy. Libeskind (2015); https://libeskind.com/work/vanke-pavilion/

3

A SPATIAL PROBE – INVESTIGATION INTO SPACE

Spatial narrative investigations

This chapter sets out to present a unique and new piece of spatial design research. It uses a spatial design probe to explore domestic interior design environments across the globe. The probe was developed and distributed to examine how special cultures manifest themselves within spaces of habitation with the aim to document and record the relationship between space and personalised cultures. There have been many forms of anthropological research carried out inside space but the results from the probe reveal a series of tentative glimpses into the relationships formed within space by culture. In *The Comfort of Things,* Miller (2008) presents a series of portraits in individual houses on a single street in south London. Each house is presented as a form of a story with the occupants and their backgrounds being revealed using the houses and the surrounding objects to present domestic culture in a clear and revealing manner. Whilst I refer to some of the narratives specifically in the next chapter, it is important to highlight the relational impact of the "comfort" of Miller's study and the spatial probe that I have developed for this book. Whilst much of the probe data is quite diverse, the comparative nature of the study and the cultural mapping conclusions (presented in Chapters 8 and 9) were taken over an extended period. Much of the probe data was sent out and gathered during the global pandemic and therefore stretched and potentially skewed the results. However, this period also found many people confined to their homes in various forms of lockdown, possibly finding the probe light relief and potential distraction.

Design probes were initially developed for use with the elderly by Gaver et al.(1999) and are collections of evocative tasks given to volunteers to elicit inspiring responses by getting the participants to return the information when completed. They usually include a variety of printed items such as maps, postcards or diagrams with requests for people to add information in the

DOI: 10.4324/9781003270393-4

form of annotations, drawings or stickers. Often they also include simple devices such as cameras or recorders with requests for certain kinds of content. Important as these materials are, it is the design of the tasks which determines whether or not probes are intriguing and revealing because there is no way to know what will be received. The best probe tasks balance empirical encounters with playfulness and surprise. For participants, they underpin ideas about research encouraging informal intimacy and creativity. For researchers, they produce observable evidence with enough uncertainty to leave room for imagination and interpretation.

By using the normative design domains outlined by Schön (1985, 44–52), a set of benchmark domains were used as a starting point to construct the probe and give a sense of spatial landmarks and cultural reference points. In the spirit of Gaver et al. (1999), and Hanington and Martin (2019, 70–72), the probe was developed as an experimental process of spatial and cultural collection and empirical encounter.

Spatial cultural probe

Between April 2019 and August 2021, a pilot spatial probe (Figure 3.1) was developed and distributed to examine how spatial cultures manifest themselves within domestic interior space across the world. Whilst this was ambitious in part, it was part of a wider anthropological study that will be conducted in the future examining domestic spatial culture. The aim of the probe was to gather data and information about the relationship between space and culture. It was designed to be introduced in a physical manner (through a posted box and contents shown in Figure 3.1) with the data returned as a series of digital applications and enclosures/photographs to shape and broaden the data that was collected. The principle of the probe was designed as a *post-out, digital-return* format to speed up and improve the data return. The probe documents cultural markers and preferences in different domestic settings across the world. The probe uses a baseline of three interior design approaches (*Designed, Emergent, Agile*; Adams 2020, 6–7) and applies this to different types of domestic and home interior space and asks the participants to judge, evaluate and document the spaces that they inhabit. Importantly, the probe seeks data on the home, what it is to have a home and how people use it to create the spaces that they live in. Rybczynski (1987, 15–49) shapes the ideas of the home through the examination of intimacy and privacy. He explores how people behave in their homes by describing the objectivity of the home and how homeliness is not necessarily neatness. He makes comparisons between the polished images in interior magazines (which seem to fascinate and repel him) and the reality of how people occupy their own spaces with their objects, mementoes and evidence of family, friends and careers. The probe set out to document real spaces of occupation, unhindered by influence or favour. There is further

52 A spatial probe – investigation into space

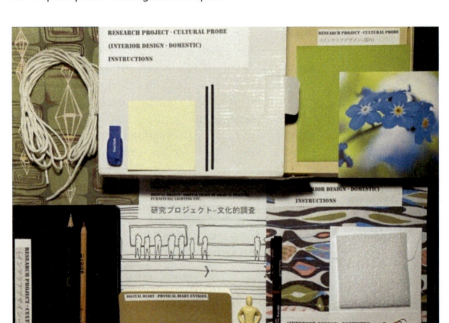

FIGURE 3.1 Contents of the (physical) cultural probe pilot – Japanese Author

discussion on the relationship between home, home working and externality in Chapter 4.

The probe is formed from three different digital data exercises (Digital Diary – physical diary entries, digital written responses (postcard); Digital Lens – interior environment imagery, digital response and Digital Object – digital image of object/feature/furniture/lighting etc.). The probe included investigations into space and domestic culture and requires the participants to record their domestic interior in different ways using the contents of the original probe box. If we directly reference the early cultural probes suggested by Gaver et al. (1999), then this probe was designed to directly stimulate responses about personalised domestic living. Each of the three main Data return elements (Diary, Lens, Object) encouraged freedom of interpretation. The most interesting aspect was the international cultural dimension where each probe was interpreted slightly differently, and each response had a distinctly different flavour. Within Table 3.1 it is possible to see the differentiation and comparisons between each of the submissions and thankfully there is enough similarity in alignment to be able to do this, however the returns were quite different. Whether this was through language and communication written into the diary and postcards or the angles of the

TABLE 3.1 Exemplar pilot probe data

Interior design cultural research probe – Exemplar 20 returns from 33

Country	Digital Diary: summary, descriptions, drawings and notes, 1 room selected (various sizes and submissions)	Digital Lens (visual reference/ images of interior)	Digital Object: cultural interior object/element that signifies a representation of interior culture (referenced to space, place and the impact on interior functions, aesthetics, styles or trends).	Additional notes (Designed, Emergent, Agile, interior)	Cultural Mapping Objects (includes cultural interior objects.) (See Chapter 8, Table 8.1 for detail.)
Australia (1/2)	Old Farmhouse in the Outback bush (1926). North of Adelaide. Used as a domestic home/ farmstead for 100 years. Kitchen	3 images (1 liage corrupted)	Interior with Furniture. (Kitchen) Farmhouse family table (Old unpainted timber table, scarred, marked and raw). Traditional turned legs and boarded tabletop (object) (Seats 8 with matching chairs) (Room size – $32m^2$)	Emergent Interior Owner-occupier. No. of regular occupants: Family of 6.	Table and 3 objects.
Brazil (1/2)	Family Flat (4 Bed) in Vila Mafra, San Paulo. 1985. Interior modern. Lounge/living space.	4 Images	Main (double) doorway between two main living rooms. Frames, embossed and differentiated. Ornately carved doors (object) (Replaced original doors from a previous dwelling.) Opening French (Portuguese) doors. Open plan living. (Two rooms – $66m^2$)	Designed interior Renter. No. of regular occupants: Family of 3.	Carved doors and 3 cultural objects.

| Canada (1/3) | Toronto flat above a hardware store. (date unknown). Originally used for storage. 1 Bed "*Maisonette Style*" flat now converted into 2 Bed with balcony over the street. Large kitchen/dining space. | 2 Images | Hybrid kitchen. Centrally placed in a big kitchen with an island. Modern glass topped table with cast iron legs (object). Seats 6. High-backed chairs. Appears quite "temporary" and open loft-style room. Large pieces of furniture, in large rooms. Lots of space. (Kitchen – **20m²**) | Agile interior Renter. No. of regular occupants: 1x Couple. | Glass-topped table and 3 cultural objects |
| China (2/3) | (a) City suburb flat. Duplex style. (1999) Part of huge "out of town" development Beijing NE. Wangjing Residential district. Living space. (b) Chinese longhouse (1850). Single story, barn-like in approach. Traditional farm building converted for a domestic dwelling. Heng Chun Bridge, Shanghai. | 6 images 4 images | Glass panel details on the wall between corridor and flat. Modern glazed vision panels/window-styled surfaces (object). Coloured patterned glass. Brings coloured light into the space. Original panel authentic spaces. (Corridor – **22m²**) Traditional farmhouse converted into two houses. Large Chinese lantern (object) houses single-story with converted living spaces into the roof (converted windows). The interior appears quite traditional, decorated with modern appliances and traditional Chinese decoration. Large kitchen. (Living space – **20m²**) | Designed interior Renter. No. of regular occupants: Family of 4. Emergent interior. Owner. No. of regular occupants: Family of 8. | Glass panels and personalised cultural objects. Chinese lantern and 3 cultural objects. |

Interior design cultural research probe – Exemplar 20 returns from 33

France (2/2)	(a) French farmhouse and gite (1901) (Lombardy). Porch/veranda. (b) Large French town/city house (1920). Rennes City Centre	2 images 2 images	Domestic environment and holiday let spaces. Quite different in terms of quality and authenticity. External veranda chair (object). (Veranda – **45m²**) Set over four floors with full-height windows. Decorative plasterwork, wrought iron staircase bannisters (object) large open staircase. Wall and hung lighting feature, richly decorated, large paintings. Traditional ornamentation and furniture. (Open staircase – **78m²**)	Designed/Emergent cross-over interior. Owner No. of regular occupants: 2x Couples. Emergent. Owner. No. of regular occupants: Family of 5.	Veranda chair and 3 cultural objects. Lighting unit and 3 cultural items.
Hong Kong city (1/2)	Small two-bed-roomed flat in a skyscraper (1965) bedroom	1 Image	Small double bedroom with window. A foldable bed (object) allows for additional storage and for the room to be used as a study when not used for sleeping. Ingenious design. All furniture is stackable. One wall used full storage. Dark colour. (Bedroom – **68m²**)	Agile/Emergent. Practical interior. Rented. No. of regular occupants: 1x Couple	Bed and 2 cultural objects.
Italy (1/2)	Italian farmhouse (1864) – (Tuscany). Lounge space.	4 images	Old blanket trunk (object). Upper story lounge. The object matched the quality of the space and was bought with the property. Timber (chestnut), metal hinged and feet. Used as a seat and for object display. (Lounge – **38m²**)	Emergent/Traditional styled interior. Owner No. of regular occupants: Single occupant.	Blanket trunk plus three items.

Japan (1/2)	Flat (1 Bed), apartment block (1969) – Asaminami, Hiroshima. Living/lounge space.	2 images	Small flat in Ccy. Straight-sided glass jug/sculpture (object) in dining space. Glass objects (Japanese glass arranged with two other glass items (French and Bolivian glass). Green in colour and influences the colour of the whole room. Swirling marbled effect. (Living space – **42m^2**)	Designed interior (small). Owner No. regular occupants: Single occupant.	Glass jug and four cultural objects.
Kenya, (1/1)	Two-bedroomed apartment in a large housing block. Living spaces. Nairobi, Africa	1 image	Large two-bedroom department with Open Plan living spaces. Sofabed (object). The lounge/dining space opens to a balcony. A colourful and bold interior with strong use of black to define the edges of walls flooring etc. Hard materials with the use of soft textiles and furnishings. (Living space – **84m^2**)	Designed/Agile Modern interior. Renter. No. of regular occupants: 3.	Sofa bed and 3 cultural objects
Malaysia (1/2)	Urban/suburban house (2010) (3 bedrooms) Bandar Peru, Penang. Living space.	2 Images	Suburban house – Television/computer screen (object) in main living space. Room focal point. No Fireplace. (Living space – **62m^2**)	Agile interior. Owner. No. of regular occupants: Family of 4.	Television screen and 3 cultural objects.
South (1/1) Africa	Terrace House. Eikenbosch, Cape Town.(1999). Lounge space.	2 images	Terrace house. Sloped hills suburban development. Range of African Art. Large canvases (4). African Art. Figurative/urban/rural landscapes (object). Culturally powerful. Bold and colourful textiles. (Lounge/living space – **90m^2**)	Designed/Agile interior. Renter. No. of regular occupants: Family of 5.	African Art and 3 cultural objects.

| South Korea (1/2) | Slimline Korean house. Daegu. Two stories, two rooms on each level. Dwelling is only 4M wide. 1985 (Approx.) Kitchen. | 2 Images | Ultra-small and compact kitchen. One wall contains kitchen storage, fridge and cooking surfaces. Food pickling jars (object). The whole room is only 2 m x 1.2 m. High ceilings. White. Small colourful graphics on the wall. Good lighting. (Kitchen – **3.5m²**) | Agile/Emergent. Practical. Interior owner. No. of regular occupants: Family of 5 (1x Baby). | Food pickling jars and 3 other kitchen items |
| Spain (2/2) | (a) Terraced Villa (2001), 3 bedroom, Lounge Balcony overlooking orange grove/farmland Sagunto, Valencia. Lounge/Living space. (b) Modern Spanish 3 bedroom house. Traditional layout in outskirts suburbs in Mostoles, Madrid. Living/dining space. | 2 images 2 images | Villa in a Spanish town. Modern complex apartment. Air-conditioned, hard materials, poor lighting. All walls are painted white, stone floors and no fireplace. Beautiful view over farmland and orange grove. Beautiful coloured objects, designer furniture (object). (Lounge and balcony – **88m²**) Modern interior with clean surfaces, new kitchen and European-style interior spaces. Plenty of light and reflective surfaces. Sculptural lighting and displayed glass (objects) surrounded by clean modern comfortable furniture. Folding doors into garden space. (Living/dining space – **68m²**) | Designed /Traditional interior. Owner. No. of regular occupants: Couple 2. Designed/Modern interior Owner. No. of regular occupants: Family of 5. | Designer furniture and 3 other cultural objects. Glass objects and 3 other cultural objects. |

UK (2/4)	(a) A small English terraced Victorian house (1899) Whalley Range, Manchester. Bedroom (b) A flat in a small English town, Stourbridge, West Midlands. Lounge space.	5 images 2 images	Small 2 bedroom terraced house. Fireplace in main living space. Carved wooden fireplace (object) (1930) Arts and Craft Style with metal fittings and edges. Tiled fireplace. (Living space – **22m²**) 2 bed flat, ground floor. Small garden. Range of comic toys (objects). (Personal collection on display in cabinet.) Modern cabinet with built-in light for display purposes. (Lounge – **17m²**)	Designed /Traditional interior Owner. No. of regular occupants: 1 x Couple. Designed/Modern/Renter. No. of regular occupants: 1 x Couple	Fireplace and 3 other cultural objects (including a dog!) Comic toys and 3 other cultural objects (including a plant)
USA (2/3)	(a)Townhouse (1916) Auburn Hills, Detroit. 3 beds. Lounge space. (b)Brownstone house – 2 Bed flat. (1920's) Brooklyn Heights, New York. Lounge space.	2 images 2 Images	Interior high ceilings. Large ornate fireplace and surround. Artwork, ceramics and interior objects. The interior is used to house a range of artistic and cultural items for hanging display. On walls, cabinets/ shelves etc. Large coloured ceiling light feature (object). Carpets/rugs on hard wooden floors. (Lounge/entertainment space – **68m²**) Funky flat with high ceilings and large windows in a traditional New York building. Eight flats in one big house. Small 2 bed flat that has large windows and supersized American pop graphics (object) throughout. Furniture all lowered to be at floor level. Thick textiles and wooden floors. (Lounge/kitchen – **56m²**)	Emergent interior (Traditional interior modernized). Owner. No. of regular occupants: 1 x Couple. 2 x Kids weekends Designed/Traditional Modern/Long-term renter. No. of regular occupants: Family of 3.	Ceiling feature and 3 other cultural objects (includes plants). Supersized American graphics and 3 other cultural objects (includes plants).
20/33 Total returned 33 (60 sent)		52 images	Rooms selected – Average size – **50m²**		Total cultural objects documented: 60

(*Designed* – Brazil, China a, Japan, Spain a/b, South Africa, UK a/b, USA b; *Emergent* – Australia, China b, France, Italy, USA, and *Agile* – Canada, Kenya, South Korea, Malaysia, Canada).

photographs or the selection of objects. All were very nuanced and had specific cultural flavours.

The probe presented documents to complete and short questionnaire material as well as a USB flash drive for recording digital images, a length of string for measuring internal dimensions, aromatic sticks for scenting the space, recording materials and instructions (translated as required) and postcards to record spontaneous remarks to include with the returned data. There was also a notebook for documenting the location (address, building type and material), and the details (rent/owner/number of regular occupants etc.) of the occupation. The interior space was described and documented. The participants were required to select, describe and document four specific objects (one primary and three secondary) that were placed in space and these are included in the results below. The probe was sent to addresses/PO boxes and included a return box for the data. The anonymous study was conducted with international participants (33/60 returns) (Australia, Brazil, Canada, China, France, Italy, Japan, Malaysia, South Africa, Spain, UK, USA). An outline of the returned data is available in Table 3.1.

Although the probe uses a small sample it does give a preliminary glimpse into cultural diversity and cultural similarity of domestic interior space, revealing small glimpses of the spaces that people live in. The probe was anonymous and focused on a single domestic setting (Living spaces, Kitchen, Bedroom etc.) and assumes that the interior space that is occupied is referenced (regionally) by cultural, geographical and architectural aspects. The total returns (33/60) from the probe are represented in Table 3.1 by an extended sample (20/33) and were completed and returned over an 18-month period. The participants were selected through contacts of secondary parties and were anonymised to ensure parity. The only fixed data was the type and location of the home, the building, the urban location and the country. All the data was drawn from each of the dwellings located in each country and there was no data collected on the users of the spaces, other than the status of the occupier (owners or renters) and the number of occupants. There were three returned data collection aspects which helped to triangulate cultural function, aesthetic, style and trend that had been used as part of the assembled interior. The information represented in Table 3.1 from the data collection is verified through the information in each of the three data collection parts. There was some uncertainty about the interior typologies within the sample, however the returns have shown a rich diversity of space and architecture. The participants were asked to (self) apply one of three typology descriptions to their interior (*Designed, Emergent, Agile*) revealing that the *designed* space category was more prevalent within the sample. *Agile* and *Emergent* were also used across the sample including a number that described the spaces as being a hybrid between two of the descriptors.

60 A spatial probe – investigation into space

Preliminary findings are drawn from the diary and visual data around the top six cultural aspects described:

- **Space** – Domestic spaces (in square metres) are determined by the architecture of the building, but the arrangement of domestic space and its organisation is diverse and actively individual. The participants selected a specific room and therefore the data represented was quite broad in terms of overall space and meterage. Within the probe, a piece of string marked to metre lengths allowed the participants to measure and calculate their selected spaces. The probe suggests huge variations in (individual) style, taste, capacity and scale (Australia, Brazil, China a/b, France, Hong Kong, Japan, Malaysia, South Africa, UK a/b, USA). However, the type, patterns and orientations space (Lounge, Dining, Kitchen, Bedroom, Bathroom etc.) are similar in type (but different in size) and all have different cultural contexts and meaning depending on their placement and spacing to each other and their wider geographical location (this was mentioned in several diary entries). Each interior has different meanings and importance depending on its scale, volume and component arrangements (again several key mentions of the placement of doors/windows, ceiling heights and positions of staircases) (Canada, Italy, Japan, Malaysia, South Africa, UK a, USA b). Spatial cultures are represented through a range of personal, familial, regional and national cultural factors, and include the mixing (or layering as suggested by one (UK a)) of cultural statements and objects (high, low, geographic, ethnic, political, diversity, corporate, popular) within the spaces shown in the probe data (Brazil, China a/b, France a/b, Italy, Japan, Malaysia, USA a/b). Significantly there are several references to international culture and the importation of *"foreign"* objects, art and cultures into the spaces (France, Japan, Malaysia, South Africa, USA b) in the visual and diary data. The diary entries and interior visual reference suggest that the sizes of the living spaces vary (this does not appear to be culturally driven), but the use of cultural reference is often displayed in different rooms across the house.

"I really don't care what people think about my taste. Everyone has always said I have good taste, but I don't know what that means. I try to show different types of style in different rooms in my house. It is important for me to create a really soothing and layered interior space to sleep in. The overall ambience of the space is important."

(UK a)

"I see my apartment as a place where I can show and externalise my personality. I enjoy when others are able to see what cultural items I have collected from my travels. I regularly rotate the items I have on display and think of it as a sort of travel diary. These items do not seem to be time-bound and keep reminding me of where I've been." (USA b)

- **Place** – In a domestic setting, place is essential and has shifted exponentially in meaning during the national direction from the pandemic lockdown. The domestic place is defined by the house *and* the home. Home (and its centrality) was a recurring theme within the diary entries (Australia, Canada, France, Italy, Japan, Malaysia, South Africa, Spain a/b, UK, USA a/b) and the development and extended longevity of the home seemed to signify the potency of the family relationships in the house (some locations appear stronger than others). The place of home is so much more than the building and physical space. The diary and visual information appear to offer a sense of pride (both national and local) (Australia, China b, France a/b, Italy, Japan, UK b, USA) and significantly the mentions of community appear in this section repeatedly. The culture of family is supported by the nature of place and its meaning to the occupants is an important factor in the construction and experience of the interior.

  "Our home is much more than the building. We have lots of things we have collected and work to display all of our treasures and artwork. It is part of who we are and our background. The interior has been designed so that artwork can be moved around to suit our mood and different styles. We move our interior around (furniture and lighting) often so the place is always new and interesting. We like to ensure the colour and lighting are sympathetic to our home and our mood." (South Africa)

- **Colour** – This is culturally referenced throughout the data from the probe (with several of the diary entries being coloured/patterned as the interior are). The colour within the shown interiors is bright and bold but do not appear to show any cultural markers or displays. Colour is significantly referenced within the probe data (Brazil, China a, France a/b, Italy, Malaysia, South Africa, UK a) often determining the activities, mood and activity in each room. Palettes are usually quite muted with the main walls often in white or lighter colours, but there are signature surface colours in several of the visuals including the use of murals. The visual data appears to show little projected colour and the main colour appears to be derived from pigmented paints. Colour is also derived from furniture, wallpaper, textiles and floor coverings. There are regular uses of deeper and more intense colours supported with reflective and textured papers and vinyl. (Brazil, China, Italy, Japan, Malaysia, South Africa, UK b, USA).

  "I selected the colour in the Kitchen because we like bright and fresh food. This makes us happy to be eating and being together" (Translated) (China b).

- **Furniture** – The data suggests movable furniture (in all forms) is a strong cultural marker within the interior, both through its aesthetic appeal, but also in its functionality, shaping organisation, movement, circulation and activity. Furniture (of all types) appears in all diary entries and visual data (all countries).

62 A spatial probe – investigation into space

"Our lounge chairs are very special to us. They feel part of the family and have lived through all the ups and downs and now I use for my working at home office." (Malaysia)

"…the dining table is the heart of the house. It gets used all the time both for dining but also work, homework and hobbies." (Spain a)

- **Lighting** – The interior always requires light to illuminate, shape and outline the space. Internal and natural lighting was mentioned in all the diary entries (12) as part of the descriptions of the house or as a way to describe space with many references to *sight, looking* and *seeing* space. This was specifically so when the data described the mood or atmosphere of the space. Generally, the older building (Australia, France Italy, Japan, UK, USA) seemed to include more descriptions of light to *"tone"* and *"control"* how space was viewed, encouraging better cultural references and experiential languages to appear. Interior lighting (and shadows) are used when describing the use of light to define space (day and night) (China, France, Italy, Japan, South Africa) and positioning of the *"ambience and mood"* of a space and were used repetitively within the diary descriptions. There were two references to the cultural referencing of natural light and artificial light (China a/Japan) to create a focus on an object or picture. The data positions light as one of the most common cultural references in an interior.

  "Creating the right lighting in the spaces is important. We have spent a lot on the lighting for our lounge space. I particularly like our uplighters which create a really soft mood with a reflected light from the ceiling." (USA a)

  "We like to use all forms of lighting in the spaces we live. What is electric lighting is important and helps us use the house at night time, natural light is important to well-being. Letting light in from the outside through the windows is an important part of living in this house." (Spain b)

- **Objects** – Occupying spaces with objects is a specific cultural form (Figure 3.1). The data suggest that the dressing of spaces with objects, personal objects and artwork provides a separate position when building and signifying cultural positions for the interior (China, France, Japan, Malaysia, South Africa, UK a/b). The objects are themselves cultural markers and the positioning/displaying of objects within the interior are used to dress and influence the space (Australia, Brazil, China, France, Italy Japan, Malaysia, South Africa, UK a/b, USA) (Figure 3.2). Objects can be brought into the space, changing the design/or aesthetics, and actively moving an interior towards different typologies (*Designed* – Brazil, China a, France a, Japan, Kenya, South Africa, Spain a/b, UK a/b, USA b; *Emergent* – Australia, China b, France b, Italy, USA a; and *Agile* – Canada, Hong Kong, Malaysia, South Korea). The data strongly suggests that the objects (both fitted and loose) within an interior are the most significantly positioned cultural aspects of interior space. It appears that the item and its display (in a range of contexts) is a deeply meaningful (and possibly the most prized) aspect of domestic interior culture. These items are surprisingly broad and include interior fittings, fireplaces, doorways and furniture, 2-dimensional (paintings/pictures) and 3-dimensional objects/ceramics/products/revealing the interests and hobbies of the occupants. These are part of the cultural aspects of the space.

"The house has absorbed all my objects and things that I have collected over many years. There are many cultures represented from my travels and it is a place that is created by the objects in it. The whole is greater than the sum of its parts really." (Translated) (Italy)

"…this is the first time that I've described what the inside of my house looks like. I regard my space as private and my objects as special to me. I have selected them all and think of them as part of me." (Translated) (South Korea)

The probe, whilst not conclusive, does reveal a more visceral aspect of the relationships between space and culture, demonstrating how humans can function and interact with their environment. A place where their personality, selections, taste and whim can be revealed. The interior space extends and introduces a more dedicated and sensorial condition, where the occupants are enticed to view and interact with the interior elements and the space.

FIGURE 3.2 Domestic apartment (Japanese participant 2020)
Anonymous

64 A spatial probe – investigation into space

The hidden cultures of space and place

Spatial cultures are defined by the way the human body moves through space and perceives the architecture enclosure, the surfaces of interior space and what is placed within. But often these cultures and spaces are not always what they seem and in many cases architectural enclosures hide or cloak aspects of the spatial experience, shaping how the space is revealed and sensed. Much of the detail, the memory and the experience can be lost. By absorbing Mallgrave's (2018, 27–37) dedicated exploration of the architectural "Culture Wars", we can understand the reference to "hard architecture" (cited from Sommer 1974, 11–24) and the tactility of interior spaces. He proposes a dynamic dialogue between the different types of cultures from the constructed environment. Pallasmaa (2012, 12–13) warns of the need to address all the senses simultaneously, creating a powerful "fuse" between the recognised self and an experiential condition of the surrounding environment. Sensorial approaches to the interior include designing better responses to and from the main senses that activate the hidden sensorial narratives of space that incorporate memory, atmosphere, and time-based compositions. An interior narrative relies on showcasing the interior, empowering the internal environmental cultures which focus on the user experience and discourse with the space. Lehman (2017, 1) suggests that dialogue with space should be two-way between the building and the user derived from the design process. This helps to define and refine the encounter within the space, providing both *"processes"* and *"sequences"* in which the interior culture can be experienced, but also encourages the *"reading"* of space through experience, promoting ideas of spatial exhibition, discovery and interrogation. Whitehead (2017, 34–37) plays with descriptions of visual cultures within space through the additions of mise-en-scène and the theatrical framing of the interior. Brooker (2016, 16) introduces the ideas of reprogrammable space and place, endearing spaces that are reformatted to fit new and alternative uses, suggesting the powerful *"tensions"* that exist between old and new elements, straining the existing spatial envelope and its reflected cultures. Abercrombie (1990, 29) provocatively suggests that seeing space individually can limit understanding and recommends that a gathered experience must be done room by room to gauge a true meaning and cultural connections within the occupied space. However, the ordinary spaces we construct and inhabit pose an interesting dichotomy. On one hand, we seek to create unique, personalised and individual spaces, that help define who we are. On the other, we seek regular patterns and conformity to the spaces we inhabit as seen in Table 3.1. Ingold (2000, 154) uses the conditions of dwelling to introduce patterns and temporality to the experience of internal space. He suggests that many dwelling environments have *"multiple layers of symbolic meaning"* that people *"cover over"*. However, this meaning creates specific cultural parameters and encourages a closeness to the interior that forms a distinctive spatial bond crafted around the activities of the user. Sloterdijk (2011, 334–335) suggests human beings are naturally inclined towards "a closeness" as part of the creation and culture of space. He suggests cultural *"Existence is always a completed act of habitation ... Spatiality is an essential part of it"*. Whilst space helps to craft the cultural limits of the interior, it is the definition of place that defines the spirit and located cultures of the hidden encounter.

As Lyndon (1994, XIII) suggests, *"Places are spaces that you can remember, that you care about and make part of your life"*. The impression of culture within space can change as we move through it from our initial perceptions of space to place. A key aspect of spatial design is the reveal; how space unfolds as we pass through it, often termed as *placemaking*. This gives a sense of "kinetics" or "non-static" existence. As the user stands still within an environment, the movement of vision (focusing and refocusing on objects or space) changes perceptions and relationships, both physical and psychological.

Cultural Trail

The spatial probe research allows a view into the cultures of the domestic home. The range and promise of this original research are compelling, but the alignment of space and culture is complex. The domestic environment allows for a more detailed personalised approach to understanding the cultures of space. In a true identification of culture, individual cultures collate to form into a community-wide perspective. This in turn influences wider society and human development. Domestic spaces present a constantly evolving kinetic environment that is created by an individual for their own expression, safety, and identity. Much of this is highly personal and private (as suggested in some of the probe diary comments) and is generally not for public consumption. The probe has presented an interesting range of results and has developed some strong comparative analyses with interesting intercontinental details. Whilst recognising there are geographical and cultural differences, there is also a remarkable similarity between the spaces and how culture is represented. The results detail the positioning of space as an agile cultural transmitter and locate the culture of objects within space, but this is highly temporal and representative through this piece of research. By assuming the research data is accurate, the results begin to reveal a pattern of selection, hierarchy and location within individual households, signalling how individual taste and cultural reference can be positioned in domestic homes. There is usually a strong transmission and acceptance of cultural patterns and beliefs (origins, background religion, politics) when people live together. Although aesthetics and taste decisions are more likely to be based on individual choices or continuous traits or cultural guidance/tales/advice

66 A spatial probe – investigation into space

passed down generationally. There is further design cultural mapping and analysis contained within Chapter 8 and the summary at the end of the book. The next chapter examines cultural ethnography and anthropology in relation to space with an outlining of a new contextual spatial cultural ecosystem which aligns cultural applications in a theoretical context.

4

ETHNOGRAPHY AND THE HUMAN PERSPECTIVE

Ethnography and anthropology

This chapter explores the cultural relationships between the design of space and the human occupants. It develops discussion around cultural anthropology and spatial ethnography and the *placement* and locations of culture within space. It is important at this stage to recognise the relationship between ethnography and anthropology. Anthropology is a wide study of humanity and includes human behaviours, cultures, societies and communications. Ethnography is considered a focused subset, primarily concerned with a systematic examination[1] of individual human culture (sometimes called cultural anthropology). Ethnography explores cultural phenomena from the point of view of the subject of the study. It involves examining the behaviour of the participants in a given social situation and through different types of interpretation. Ethnography relies on participants and researchers contributing together using qualitative methods that document patterns of detailed social interaction, including the perspectives of participants, and their local contexts. This includes a detailed cultural analysis of location, place, space and habitation. Both fields use past, current and future perspectives as the context for knowledge. Further subdivisions within anthropology include socio-cultural anthropology, biological anthropology and physical anthropology which study different aspects of being human.

Tim Ingold (2018) has consistently positioned anthropology as a broad discipline which encompasses an unfolding mirror to human beings and enquiries to the way we live.

> We call ourselves human beings, but what does it mean to be human? The name science has given us, as a species, is *Homo sapiens* but in what does our alleged sapience, or wisdom, consist? How do we know,

DOI: 10.4324/9781003270393-5

68 Ethnography and the human perspective

> think, imagine, perceived, act, remember, learn, converse in language and live with others in such a distinctive and yet various ways.
>
> *(Ingold 2018, 3)*

Significantly, Ingold (2018, 88–90) positions the divides and alignments across what it means to be human but also highlights how cultures drive behaviour that helps adapt humans to their environment. This chapter introduces a new cultural framework which helps locate the relationship between human cultures and space. This framework is presented through the Spatial Culture Ecosystem, which is a process and a method of being able to align culture application and spatial enablers in a theoretical context. Using ethnographical social research, the Spatial Culture Ecosystem (Figure 4.1) examines the type and application of cultural provision within space and society. It recognises different forms of cultural application with key spatial enablers to develop space that is functional, aesthetic and protective. It supports and guides the behaviours of the inhabitants in each social situation and provides context for individuals and groups to develop. The top part of the ecosystem relates to the space typology and the cultural dynamics of space set out in Figure 1.2. This is aligned with the core themes and spatial descriptions that are used throughout the book to contextualise the cultural relationship to space. The central section aligns the enablers with the applications that build discovery throughout the book and are expanded on in

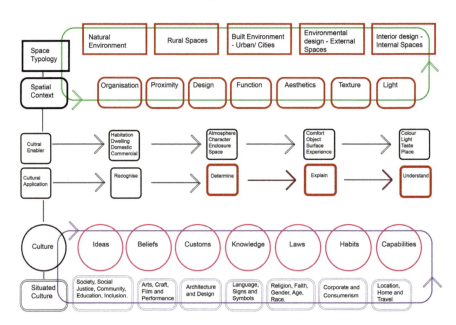

FIGURE 4.1 Spatial Culture Ecosystem
Author

Ethnography and the human perspective **69**

Chapters 5, 6 and 7. The lowers part of the ecosystem expand on the origins and sources of culture and reference them directly to the situations where culture develops.

Situated culture

Human beings mostly need to be surrounded by human beings. History dictates that as a herding species, we achieve more through the collaborations between people, building societies, forming communities and generating a mercantile society. The culture of space is an active part of this matrix and how humans form space for their use is a critical component. There is a direct marriage between how spaces are formed and used and human behaviour. Indeed, there are many examples of how humans directly impact the spaces they create. An example of this is the "inscribed" space (Low and Lawrence-Zuniga 2003, 13–14) where humans inscribe their presence into an environment that they create. This inscription can be described as developing a meaningful and integrated relationship between humans and the environment. This is often described as the transformation of space into place. This is either through a space being populated, adapted or designed for a specific purpose. Other forms of situated culture are presented through the notions of "fielded" space. By using Lefebvre's (1991, 60–61) concepts of "field of knowledge and action" as an embodiment between humans and space, Munn (1996, 94) creates a *mobile spatial field* utilising a notion of performance and the relationship between actor and stage to describe a "situated" and "mobile" relationship between humans in space. This concept has a strong resonance with the mobility experienced in most forms of commercial and domestic spaces.

Culturally, the way space is used is determined by the way that we use and experience space within our "home". Our homes are a critical part of our understanding of space. Instinctively we develop being surrounded and fed by the womb, protected and nourished by another human. Whilst we are unaware of our early development, this protective space forms an inherent and instinctive bond between our body and the surrounding environment. A mother's womb is an important part of a physical understanding and tactility of space, developing closeness and enrichment for the bodily senses. Sloterdijk's (2011) sphere theory uses intimacy and the relationship between mother and baby as a metaphor for protection, but also to explore spatial contexts opening to wider relationships within the built environment:

> The unified to become related to third, fourth and fifth elements as the singular line ventures out of its initial shell, additional polls and larger special dimensions open up, each defining the extent of the developing and developed connections worries and participation. In fully grown spheres, forces are at work to draw the individual into the illusion shared

70 Ethnography and the human perspective

by millions. It seems impossible to live in large societies without yielding in some measure to the delirium of one's own tribe. From the outset, therefore, spherology examines the risks involved in transference process from micro- to macropsychoses.

(Sloterdijk 2011, 61)

He continues by describing the transference between spatial states:

The exodus of the living [is] from the real and the virtual mother's womb into the dense cosmoses of the regional advanced civilisations, and beyond these into the non-round, non-dense foam worlds of the modern global culture.

(Sloterdijk 2011, 61)

Culturally, this movement between the immediate proximal environment into the external world provides an early awareness of comfort and protection that changes but also replicates the early experience of space. Our homes are often driven by an early understanding of this environment and this explains why some cultures and places are developed around the idea of proximity and closeness to others. Some domestic densities of housing seem difficult to fully understand but are preferred culturally by some populations. Living spaces help to frame a sense of place and privacy. Most homes are never seen or viewed by others. They are only for our personal gaze, as privacy is a fundamental part of the home.

The centrality of the home is as much about place as it is about space. *The Poetics of Space* (Bachelard 2014) considers the house/home as a sanctuary and primal space that acts as the first world or first universe to the occupiers. The home is an intimate space for personal intense experiences of space. To Bachelard, the interior arrangement of the house constitutes not one homogenous place but rather a series of places where the occupiers leave personal traces and residues of occupation with their own memories, imaginings and dreams. Miller's (2008) expose of 30 identical residential homes in South London develops the theme of "comfort" and reassurance of the home. It individualises and diversifies the highs and the lows of the home over 17-months. All of the 30 "portraits" are very different, describing a range of activities, aesthetics, tragedies and future trajectories. This anthropological study is highly revealing about the diversity that happens within people's homes and demonstrates the differing cultures and approaches to living that occur in everyday living and working spaces in Britain.[2]

Working life has fundamentally altered since the onset of COVID-19. It has shifted the focus and emphasis of working to a state of hybridity, where most working is super flexible and migratory, and many businesses reported lifted levels of productivity through the COVID era. The workplace is no longer considered a geographical anchor, where the divisions between home and work were clear. Social media and technological communication have altered the speed and immediacy of the work situation, enabling a more dynamic hybrid working model to emerge. However, a new and sustainable model, balanced between home working, office work and potential third-space[3] working, is still emerging, demonstrating the complexity of the impact of the pandemic on the spaces we work and live in.[4] Companies are working with employees to establish a workable balance between sustainable in-person and home working environments, where businesses remain profitable, and workers remain committed and happy. This new form of spatial work culture is becoming become normalised as the impact of the pandemic subsides and new working practices have taken hold. This is a good example of how cultures within space can be altered. Such a large-scale event that impacted the globe has forced a complete rethink of highly established and embedded spatial practices. As the direct impact of the pandemic begins to slowly subside, there are much deeper considerations and implications of space. Many of the pandemic decisions happened immediately due to the unknown effects of a global pandemic. It was an emergency where humans adapted their behaviours to ensure the continuation of their livelihood, families, and communities. Whilst this was unprecedented in scale and impact, it enabled considerable reflection on the importance and use of all spaces and their associated cultural relationships.

Designed interiority and exteriority

One key spatial aspect of the research that has been considered in the preparation of the book contextualises internal and external space. All have a slightly different dimension of how space should be perceived, understood and interpreted. Whether this is the examination of *space* and *place* or the development of a new relationship between interior and exterior experience, an understanding of the interiority and exteriority of space has become documented and wide-ranging. There are some interesting divisions and categories regarding different forms of space. If we explore urbanism then there are divisions around the *hard* and *soft* sciences (Plunz 2017, 15) that are in play in the urban environment. The hard divisions are driven by architects and technicians who explore the physicality of the urban environment. The soft aspects relate more directly to the human perspective and an understanding of the psychological and social aspects of being inside or outside. This is also affected by the notions of privacy, solitude and socialisation.

According to Schneiderman and Dzis (2022 referencing Merwood-Salisbury and Coxhead), the contemporary city is now as much about an interior condition as an exterior one. They give some examples of exterior spaces with "interior conditions" where a blurring of the relationship of traditional or *standard accounts* (Sennett 2016) of spaces occurs. Sennett (2016) draws

72 Ethnography and the human perspective

a clear relationship between the interiority and exteriority of the urban environment through spatial fluidity or the porous nature between the inside and the outside (echoing the divisional transparency described in Stone 2020, 15). He describes some interesting case studies across the world where interior activity (and domesticity) openly happens in an exterior context. He draws on historical examples (Shanghai courtyards in particular) that have helped maintain social order and the fabric of the community by moving fluidly between the insideness and outsideness of human activity. Bradbury (2021, 93–96) describes Fallingwater (Frank Lloyd Wright 1937) as having constant synergy between the interior and exterior environments. The glazing allowed frame views of the water and the woods beyond creating a series of levels on the building halfway between the two environments. He suggests that the boundaries between the house and landscape become "blurred" and continually intersect as you are moving through the architecture, experiencing the terraces, pools, walkways and viewing points. Further descriptions of this are found in Richard Neutra's philosophical approach called *Bio-realism* (Figure 4.2) which deepens the relationship between the building and the site, blending the inside and outside atmospheres, forming a more heightened and liveable approach for the inhabitants. Bradbury (2021, 106) frames this architectural approach as a form of "prescription" for good living. This is also supported through the extraordinary houses produced by the architect John Lautner (Hess 1999, 203–211) where he produced unusual and sublime domestic spaces that focused on bringing natural light into the architecture by actively drawing external materials (rocks, boulders, planting and water) as part of the internal experiences. Interestingly, both Neutra and Lautner were students under Lloyd Wright in the Taliesin fellowship programme in the 1930s.

Much of this activity has a human description and uses the body as a measure to understand the transitions between the inside and the outside. Lawson (2001, 2–12) frames a set of spatial languages that offer critical insight into the exploration of space. He determines the basis of this interpretation through historical values of architecture and, in particular, outlines the use of anthropometrical data by Le Corbusier and his Le Modulor scaling system (1943). This system is figural in approach, but in using this system his buildings were designed to accommodate this strangely mis-proportioned anthropometrical figure. Le Corbusier used this to design his architecture, believing it to be a way of user selection and creating modern design. His use of this figure was symbolic and has a perception of human form implanted in the built environment. He often cast the figure in the side of his architecture to reinforce the human dimension. Lawson (2001, 91–92) suggests that by using two modes of spatial perception (formal and symbolic), it is possible to interpret spaces in different ways, allowing symbolism to be represented in the exterior territories of the city and the internal enclosures using volume, light, colour or materials material selection and this manifests itself through the design process.

FIGURE 4.2 Bio-realism – Richard Neutra Design Philosophy that blended spatial atmospheres.[*]

* Photo by Daniel Kim. [Generic (CC by 2.0)] https://flickr.com/photos/119658633 @N07/34377421235/in/photolist-UnPgDe-T9dDv4-TMQ5Uf-pT3PAb-yVBt6a-xZ Pf7ze49KW7-vSnF5-x8ik5b-zCLLVL-xbAeNs-2k4Yi9f-V2US5Y-qJCNmW-2k4Yi9 k-8QyWVd-jXxk3t-2jXKCVh-jXwSYp-T6qAPC-TMQLTU-Ujas2o-T9dLQz-T9dnYH-T9d23V-8Pfmq6-kJaPq-PJM98Q-Nimgcb-saceRL-yCehaL-rdkzfm-vSnkc-2jXKCTy-x cyy1b-tGqhW-7goKUn-rSLsxS-ySLDus-21vKWb-xnVUu7-e6GQw8-xHo39B-tGqe e-pGv3qD-xWTavH-yZCvNE-yBaWuf-ySLW5w-2jXKCRj

74 Ethnography and the human perspective

Understanding the differences between the interior and exterior of the built environment is usually defined through a notion of territory. Whilst this can be multidimensional, human beings are particularly sensitive to the ideas surrounding boundaries, borders and territories. In a spatial context, a defined region by its very nature has a boundary connecting or overlapping with other regions and usually some form of centralised point of focus. This might be a continent with defined countries, a country with a capital city, a city with defined "quarters", city districts with parks and squares or specific buildings with businesses and living spaces. Once you get down to specific buildings and dwellings you move into the specifics of the interior parts of the building and a more dedicated human scale. This *movement* through the permeable boundaries of the building exteriority is a critical component of spatial culture and human understanding of space. This has become much more than a building just protecting and isolating human activity from the outside. At this moment the interior begins to take on a more emotive and impactful role, developing a sensual aspect where humans can interact and respond to their environment more directly. In most human societies, having a sense of location and belonging within a boundary is an important part of human sociology and psychology. Having that central focus within that boundary is important for building narratological and spatial understanding when considering the dynamics of human cultural territories (Figure 4.3).

As part of developing spatial culture, the emerging experiences that develop between the external environment, the architecture, and the interior often move beyond the ordinary perceptions and understandings of space. There is often something much more fundamental that drives humans to break through and expand existing spaces forging new territories which extend the natural human instincts for survival, safety and function into emotion, love, respect, and self-fulfilment. The cultural space enriches the purposes of the environment that surrounds us. Pallasmaa (2012, 71–74) overturns a dereliction and precedence of the eye and the gaze in favour of the other senses to promote a holistic spatial experience that embraces all the senses. He argues that smelling, listening, tasting, or touching something brings you closer to the real cultures within space, enabling it to fully invade your sensory experience and build memory. He promotes that it is a more genuine or authentic experience when something is felt by the skin, smelled, or heard, as opposed to being seen.

> Touch is the sensory mode which integrates our experiences of the world and of ourselves. Even visual perceptions are fused and integrated into the haptic continuum of the self; my body is truly the navel of my world, not in the sense of the viewing point of the central perspective, but as the very locus of reference, memory, imagination and integration.
>
> *(Pallasmaa, 2012, 12)*

Ethnography and the human perspective 75

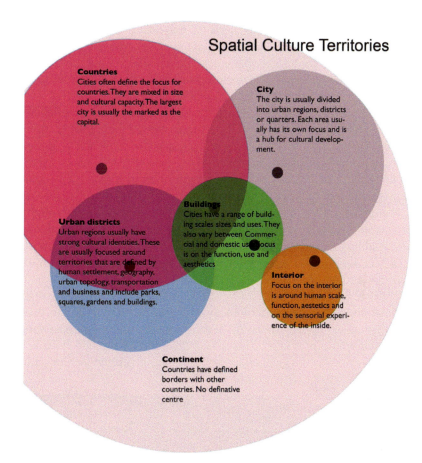

FIGURE 4.3 Spatial cultural territories
Author

He suggests there is a strong relationship between the human body and the spaces that the body occupies. He uses the mimesis of the body as a way to explain an embodiment within space, suggesting spaces are filled with the traces of the creator, whether this is by an architect, designer or person that has documented and formed the space. The way a space has been created and arranged is a form of *communication* between the creator and the person that encounters and experiences the space. According to Pallasmaa, architectural and interior space help shape experience. He suggests that the environment enters you, and you enter the environment. As your home changes, and perhaps as your personal spaces change, you change. He shifts the emphasis away from the eyes to argue that the human condition is to use the other senses to create an alternative understanding and interpretation of the interior: "They define the interface between the skin and the environment – between the opaque interiority of the body and the exteriority of the world" (Pallasmaa 2012, 45).

It is important at this point to look at the relationship between spatial experience and narrative storytelling. Both seek to extend what the bodily senses tell us about the spaces that we occupy. They provide further context for the experience of space and seek to enrich the descriptions and experience of all environments, both at a spatial, cultural and personal level. Pallasmaa (2012) asks questions about our bodies and promotes experience as a priority within the architectural situation. Whitehead (2017, 86–109) describes the perception of space as an "intrinsically subjective experience" describing an individualised approach to the perception of space. She also strengthens the idea that as the spatial atmosphere is created it becomes a shared experience, helping to condition a shared cultural and spatial narrative. Zumthor (2006) extends this architectural storytelling through the examination of detailed and immediate responses to the experience of space, enabling an emotive and cultural experience of space. It is a personalised account and aligns with Pallasmaa's (2012) theories on using knowledge and emotion as templates for measuring the quality of a space.

> Something tells us an enormous amount straight away. We are capable of immediate appreciation, of a spontaneous emotional response. Of rejecting things in a flash. This is very different from linear thought.
>
> *(Zumthor 2006, 12–13)*

FIGURE 4.4 Theme Vals Spa by Peter Zumthor (1996), setting a powerful cultural indicator of space using atmosphere
[Generic (CC by 2.0)] https://flickr.com/photos/anonphotography/6379409381/in/photolist-KKm6Vr-pZyUVZ-aHJbuT-aHJaWr-8BUL8C-aHJ99V

Zumthor has created several architectural works that propose a porous relationship between exterior and interior space and how experience can transfer between spatial states setting new relocations for culture. These works specialise in the creation of spaces that, through the use of volume, materials, light, surface and consideration of the user in the experience, are highly crafted, symbolic architectural statements (Figure 4.4). Zumthor's Therme Vals Spa building, built over thermal springs in Switzerland is designed to craft a complete sensual experience of the situation, space and architecture forming a powerful cultural and physical experience.

Whilst Zumthor (2006) promotes a narratological approach to space and ensures that the human experience is at the heart of his work; his spatial descriptions build relationships between places, memories, moods, atmospheres, films, art and theatre. He connects all the key elements by framing the cultural significance of the space by binding the associations and components together.

Cultural regionality

It is difficult to completely define clearly all the cultural attributes of urbanised environment work as most cities are complex often priding themselves for being multicultural and diverse. This diversity often manifests itself either through the development of cultural regions or enclaves. A culture region is an area inhabited by people who have one or more cultural traits in common, such as language, religion or *system* of work or livelihood. It is an area that is usually homogeneous concerning one or more cultural traits. Urban areas start to embrace several cultural groups that overlap and start to form new types of cultural identity. Because cultures overlap and mix, such boundaries are often highly permeable and are defined by cultural border zones, rather than lines. The zones broaden with each additional cultural trait that is considered because no two traits have the same spatial distribution. As a result, instead of having clear borders, cultural regions reveal a centre or core, where the defining traits are all present. These cultural traits are often quite complex and multifaceted. This includes employment, economy, services, music, arts and entertainment. Away from the central core, the characteristics weaken and disappear revealing a form of *urban blur*. The cultural aspects of the city are the elements that often define the city but also ensure different communities create spaces that help to promote and signify cultural differences. These differences are also apparent when they are externalised both through street activities like festivals, parades and religious celebrations, but also apparent through better urban transparency, encouraging better openness and diversity in the city spaces.

Designed proximity

It is very easy to assume that once the city has been dealt with and constructed that it effectively stays as designed and constructed ad-infinitum.

78 Ethnography and the human perspective

According to Fry (2017, 23–24), the city is a specific "draw for people seeking work, wealth, pleasure, exotic, erotic, anonymity, friendship, hope, shelter, drugs, fame" and therefore is in constant flux. Fry makes the point that even when a city (or part of it) is created for a specific purpose, it is poised to change and never holds onto its "posited destiny". As part of the definition of culture for the city, he suggests that the city is unviewable as a whole and only seen as fragments of streets or through an aerial abstraction. The cultures of the city are fragmented spatial practices that are constantly shifting.

> the city is also a socio-political landscape where ethnicity ans class are territorial determinants, and together with gender and religion, are generative of its cultures and the variability and viability of its communities.
>
> *(Fry 2017, 24)*

A specific area of focus for culture is an examination of population proximity where different human cultures can display cultural approaches to occupation, to social and cultural activities and to the designed and organised spaces that are focused around need. Different human groups treat their proximity to space quite differently. Humans make a claim to their living and working territory with a demarcation of a recognised and respected "bubble" of personal space (see Chapter 1 and Chapter 2). As humans, we carry a personal space around with us as we move and live and work. Depending on the situation we are in and our familiarity with both the space and the other humans that are near us we behave quite differently. Some cultural backgrounds are more comfortable with closeness to others. Different forms of culture encourage different approaches to proximity. A critical area is the distance of our arms that determines the zone around us; it is deemed as the personalised (and cultural) boundary or territory around us that we "own" and use to both separate us from others and the environment around us.

This moves with us as we endeavour to keep this space free to allow us to circulate properly. Different cultures have different approaches to how this personalised space is used and what is acceptable. In our domestic spaces proximity is less of an issue as the people we usually live with are known to us, and therefore more accepting. There will always be people who invade our "personal space" and, generally, this is unpleasant with humans we do not know. Edwards (2011, 128) describes these feelings of proximity as uncomfortable and unless forced upon us in an urban setting (lift, train, etc.), it is something that humans do not readily accept. Edwards also highlights the aspects of privacy and how personal spaces (work or home) can be adorned with personal effects and emblems on desks and work surfaces. This becomes a spatial identifier and forms new cultural aesthetics (particularly for office cultures).

Ethnography and the human perspective 79

To fully understand the contexts of culture and spatial closeness, it is important to review the use of the science of proxemics in context. Proxemics is a sub-category of non-verbal communication and was framed in several publications by Edward T. Hall, including his text *The Hidden Dimension* (1990, 113–125). Originally published in 1966, this text contextualises a set of spatial principles (Intimate, Personal, Social and Public distances) of how humans use and understand space. It describes the spaces of sociability, circulation and environment through a set of mobile bubbles that surround the figure (Figure 4.5).

Although Canter (1975, 142) cautions against the absoluteness of Hall's categorisations, suggesting that the proximities should contain more flexibility to allow for human and cultural differences to develop. He describes regulating distance with the proxemic zones as "inappropriate" in some situations. However, Hall's (1990, 101–178) classifications of these distances can be directly interpreted when determining a range of situations. Munn (1996, 92–109) used Hall's proxemic fields to develop a more flexible and inclusive *Mobile Spatial Field* by using and centring the human body. Munn seess this field as extending away from the human into space, describing this as a "culturally defined" corporeal field "stretching out from the body in a particular stance or action". She describes this field as having a performative *indexical* process embracing a situated body within expansive movements and immediate tactile reach. This then extends beyond the bodily centre using vision, vocal reach and hearing. She positions the body as a distinct

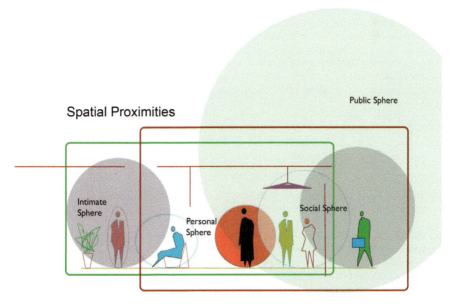

FIGURE 4.5 Spatial proximities
Based on proxemic spheres, Hall 1990. Author

80 Ethnography and the human perspective

centre of the spatial field, propositioning a new form of spatial field that alters and flexes as the body moves through space. This form of "located culture" shapes and affects the spatial relational contexts of any selected environment.

Cultural Trail

As the chapter introduces a Spatial Culture Ecosystem that collates the conditions for space and culture to intertwine, we see a forged symbiotic relationship where space creates the settings for culture to exist and change. By using anthropology as "philosophy with people in" outlined by Ingold (2018, 3), it becomes possible to explore human behaviour through analysis of space, positioning it as a kind of vessel where culture exists and develops. The ecosystem operates very much like the spatial field that Munn (1996, 92–109) outlines, but constructed through the use of constructed design thinking to consider the relationship between space and culture. Each area of the ecosystem is designed to be read systematically and comparatively to understand the complex relationships of design, emergence and agility at play. Whilst the situated cultures are represented as fixed, the cultural enablers, when located in commercial and domestic settings, are highly flexible and significantly, mobile. These are discussed and investigated as groupings, themes and realms in the next three chapters.

Notes

1 Ethnography explores cultural phenomena from the point of view of the subject of the study. It is a type of social research that involves examining the behaviour of the participants in each social situation and understanding the group members' own interpretation of such behaviour. As a form of inquiry, ethnography relies heavily on participants and researchers participating in the setting or with the people being studied using qualitative methods that document patterns of detailed social interaction and the perspectives of participants. This often includes a detailed cultural analysis of location, place, space and spatial habitation.
2 Miller (2008) is a powerful compendium of 30 personal portraits that reveal true diversity in one single street in South London. It is an excellent piece of anthropological research that snapshots a period in time in one street. Three good exemplar portraits are number 3 – a Porous Vessel, number 15 – Rebirth, and number 28 – the Carpenter.
3 Third-space working is effectively a form of working action where people find space to conduct work online between the home and a formal work environment. This includes coffee shops, restaurants and cultural locations like theatres, but many cities have established Coworking zones where offices are set up for people to drop in and work as they move through the city. This has become a popular model for a new way of working. https://www.weforum.org/agenda/2021/07/third-space-remote-hybrid-working/
4 A good place to understand how hybrid working is growing and impacting human interaction and working spatial culture is this article by the BBC. https://www.bbc.com/worklife/article/20220628-the-six-big-things-weve-learned-about-hybrid-work-so-far

5

DETERMINING SPATIAL CULTURE

Atmosphere, Character, Enclosure, Space

The next set of three chapters sets out a series of grouped realms (Figurative, Sensory, Textural) that help explain a connected narrative for spatial cultures. These realms set out a series of themes that reveal the relationships between space and culture. This chapter will explore four figurative thematic sections Atmosphere, Character, Enclosure, and Space. These themes will create a context (in some cases the settings) for cultures to emerge and be established. Through each of the themes, there are examples and case studies which help to expose the variety and detail of how culture is located and interwoven as part of the human spatial environment. The themes have been carefully selected to incrementally reveal the complexity and variety of where and how culture is positioned. They deliberately use recognisable spatial language to capture a broad perspective of the realm. Brooker (2013, 5–19) suggests that the "understanding of space can involve a broad and expensive enquiry" suggesting it would include "buildings, the environment, human occupation, scenography, performative environments" splitting the classifications between pragmatic and esoteric. Brooker (ibid.) and Bruner (1991, 9) conclude that spatial formulation and human perceptions of space are mental as well as physical.

To capture and explore definitions of and relationships within spatial culture, Norberg-Schulz (1985, 99) locates the human as a "Spatial Organism" which provides a narrative of a temporal and figurative context for an evolving spatial phenomenon. This builds purpose for habitation, determining the natural occurrences and fluidity of spatial relationships where "humans and environments can have influence over each other". Ingold (2018, 99–101) determines the cultural separations between person and organism by suggesting that humans are inherently "biosocial" beings that draw together the mechanics (and structuralism) of the body with the social, cultural and contextual settings for living. Charles Eames propagated a genesis for this

DOI: 10.4324/9781003270393-6

FIGURE 5.1 The Eames House. Case Study House No. 8, Los Angeles
Photo by Paolo Gamba. [Generic (CC by 2.0)] https://flickr.com/photos/abukij/
21076589233/in/photolist-y7t2Fx-yLJNU7-z23k5A-dcDr5L-yLKnx1-y7sTfV-xuFk
N-nDgcDf-4yv5sV-4yv5oz-dcDo3p-qFSLfq-7mg8ct-7mk2y9-Xd8hyY-z4kCJB-
22Bm3Ao-CZhcV7-CztevC-3TVGH-3TVH3-9tJFHS-3TVHk-K75j2A-z4kwTD-a
23RwS-xuMmN-cT1hrw-HQAxgf-HZkjKH-UyAqbf-6FKZh-cT1hLj-23Szoin-
cT167C-9HxQQq-djDyEq-dmB2V8-UyAqad-cT15dj-cT1biE-dmBd7b-cT1AAY-ei
LUEG-dmB4BT-dXrw6Y-dmB8BL-dXrw3q-dmB2HR-cT1aY7

organism through his conceptual design development activity and spatial planning (in this case his own house); he creates designed "boundaries" which set out the limits of space through different layers and thresholds, constructing and deconstructing space where spatial narratives (users, clients, guests, society as a whole) intersect (Figure 5.1). Eames does not make a distinction between 2-dimensional (plan) and 3-dimensional (volume) thinking and allows the interlinked layers and surfaces of the building to encourage a patternation of zones and spaces. His house was designed to be a highly flexible container that adapted and changed depending on the figurative need.[1]

Atmosphere

One of the most complex and transient elements of spatial culture is the atmosphere. In scientific terms, it is described as the air/gases that surround the planet, protecting humans from the vacuum of space. In spatial terms, it is indistinguishable, complex and often highly subjective. As Zumthor (2006, 12–13) reminds us, atmosphere is primarily detected by our "emotional sensibilities" and human beings can quickly decide on key decisions about the spaces they occupy. Our innate senses feed our decision-making processes on whether the space can be occupied for any length of time. The spatial atmosphere is not necessarily defined by space, volume, location, or the quality of the air, but it is driven by the relationships between people and place. The atmosphere can be detected in city vistas, huge sporting arenas and urban piazza (Böhme 2017, 125–135). This can be through a historical event triggering national mourning (an example would be Deeley Plaza in Dallas, the location of the assassination of President John F. Kennedy in 1963), the site of extraordinary human endeavour (like the Olympic Games) or more intimate ceremonial events like a birth or wedding. Whatever the event, atmosphere is created through the memory and circumstance of people in a spatial setting. Low (2017, 156–157) describes a theoretical concept of "affective atmosphere" where the atmosphere is "located, circulated and transmitted" through space and warns of limiting the understanding of the atmosphere using only direct emotional responses. However, the most highly palpable spatial atmosphere is more regularly detected within enclosed spaces, often within architecture, alerting the senses to a contained and interiorised atmosphere. The power of this is defined by many factors. One of these factors is the way the interior "feels" and we are guided by the way our senses inform us quickly of our surroundings and the spatial "mood". Stewart (2011, 452 in Low 2017, 157) describes atmospheric space as a form of "force field" that "pushes a present into a composition, and expressivity, the sense of potential and event". The other is the familiarity of the surroundings and where we feel comfortable/understand what is going on. A simple example of this is to consider how humans perceive restaurant

84 Determining spatial culture

spaces (arrival and entry, occupation, internal movement and seating positioning and exiting) which is part of the human food experience across the globe every day. But this has huge variants in culture, society, cuisine, climate, location and spatial experience, meaning that every restaurant interior is different and individual, every day. To control this, part of the designer's

FIGURE 5.2 The Rabbit Hole Restaurant, Durham
Author

role is to coordinate human experience through the formation of physical factors and the creation of different levels of interior atmosphere.

Formulating an understanding of interior atmosphere is inherently connected with spatial culture. It could be argued that the atmosphere of interior space *is* the interior (Figure 5.2). It is the embodiment of the interior and the space. Interior atmosphere is the changing mood and ambience created by the users of the interior. The users themselves play the role of interior regulator, tempering and engendering the disposition of the interior. This changes through the location and time of day. The atmosphere is strengthened by adjustments in light (natural and artificial), sound, colour, or modifications to space and volume and environmental control. However, interior atmosphere is also created through the composition of beauty, aesthetics and tasteful[2] applications within space. (See Chapter 7.)

Developing an atmosphere in an interior space is usually formed through detailed knowledge of how people behave and react to the interior space, whatever the design. Humans are often the main components of the atmosphere (and might not be a crowded space), moving and gathering in space, forming "communities of activity" that help other users understand how to behave. Sometimes only when the interior is full of people and being occupied is it said to have an "atmosphere". A good example of this is the nightclub or bar, where the interior is created to attract people. As these people arrive, they create the interior mood, forming a hive of activity, moving, circulating and communicating in a social way, allowing the atmosphere to be self-determining and forming. In contrast, reflective spaces can also provide powerful but still atmospheres where isolation and contemplation can develop an alternative culture. By inhabiting space, individuals can sense the atmosphere that surrounds them, stimulated by the senses. This is a complex and highly individual assessment which is created through the environment, building and objects. The atmosphere is usually determined by the people that occupy the space. "Atmosphere is something we inhabit, we experience it through our bodily engagement with the world around us" (Whitehead 2017, 17).

Character

When attempting to intertwine character and space, we move into a specific and quite subjective arena. Key characteristics of space become clear when we explore the distinction and uniqueness of different forms of space. The character of space is defined by a range of human and physical factors. There is a range of spatial identifiers that help build an understanding of space. This understanding is derived through uniqueness and individualism. Character is often derived through a singular quest to create a unique space. When we consider architecture, we can see that this distinction is formed through shape, aesthetics and form. A unique character with architecture is also its positioning and site which creates a unique form or setting. This setting can be considered when viewing the architecture externally, but also inside the building looking out on specific vistas where the external features are brought into the building. Character and uniqueness are also emboldened in the shape and form of the building. Whilst there are many examples of architecture and architectural styling (examples include mid-century utilitarian and suburban housing) that provide a context for the built environment, most lack the distinction, character and uniqueness that architecture usually strives for. Often the character is installed into architectural developments using colour, dressing or flamboyant additions that nourish the overall aesthetics. An example of this is when you have a row of identical houses, and the owners take it upon themselves to colour them differently. This individually changes the nature of the exterior surface of the house and the entire street. Having differences and identities is an important part of the spatial continuum. Each house will be very individualistic inside, but this idea of an external display is an important component that creates the character of a street or a town (Figure 5.3).

FIGURE 5.3 Tobermory Harbour, Isle of Mull, Scotland – an example of spatial character "of place"

Photo by low cloud on flickr. [Generic (CC by 2.0)] https://flickr.com/photos/25709664@N00/274154942/in/photolist-qe7Hm-39Fszg-2bLrVgX-CMRsSa-2bLsfgv-CoY4z6-adjEaL-agsuoN-CoQXfN-PoVgtD-9i4K8v-2aJKu6X-2aJKMjV-agpEcM-agsnVC-W5rz-CMRyvK-cLTJz9-CoRfgb-8zyk8-28nc9f4-agsztu-QxtA sY-Dj34wY-29DtFxs-29mxKre-27Z4oP7-2aJR9Rx-27YWnWQ-29DskjU-2a EvKB9-2aEw4VU-2aJTf9T-7YFULY-RzeZfq-LYTNZZ-RWrTrc-LYSRBp-S4Kwoh-2a Ev1PW-27Z295b-2yh8EE-RxJvcW-fSnQfQ-GDW2gs-2aJP5vT-29mq23R-6ZKy nA-2aJSNyz-NBbvzm

These spatial characters (of place) can be stimulated by the urban fabric, architecture or design but also include demographics of the population, weather, geography, geology and climate and communications. It is the mixture of these factors interacting together that make places unique and change our sense of place. These unique factors (that often sit in the background) also dictate decisions on how places develop and change and are termed endogenous and exogenous factors. Endogenous factors are the characteristics and identity of the place itself or factors which have originated internally and can be attributed to design, construction and where the inhabitants have altered (or designed) the environment. This includes the local place factors like location, topography, physical geography, land use, built environment and infrastructure, demographic and economic characteristics. Conversely, the character of a place does not exist in isolation and is influenced by the connected relationships to external places, factors and locations, termed exogenous. Exogenous often includes the impact created by large-scale migration, changes in the global economy or the development of technological change. Both factors work together to form the character of place.

Any pop-up market, event or festival relies on the idea of a diversity of cultures being brought in to influence the character of the place (Figure 5.4).

FIGURE 5.4 Glastonbury Festival – character of place
Photo by Rachel D. [Generic (CC by 2.0)] https://flickr.com/photos/fussyonion/
35573133015/in/photolist-WctB6z-CBiA8H-8Scyi-vziqWF-4YWzdi-vwCyHC-
urVz62-6Zet8R-9WJDpJ-W4G7EV-8mi5We-f3meW1-2T4ix-cgZSBd-8m
j1vr-6Zit6h-8miUba-8miTin-8mj5DP-8miMM4-8Sd6k-8mmZn1-8miFMM-8mm
KJ1-8mn7pw-8mmNF1-f3mcvN-f3mafo-vzipJv-8mkYG1-uvhfLC-f3m
f6C-f36ZnK-f374b4-f373Cz-f3mgeL-8mnedE-8mngDW-f374FR-f373Kn-f3maBm
-f373dt-f373Tt-f3mgmj-f372mZ-f3mfDs-f3m8XQ-vwLHE5-f3741z-f36VAZ

88 Determining spatial culture

This can be directed by different demographics like age, gender or religion. The character of a place can be determined by diversity. Having a range of cultural influences in a place can be the critical mass that creates the character. Another important aspect of the character of a market or a festival is its external setting, which can imply more freedom. Mobility also brings character as both markets and festivals have a strong sense of agility brought on by their temporal nature. This drives a strong sense of appeal and desirability. These live characterful spaces are often described as cultural hubs and help to define regions of cities and large summertime activities.

Enclosure

The process of enclosure starts as humans form in the womb (see Chapter 4). This sense of how space wraps and protects is inherent in human beings and is the basis for the methodology of developing space for occupation, dwelling and work. Enclosure is at the heart of many of the symbolic and figurative representations of space enclosing the human figure and soul. A dichotomy is created between the histories and development of architecture (from caves to skyscrapers) where early curved spaces are directly at odds with most modern right-angular building fabrication. Beyond the early caves, the curve in architecture only became common when materials and processes were created that enabled buildings to take on more complex external and interior forms.

Inherently, humans feel more protected when the spaces that enclose them are curved. Early cave dwellers quickly understood the importance of naturally protected spaces and were not restricted by the use of squared furniture. Whilst understanding that adding curvature to the built environment adds strength, squared spaces (and furniture) are faster to produce and allow for more rapid preconstruction. But, having a sense of enclosure of space helps determine much of the cultural reference that is present and forms a humanistic process of layering the body as a way of copying natural structures and biological physics through types of biomimicry (Pawlyn 2016, 2–44). Curved or bubble-like structures are becoming more common, often used in extreme environments like submarines and spacecraft as super-enclosures that defend the spatial requirements needed for survival. Curved living environments are often treated as fantasy settings and child-like spaces that are usually grounded in the earth (consider The Hobbit house in J. R. R. Tolkien's work) or unusual signature houses (Figure 5.5). Curved spaces for living are quite unique and create signature cultures of their own. For example, acoustics and sound move around space very differently to conventional rectangular spaces. Sound bounces and transmits quite differently, and more completely when the walls are curved. Air moves around spaces without corners more completely, allowing for better ventilation. Wrapping space around us suggests a closeness between the body and the building,

FIGURE 5.5 Pierre Cardin's Bubble Palace, in Theoule sur Mer, France (1975)
By Frans-Banja Mulder, CC BY 3.0, https://commons.wikimedia.org/w/index.php?curid=46718076

developing a more sinuous and connected space. Small spaces are used in many building forms and are often used in domestic settings to create a strong sense of protection and containment. Many commentators suggest a powerful connection between contoured spaces in the human body. Taylor (2007, 155–164) introduces Hertzian space, a term taken from the use of radio waves to map space to individual bodies and activities. Sennett (2016) includes discussions around spatial interiority, describing many architectural spaces but also introducing a form of "bodily comportment and bodily dress" interiority of the body.

However, inclusion in a spatial sense can also be considered through the idea of a boundary or threshold. Passing between an exterior space and a piece of architecture changes spatial understanding and perception. A sense of enclosure is a powerful human condition and echoes previous references to the transmissions between the insideness and outsideness of space (Introduction, Chapter 4). Cultural reference to enclosure appears in many different historical reference points. This includes many of the classic sixteenth-century Renaissance paintings which often indicated thresholds between an interior and exterior within a new single painting.[3] These settings show the importance placed on the relationship with the outside, developing an early

90 Determining spatial culture

understanding of an in-betweenness of space and the relative luxury of being inside. This threshold is an important part of spatial cultures and represents one of the areas where space has been altered and changed. Early buildings in Europe were taxed on the size of their windows and the cost of the glass, reducing the scale of the view to the outside. Other human eras and building styles have either enclosed buildings to create higher levels of privacy or later architectural innovations have removed the solidity of buildings using glazed walls, re-introducing a more dynamic visual relationship between the inside and the outside.

Much of the Arts and Crafts movement (1860–1910) reacted against the industrial revolution and focused on the relationship to materials. Their interiors often drew direct inspiration from nature, bringing the exterior into the interior, developing sensitive and considered enclosures. The relationships between exterior and interior environments are a repeated theme that is observed over the centuries in different forms of spatial settings. Enclosures are either designed to act seamlessly between the different spatial forms or react against them. Modernism was developed on the basis that inside space should be actively separated from the Earth. This is demonstrated by much of the international style that was elevated up on pillars from the Earth, separating the exterior and the interior. This was then complemented using large sheets of ribbon or curtain glass to draw in as much light as possible, whilst being separated from the outside. The purposeful and sharp lines of any modernist building are the direct opposite of the organic nature of the Earth. These glazed boxes interned humans, away from the Earth, providing a controlled environment of separation. Enclosure provides a critical commentary on the relationships of space while simultaneously providing an environment for new aesthetic cultures to be located. Enclosure creates spaces that can be environmentally managed, where plants can grow and gardens are created. In cities, redundant road and rail spaces have been converted into new forms of civic gardens. The New York High Line[4] was one of the original city spaces created to reintroduce planting into the city landscape, encouraging people to promenade at an aerial view over the city. It became increasingly popular as a way of re-greening the cityscape. Other more recent examples include the Washington DC Bridge-park by OMA Architecture which connects two halves of the city, and the new Castlefield sky park[5] in Manchester, UK which has been developed by the National Trust and reuses an old elevated Victorian railway and bridge becoming a green "sky-park" spanning part of the city. This new sky park has a strong sense of enclosure from the Victorian steelwork and architecture, but also offers expansive views across the industrial landscape.

An internal enclosure also means more dedicated control, where all the conditions of the interior can be monitored and adjusted. The air can be recycled, heated or chilled to create a perfect environment for living and working wherever the building may be located. This environment creates an artificial condition that is "perfect" for humans to operate in.[6] Enclosed environments also control sound, often alternating between dampening loud sounds and adding in artificial sound to create spaces and places that feel comfortable to live and work in. The different scales and sizes of space that people live and work in influence how the enclosure affects human behaviours and the relationships to spatial culture. This is reflected in other chapters when examining different sizes of domestic spaces, particularly the living/main reception environments that people live in and the proximal relationships to the service environments like bathrooms and kitchens (Chapter 2 and Chapter 4 and Figure 4.5). As living trends change, it is important to note the developments in kitchens and bathrooms. These spaces were traditionally enclosed, having a specific function for either the preparation of food or the cleanliness of the body. The kitchen (and food) has been specifically "opened up" moving to be combined with both dining spaces and increasingly living spaces. These agile living environments have been gradually becoming fully open plan over the last 10 years, removing walls and having more open space to be able to live, work and eat. This removes the idea of privacy in the home, allowing for spaces to become more hybrid and flexible in their usage. Open-plan living is much more acceptable when there is a sole occupant, but when there are others, spaces can become crowded and conflicted when used for different purposes. But, the bathroom stands alone, usually as the only private and lockable room in the house. This space has moved from a series of individual sanitary products (sink, bath, toilet) to fully fitted environments where baths, showers and indeed whole rooms become wet spaces for complete immersive cleanliness. Ashenburg (2007, 265) comments: "in the 21st-century, these rooms have become the inner sanctum, the place where hedonism, narcissism, over-the-top luxury and hygienic scrupulosity meet".

Space

The act of designing and choreographing space is humanistic and is formed through a series of recognised spatial typologies (Figure 1.2) that are repeated throughout the world. These spatial types help to both define and locate culture and other human activities. Space represents and defines the structures and places of human habitation, helping to frame and enrich the cultures within the different human communities. It instructs and coaches figurative behaviours that form relationships with the internal and external environment. It can form social constructs and represent how humans create space as a lever for the construction of society. For context, Lefebvre (1991, 33–53) defines spatial practice around social space. He divides space into three "moments" and representations of space, described as conceived space, perceived space and lived space. This active "triad" embraces many of the perceptual understandings of space crossing through many human

92 Determining spatial culture

perceptions. He moves between psychological and physical references and presents this "production of space" as a positive representation of how humans inhabit space, highlighting and explaining the contradictions between the experiences of perceived, conceived and lived space. He strengthens the idea that humans are social beings and are continually in flux, dynamically changing their location, places, relationships and social practice. He describes social space as incorporating social actions and specifically around the idea of "subjects" and "social acts". He specifically documents how every society produces its own kind of space which shapes its social and implied cultural existence.

Alexander et al. (1977) set out a patterned language for space by identifying different kinds of spaces. This groundbreaking text examines the relationships between each of the spaces and how they clustered in patterns in different forms of living environments. It specifically groups patterns (all 253) into manageable forms so that the built environment can be seen as a series of patterned identities where cultural characteristics can be observed. Many of these patterns are seen as ideals and are embedded in many of the towns, cities and neighbourhoods that are designed today.

The design of the urban fabric, cities, architecture and interior design are usually undertaken by defining two key aspects. The first one is usually about developing and "plan of works" or a "brief" that the architect or designer work to. This is often defined by a client, who instructs the details of the brief around what is required. This can be in a civic, commercial or domestic setting. How that brief is interpreted is usually at the will of the architect or designer. Connected with the brief is the consideration of the site. Across the spatial disciplines, the notion of the site is similar in principle (this is usually the location for the design to be implemented) and is widely diverse in detail, depending on the project, geography and detail. However, the site shapes the condition of the project and develops both the location and the elements for the design. The outcome is determined at the point where there is an agreement between the client and designer and the design is "handed over". This is part of the professional practices that have been developed over the last 300 years. However it must be noted that in many special design situations, the design, whilst planned and arranged carefully to a selection of tight criteria, often only reveals its quality (and failings) through human use. This may well be a section of a town that gets redeveloped through alterations to urban planning. As the population changes there is pressure to alter housing and commercial businesses, changing the way the urban landscape appears. This is often a slow process, and the redeveloped part of the town can look quite different to the way the urban planner initially intended. The same can be applied to architecture and the way buildings get altered and extended as the needs of the occupant change. This might happen more quickly than in the urban environment, but it still might be a relatively slow process. This will be impacted by trends and different emerging styling tropes. Architectural styles remain in city environments for a long time often becoming signature buildings (Figure 5.6) which, when combined with modern styles, help to drive new urban aesthetics that enrich culture. However, some urban changes are visual and are applied to the urban landscape through unsolicited graphical imagery like graffiti or

FIGURE 5.6 Brutalist Architecture – Newcastle Civic Centre by George Kenyon 1968
Author

94 Determining spatial culture

flyposting, and old buildings can be recladded in new surfaces, paint and textual render which helps to revitalise the urban landscape. New lighting can also refresh the skyline and completely alter the perceptions of most buildings. Culturally, internal spaces are diverse and more responsive to trends. They are quicker to refresh and repurpose and this can be achieved with less effort and complexity.

The design and organisation of spaces are driven by the commercial needs and domestic practices of spatial users. This is determined by differing styles, trends, designs and organisation of all the elements of the environment. These need to work in harmony and juxtapose with the qualitative aesthetic to build a form of "storytelling" or "narrative" element that reinforces the relationships of the individual experience. within the spatial experience. This element of space is a complex feature and something that is not regularly recognised/ considered by users as they pass through or engage with it. The narrative should connect all the main aspects of space (and related place, see Chapter 7) together and is a key component when considering space as a transmitter of culture (the space itself is a wholistic cultural statement) or as a cultural container (the space holds and encloses cultural objects or activity). Petersen (2021, 35–47) set out a compelling narrative of life in a Copenhagen building. Her opening account explores "how built environment and human subjects are deeply entangled" through the porosity of the walls in an old building. She frames the relationships between humans and building components like walls and floors, outlining how sound moves through space and into her environment. Her narrative is expressive and honest and gives a dedicated account of the cultures of domestic city living. This traditional narrative context is viewed as a connector of events or *nodes* of experience which are connected through the building. The city can be viewed similarly through the network of pathways which are either physical elements of the urban environment (paths, roads, rivers etc.) or figurative aspects (often subjective realms) that are described in this chapter. A spatial narrative is a connected experience that humans compile as they pass through space. It is a recounting or a discourse of the story of spatial use. This weaves directly with the positioning of culture in space and its representation. As an example, a conscious narrative process (using phenomenology[7]) draws on real knowledge from the phenomena of a direct spatial circumstance that captures a certainty and honesty of the experience. This narrative can unfold over time and be recounted and remembered both in a more structured linear fashion through experience or a more random non-linear manner, which often reflects how humans remember the experience. Culture weaves intrinsically through this spatial condition, influencing the conditions and organisation of space. This is specifically present when culture is presented as a primary focus of space. A good example of this is the presentation of history and heritage in the museum. The museum acts as a vessel of culture. It is a historic and curated collection that provides reference and research into human history, usually in an ordered and designed manner. This design provides a natural route through the collections, spacing and presenting the collections in a way that will be both memorable and build new knowledge of the past.

Because most museums have strong research-related cultural contexts, most visits to museums contain key experiences and highlights but are often quite blurred in terms of memory. Human experience collates phenomenological codes where historical and cultural knowledge is absorbed in real-time. Cultural knowledge is based on the "passing-on" and acquisition of knowledge, which is more nonlinear in approach and is produced as culture is established and revealed. Importantly the experience of gaining cultural knowledge has a wide-ranging impact and a visit to a museum might just be part of this understanding. Culture can be implied by an individual or community, but it is often only really recognised when a cultural institution like a museum recognises it. The idea that something gets accepted into a collection at a museum endorses its cultural significance and appeal. Importantly, this is based on physical objects and artefacts rather than behaviours, but it is a way of being able to record and register different cultures and how they are represented. This is specifically used by museums that continually update their curated catalogues to reflect the changing nature of human culture and innovation (Figure 5.7).

Space contributes directly to the understanding and positioning of culture, but this also would include an emotional and aligned response to space. A cultural narrative of space documents emotions, thought processes and feelings, often blurring the physical detail of space but leading to a broader understanding of the physiological intricacies of space. The relationships between the urban fabric, architecture and interior space are fundamental to the development of society and its related cultural histories and experience. Without the development of a mercantile society, the city and the urban fabric would not have materialised. The developments in ambition and materials set the scale and complexity of the built environment. A human need for architectural protection triggered the desire to soften the enclosure of the interior. Without an interior, architecture would not fully develop an engaging social experience for the user, losing the symbiotic relationships needed for an interwoven spatial culture.

Whilst architecture often creates a contextual volumetric experience, the interior coats the architecture creating tactile, flexible, comfortable and acquiescent user experiences. Design practices use spatial cultures as part of the design development process, translating traditional and modern cultures into new and recognisable interior spaces. Spatial practices and perception differ in various regions of the world and the bound relationship between architecture and interior design is often dependent on ancient precedents, tribal histories and community values. Often the margins of the relationship are formed from the level of enclosure, location and climate, and how this

96 Determining spatial culture

FIGURE 5.7 Science Museum, London
Author

affects the user experience. The cultural relationships between the inside and outside of the building also influence how the spatial culture and the narrative of space and place are entwined. Cresswell (2015, 52) uses the process of "gathering" of place as a way to differentiate between the inside and the outside. "the process of gathering (things, emotions, people, memories, etc.)

suggests a significant relationship between the inside of place (which gathers) and an outside (from where things are gathered)". (Please refer to Chapter 7.)

All the bodily senses gather information on the occupied space and feed this back so we can process our position. It is generally accepted that vision helps us understand a broader context of how space surrounds us. It is often the layers created by the architecture and the interior design that help us understand the context of our position and the position of objects around us. These spatial *layers* are perceived as generally running from the exterior through the architectural envelope and into the interior. By using glazed surfaces, we can contextualise what our position is concerning the outside and the inside. This is important as we have an inherent need to understand our position, what is in front of us, what is at our periphery and significantly what is behind us. The building, whilst protecting and reinsuring us, also needs to offer a physical and psychological means of escape. The art of designing internal space is combining the human need for understanding the phenomena of our surrounding environment, the spatial volumes (to ensure that we are confident we can get in and out of the space if we need to) and how the space forms a refuge. According to Appleton (1975), *prospect-refuge theory* describes a universal, human behavioural and psychological need for places that allow a person to see, but without being seen. It is an important theoretical concept that was developed to explain why humans always seek out a protected place to work, eat or dwell (in space) when given the opportunity. Whilst this theory is focused on individual choices, it also has direct relevance to group dynamics and the building and forming of a community. At the heart of prospect-refuge theory (Dosen and Ostwald 2013, 9–23; Kopec 2006, 82–84) is the idea that the qualities and attributes of a space (particularly including volume, configuration and access to natural light and outlook) can significantly influence a person's emotional response to that space. The theory positions that an enclosed or sheltered space will evoke a feeling of safety, relaxation or protection, while a view out from that space (prospect) can add levels of stimulation and excitement when feeling protected (refuge). Having a clear understanding of how humans perceive and use space is an important aspect and impacts human development and culture. Spatial cultures are developed through being able to be content in space, but also being able to communicate and view other humans during their activities. Usually, there is a delicate line between creating the right levels of privacy and communicative spaces for the community. Most public spaces apply a mixed-use approach which allows for individuals and groups to operate. Workspaces encourage both dedicated individual work and team/collaborative working and require a strong mixed economy where workers can be viewed working individually and also actively communicating as a team. Most modern new offices concentrate on this. They usually have clear sightlines to daylight and limits to how deep

98 Determining spatial culture

their design footprints are to allow as much natural light into the office as possible. They use much glazing to surface the internal spaces so that long vistas through the building can be created. The use of atria is also an important feature of bringing the light down from the roof into the office levels.

One significant feature of the design of space within cities is its level of control. By exploring other futuristic interpretations of space like the futuristic society imagined in 1931 in Aldous Huxley's (2007) *Brave New World*. His promise of technology and efficiency forces a level of control on the population. His big brother society used space as a metaphor for control in a new sinister society where the *World State* organised the world of mass production, standardisation and predictability. He presented a new world where space, technology and human freedoms were integrated. Today, Huxley's dystopian ideal for the city has been realised through some of the initiatives around smart cities and architecture. When this is combined with modernist ideology, a strong metaphor for the city as a *thinking machine* can be shaped. Technology has enabled buildings and space to collate knowledge and to *think* for themselves, responding, reacting and altering to the presence of humans. This bond between humans and technology is triggered through the developments of spatial automation, surface and soft robotics and augmented realities. Hnilica (2020, 68–83) creates an interesting discussion around the city and body as the machine, and positions future human behaviours somewhere between "cybernetic hybrids of organisms and machines" (Gandy 2005, 26–49) and a collective swarm intelligence that adjusts the nature of the city through humanised data and "technical systems". She develops ideas of city intelligence with a "memory-like storage system" that can "pass on complex cultures from generation to generation thanks to their storage facilities in buildings, street patterns, monuments" etc. By utilising emerging urban intelligence and knowledge, new agility and urban acumen to the cultures within a city can be explored. This secures and promotes a new articulation of how spatially arranged knowledge can be used to futurise the cultural landscape.

Cultural Trail

By using the figurative realm this chapter has formed a bridge between the ethereal and the physical. By exploring the atmosphere of place, it is possible to be able to recognise the importance of spatial character. By centring the descriptions of *Genius Loci* (Exner and Pressel 2009, 18–19; Norberg-Schulz 1980, 3–18) the annotations of spatial atmosphere as a "force-field" sharpen the figurative terrain of cultural space. Whilst atmosphere can be described figuratively, it can form through exposure to cultural aspects and experience. This chapter gives a series of examples and case studies that reveal the crossover between space being seen as a wholistic transmitter of culture or as a cultural container (of objects and activities), whilst many of the figurative descriptions in this chapter aim to dispel the idea of spatial territory and instead focus on the sensory movement and diversity of culture through space. The scale at which most festivals or street parties operate indicates that cultural diversity forms both a strong sense of belonging and a form of *tribal* herding. In many cases, the festival event is as much the culture, as the collective culture it is trying to promote. By developing the nature of enclosure concerning culture, it is possible to separate how different internal spaces have different cultural dynamics. If you begin to explore the cultures of working, living, bathing and relaxation spaces you are able to begin to understand the context of how people wish to live their lives. This leads to exploring the methods and processes that spatial cultures change and alter. Many of these methods naturally evolved, where humans alter cultures attached to space through new uses and a more evolutionary process. Other methods are more influenced, enforced and controlling, often driven by technological developments which are changing the understanding of space and time, further accelerating cultural change. The timeline for these is difficult to either predict or form, and suggests that the relationship between space and culture in a figurative manner is constantly evolving. The following chapter explores four themes based on a sensory realm.

Notes

1 A collection of works by the Eames studio is available in Ince (2015, 35–67).
2 A rich source of discussion around Taste within a spatial context can be found in Plunkett (2020). Of particular note is the opening discussion within the prologue which highlights the individuality of spatial taste and cultural reference in the domestic space.
3 A good example of a Renaissance painting with an inside and outside reference is the image of St Jerome in his Study by Antonello 1479 in Casson (1968, 4). (Courtesy of the National Gallery).
4 The High Line can be accessed here: https://www.thehighline.org/
5 The Castlefield sky park can be accessed here: https://www.nationaltrust.org.uk/visit/cheshire-greater-manchester/castlefield-viaduct
6 World Health Organization recommends a temperature of 18°C for well-dressed healthy individuals. For reference: Lane, Megan (2011-03-03). "BBC News Magazine: How warm is your home". BBC News. Archived from the original on 2017-12-31 or *WHO Housing and Health Guidelines*. World Health Organization. 2018. pp. 34, 47–48. ISBN 978-92-4-155037-6
7 An introduction to phenomenological processes of experience is available in Zahavi (2018).

6

EXPLAINING SPATIAL CULTURE

Comfort, Object, Surface, Experience

This chapter explores four thematic sections (Comfort, Object, Surface, Experience) through a sensory realm and their connected spatial relationships with each other and the human condition. It explores the optical and haptic senses concerning these themes explaining tactile material aspects of spatial culture. The themes are descriptions of mostly physical aspects of spatial experience (urban architecture and interior) and therefore are more tangible (bringing a sense of reality) to the descriptions and how culture is determined and located. They are used when planning and completing the design of space and are reinterpreted in this context to demonstrate their impact, effect and contribution to the experience and assemblies of space. The chapter includes the use of spatial case studies that explain cultural meaning amongst the diverse types of human occupants and the spatial environments.

Comfort

As a way to explain a human dimension to space, the use and application of comfort in space are directly related to its use and purpose as a place. Using the common parlance of "being out of my comfort zone" it is possible to explore what is comfortable and what is not. The phrase suggests that being out of your comfort zone is a place which is generally uncomfortable but palatable enough to be able to succeed. This is a decision that individuals make and the overused phrase tends to suggest that most humans are often in a place that is generally uncomfortable. This is not strictly true, as most humans usually insist on being comfortable. Rarely does any form of architecture or design actively make space an uncomfortable experience. There are of course exceptions and certainly, the work of Daniel Libeskind (2018, 154) and his architectures of the holocaust are designed specifically to make

DOI: 10.4324/9781003270393-7

the visitor experience uncomfortable. He describes good building design as having a sense of "strangeness" or "otherness", making it "surprising, thought-provoking and meaningful". Others use design to explore the boundaries of human experience, pushing humans to explore new experiences. Theme parks and funfairs with a culture of "fun" often push the boundaries of un-comfortability or even go as far as jolting the pain barriers. But most spatial design solutions consider carefully human physiology and specifically the diversity of the human body and its receptiveness to motion, stillness, transition or other forms of targeted use. This can apply to both domestic and commercial settings. If you consider this in the context of the workplace, employers are targeted to ensure that the spaces in which workers are employed are safe and flexible enough to be usable and "comfortable" for the widest diversity of the population (ideally more than a 95 percentile of the population).

Humans strive to construct living (domestic) spaces to be exceptionally comfortable. The culture of home design is based around usually making it as comfortable as possible, suggesting that individual comfort is part of the culture of the home. It is important here to separate the difference between comfort and luxury. The comfort of space is about providing a minimum and a range of support for the senses (usually to do with softness) and the body (in varying degrees to personal specification) to make the time spent at home restful and relaxing. Luxury is about comfort too but is usually associated with a higher level of opulence and quality which can be associated with unnecessary need or cost. But comfort is not necessarily about adding softness to a space, it is about a reassurance that the space can become comforting (both physically and mentally) to the occupants who are in it. Highmore (2014, 1–11) moves the direction away from traditional cultures of comfort instead suggesting that it is the kitchen that offers a perfect condition of the comfort of the home. "The kitchen combines industrial precision and homely comforts". He explores both the physical comfort of the space and introduces the comforting notion of food through production and consumption.

Comfort can be achieved both in an exterior and interior context and has a multitude of applications for the body. The climate, weather or man-made exterior environment can be pleasantly comfortable for human beings. The warmth of the sun, the softness of the sand and the calmness of the water all provide comfort. In the urban environment, the parks, gardens, beaches, riverfronts, cityscapes and urban walks provide a comforting richness to being in the city. Hard surfaces can bring comfort and reassurance to the built environment by providing solidity, organisation and structure to man-made spaces. By contrast, internal spaces are usually fully controlled with comfort levels increasing and changing as they switch between the more permanent hard-surface cultures of the exterior, to the more agile and responsive surfaces of the inside. Internally the concept of comfort changes

102 Explaining spatial culture

and it moves from the environment surrounding the body to touching and supporting the body creating comfort and "a sense of humanity" (Crawford and Thompson 2005). Casson (1968, 17) positions two distinct approaches for the spatial designer. One was an "integrated" process where the interior design is integrated with the structure, form and texture of the architecture. The second is "superimposed" onto the architecture, where the agility and flexibility of the interior add new levels of comfort, transforming the architectural space. This superimposed comfort level is part of the layering process of the built environment which helps develop an emotional response to the space, in turn impacting human psychological needs (Kaplan and Kaplan 1977, 43–45). The soft elements of the interior provide a richness of comfort, enclosing and wrapping the user within the interior space. Consider the lengths that hotels go to ensure their guests have a comfortable stay. The variations in the softness of the pillows and different firmness of the mattress all ensure the guests enjoy a personalised stay. Work environments are also protected through governing laws to ensure that the comfort of their workers is controlled. Businesses need to ensure that both the work environment (air quality, building sounds) and environment control are fully considered. These are specific kinds of cultures manipulated through spatial practice.

The furniture company IKEA has reinterpreted Sweden's attitudes towards domestic living, design aesthetics and national identity to build a successful furniture design brand. By reviewing the principles and processes of comfort related to their furniture, it is possible to identify how specific Scandinavian design traits and cultural sensitivity have specific aesthetics. One is very clean and modern (as is much of IKEA's styling) with crisp styling and clear open spaces. This modernity comes with the use of hard but often shaped materials which encourage hygienic, purposeful and colourful spaces. The other aesthetic is soft using textiles fabrics in a layered technique to introduce a deliberate softness and curve to the spatial aesthetic. The Scandinavian climate encourages a temporal nature to comfort by introducing and reintroducing layers as the temperature changes. These changes are introduced gradually (much like the seasons) and are specifically placed within the interior setting to focus on areas of comfort. This deliberate methodology separates the areas of function (working, eating etc) from the spaces of leisure. IKEA has actively influenced the cultures of space through two distinct innovations. One is the ubiquitous laminate floor which allows a distinct flexibility of comfort within the home. The other area is stackable storage, where seasonality for clothing and items for the home are regularly placed in storage and brought back out depending on the comfort levels required. These two areas have actively influenced the cultural use of the comfort of the home.

However, what is specifically revealing about the examples discussed above is that comfort is very much an individual constituent. It might be argued that comfort levels can quite easily be aligned with Hall's (1990) personalised distance and proximity rings. The intimate ring allows for items to touch the body and the other rings provide a graduated level of ambient comfort. The philosophy of comfort within space allows a level of perception and anticipation of where and how comfort is appreciated. If we consider a seaside bench overlooking the sea, the bench itself could be made from hard timber or stone and not necessarily be perceived as being comfortable and more as a temporary perch. But with the associated sea view, the bench in its location takes on a much more relaxing and comfortable setting. The view and the spatial expanse of the location help to add additional levels of comfort/pleasure to the mind as well as the perceived comfort of the seating. Conversely, a battered sofa with exposed springs initially suggests comfort, but would not be able to support the human body correctly and is a non-comforting experience.

An example of an application of comfort is through the architectural masterpiece by Mies van der Rohe called the Farnsworth House (Figure 6.1).

FIGURE 6.1 Farnsworth House. Mies van der Rohe 1951
[Generic (CC by 2.0)] https://flickr.com/photos/julielion/52344533384/in/photolist-2nKvq7U-2jR7dCU-ghkuhG-5stsdg-ghkPKw-2jR2Lrp-2hF7fMt-2jR7dD5-2jR2Lre-2hF7gjq-2hF4vAE-7SKviF-5Gd7zN-2jR6juV-2nKw4fN-2kKU6Gu-bMb88T-bMb8n6-2MRUs7-2MRW71-9Gbugw-4HnWXA-2MRSCL-9G8zBn-2MS5iW-2MS56h-2MRUFL-2MMtDX-9Gbu2S-2MMBDk-9Gbuko-9GbtWm-2MMH3p-2MMvUX-2MMGCV-2MRUcb-2MMvEr-2MRTdY-2MMxM8-2MRVWU-2MMG3e-2MMxfc-2MS6j7-2MRSoY-2MRVGN-2MMFMZ-2MMFnr-2MRRyW-2MRWjG-2MMGQi

104 Explaining spatial culture

This architectural gem was designed in 1950 by the architect for Edith Farnsworth (a wealthy American). The brief was to design and construct a small summerhouse on her grounds but caused much friction between the architect and his client. Much of the disagreement was around the nature of comfort. She was very keen for a relaxing weekend summer house to be built in the image of a small cottage. It would be welcoming, warm and comfortable. Van der Rohe had other modernist ideas, producing a ground-breaking modernist pavilion elevated from the ground made of glass, concrete and steel. It was highly minimal and had almost no softness to it at all. It was described by Stephen Bailey (2021) "as visceral as intellectual". Regarded as one of the purest examples of *international style* modernist architecture, it was beautifully crafted, but once completed was filled with soft textiles and unsympathetic but comfortable furniture on the inside, jarring with the crisp plains of the architecture. The two of them were conflicted and the project was beset by controversy.

Comfort is decisively individual but this naturally changes with alterations to the body, age and preference. It can be seen as a way to entice and enrich the spatial setting. It can be free-flowing and open to interpretation and is also controlled and measured. Some spaces are not designed to be comfortable and require only minimal contact with the user. Some spaces are actively designed to only be comfortable for certain periods. Others are designed to positively support the body and ensure that it is as comfortable as possible whilst allowing for the body to continue to function normally. Comfort can be used psychologically to encourage humans to dwell or stay within space, enveloping the body haptically through sensory receptors or something more figurative and interpretive like atmosphere. In commercial settings spaces are required to be comfortable and human-centred, encouraging interaction and use. If we consider an interior culture within a bar, comfortable seating will encourage customers to stay, socialise and spend more money. But this would have to be combined with other cultural phenomena like a positive atmosphere and good service. In this setting, comfort is important in setting the physical scene, but other types of spatial culture are required to form a more complete experience. A further example is the use of carpets within retail department stores. Whilst carpet is a commonly used surface in retail environments, it presents many powerful psychological statements. Firstly, carpeting represents a higher level of quality than a hard floor and when a carpet is laid in certain parts of the store it actively slows people down as they pass through the retail environment. So hard-set passageways through department stores tend to encourage passage through the spaces to get to somewhere else. Carpet, encourages much more leisurely movement, making people pause, stop and circulate. This design is intended to encourage retail purchases.

Comfort can be perceived through the tactility of the skin. Pallasmaa (2012) asks us to consider the other senses within the body to understand space. If we walk into a hotel, there are usually three key concerns that we consider carefully as we arrive at our new hotel room. First is usually around the space and light of the room. Many hotel rooms are set out in a formulaic fashion with the main room being an L-shape and the bathroom usually being tucked in by the entry door completing a rectangle plan. However, the other two key considerations are usually the cleanliness of the room (usually the bathroom toilet and the bed). This is certainly an important consideration as hotel rooms are used repetitively and guests are keen not to see any form of traces of the previous occupant in a hotel room as they arrive. The final consideration, and usually the one that emerges more slowly as you work your way into the room is the level of comfort. Importantly, in hotel rooms, comfort is also directly associated with luxury (see descriptions above). Luxury is usually associated with the level of cost of the room. So, the comfort of the bed (hard or soft) is critical to individual satisfaction, but so are all the seating, cushions, curtains and towels. These textiles add significantly to the levels of comfort/luxury and set a certain level of expectation of the spatial culture that is presented within each hotel.

Object

> Most household objects began their lives to fill a need … Something to lie on, sit on, cooking from, drink from, chase away the dark. That doesn't mean they were always plain, humans being seem to be drawn to beauty. Once the basic need of food and shelter were taken care of, people had time to enjoy at the impulses to decorate the living spaces. Utility became luxury.
>
> *(Azzarito 2020, 7)*

As a way to begin to consider objects as elements of spatial culture, it is critical to consider some historical contacts for how and why objects were placed in space. From the early forms of shelter, space that was created for protection was adorned with practical and personal objects, forming part of an ancient human condition. Objects and adornments help identify and improve the environment, making it more suitable for dwelling and conditioning the beginning of the human experience. More permanent settlements formed locations for towns and cities, encouraging a more stable view of habitation which further anchored living and working to build more established communities. This would happen locally, slowly building regional communities around agriculture, industry, commerce and manufacturing. Cultures began to form using the activities and objects of farming. But through the Industrial Revolutions of the nineteenth century, the need, style and aesthetics of manufacture influenced production and progress for objects and "things" for the spatial setting.[1]

Industrial housing was produced as a way to improve the conditions of the workers and encouraged the development of the interior as a more

106 Explaining spatial culture

permanent, individual and normal part of everyday life. (See Bournville references in Chapter 2.) Whilst the architecture was similar, the workers improved their living conditions by making their homes as personalised as they could, bringing the ideas of individualism and separation of space. Many of the objects produced were used in domestic settings as markers and talismans of success or celebration. This included the use of religious iconography and the need for furniture, developing objects that could be sat or lay upon as part of the development of civilisation and hierarchy. If you could sit on something that had been crafted and manufactured rather than a tree stump, then you were seen as having higher status. Furniture was used by royalty and elevation as a mark and symbol of their rank. Indeed, the furniture was used to physically elevate the king to ensure that he sat higher than anyone else. Much of the anthropology and culture created by ancient objects are key to understanding much of the spatial cultures around today.

However, the object in space is not confined just to the chair in a room, a vase on the shelf, or the artwork on the wall. By definition, an object is the opposite of a space. It usually has a convex surface as opposed to a concave one. It is also determined by different forms of human scale. In Miller's (2008) account of domestic portraits in London, he outlines the importance of the object in space. He describes how each object, or collection of objects in each of the domestic portraits is used to express personal perspectives. He describes what an object is and how its temporal nature is changed regularly to suit different situations and moods. He describes the attention to detail presented by each household.

> They put up ornaments, they laid down carpets, they selected furnishings and got dressed that morning. Some things may be gifts or objects retained from the past, but they have decided to live with them, to place them in lines or higgledy-piggledy; they made a room minimalist or crammed it to the gills. These things are not a random collection. They have been gradually accumulated as an expression of that person or household. Surely if we can learn to listen to these things, we have access to an authentic other voice.
>
> *(Miller 2008, 2)*

There are powerful sensorial relationships formed between the formulations of space and objects; these relationships are often symbiotic as well as contextual. The quote above positions objects in space as having a temporal context, a personal timeline that gets altered and adjusted as time passes. This feels highly personal and Miller's work reveals the importance of individuals and their collective lives. It also brings into focus the importance of *collections* that surround people and how this gives a strong sense of wellness, familiarity and reassurance in spatial settings (Figure 6.2). This gives a strong sensuality to space and the movement of objects (within space) helps

Explaining spatial culture 107

FIGURE 6.2 Object collections from a domestic dwelling
Author

to frame and locate space. By occupying space with objects, the space becomes performative and curatorial, allowing it to become a representation and presentation of the self. This further reinforces Lefebvre's (1991) representations of space (perceived, conceived, lived), deepening the connections between personal (and social) space and objects. Hicks (1979, 79) highlights

108 Explaining spatial culture

an evolving process using objects in space. He describes objects as having a particular interest to him personally, building a sense of desire or wonderment. As part of his design practice, he constructed a series of "tablescapes" which presented objects as a collection and described the method as grouping objects of "vaguely similar texture, colour and character" as a way to culturally theme space. He continues by suggesting blank (table) surfaces are better than the wrong objects (at the wrong scales) placed together. In his descriptions, he promotes the idea of importing cultural iconography into spaces (like museums), which is both used holistically to dress the space and to use the history (and culture) of the pieces to bring a level of authenticity to the space.

Each of the objects (in Figure 6.2) offers different cultural representations (individually) and meaning (collectively) and is defined by the objects that are placed in space. Hillier and Hanson (1997, 9) suggest that this relationship can be humble and that the social "subject" and the spatial "object" act as distinct entities, concluding that social behaviours are derived directly from the construction and ordering of space. He introduced the idea of the de-socialisation of space and the de-spatialisation of society as a newly constructed spatial syntax. These relationships power the structures between a city, community, architecture and the interior and are important to determine the holistic user experience. Architecture forms the spatial enclosure which facilitates the existence of the interior. It is a fundamental aspect that determines the space in which the interior is used. The interior is the dressed human interface with the architecture. It is the narrative by which the space can be identified, used and occupied. Conversely, how the architecture is formed also affects the interior experience. Internal interventions like columns and walls divide and influence the space. External windows and doors also create corridors and access points through the space and influence the available internal volumes. Other architectural aspects like floor plates, atria and building floor configuration all impact the design and the interiority of the space.

Surface

Surfaces have become the constructed, visual, communicative and interactive objects of the built environment. As Adamson and Kelley (2013) suggest, they are "a site where complex forces meet", which summarises neatly the way a surface should be considered. When designing space, surfaces are a useful tool, they are a coating and a structure. They are "membranes, protective shells, sensitive skins" (ibid.) which populate the architecture of cities and towns. The surfaces have become part of the built environment, ever more sophisticated and uncommunicative. But they can also represent other cultural references in other forms of life. Surfaces dominate the built environment, design products and fashion. They are part of most of the reactive products that we use in everyday lives, they package our food and make transportation streamlined and beautiful. Surfaces, protect and preserve, they receive and respond to our touch, they feed back and have become self-healing and self-cleaning. In many ways, the surface has become the visual totem of the increasingly digital and modern world.

The culture of the surface is primarily a sensory realm which has been revolutionised from the humble natural material through to the use of digitalised products and mobile technology. By extending the nature of a human haptic response, space and culture have been revolutionised. This has been at various scales starting with the finger as a tool with a mobile phone. These haptic surfaces have expanded the definition of sight, touch, shape and texture. Surfaces are a significant part of the built environment and have moved from the solidity of ancient architecture (consider the mass and surface of ancient Egyptian pyramids) to the delicacy of flexible and reactive films that are used in outside venues as screens. Spatial culture has been and is being continually adjusted through the use of surfaces in space. Decoratively, the surface is used to clad, colour, ornament and paint the finishes of architecture and design and has often evolved as a method of concealing the working mechanics or construction, or, conversely of revealing them; consider examples of high-tech architecture where the surfaces are on the inside and the services on the outside (notably the Pompidou Centre, Paris and the Lloyds building London).

Most surfaces are used to cover an object, building or vehicle. They are used to pictorially decorate buildings but also are often used in repetitive pattern formations to create statements both cloaking the building (Figure 6.3) and also for establishing architectural landmarks.

Recent innovation surfaces include movable surfaces that react to light and touch. There is also a large scale surface application for architecture that adjusts to alter the shape of buildings (or their surfaces at least). The "Aegis" hyposurface[2] is a flexible metallic surface that can be manipulated to deform physically by electronic stimuli from the environment (movement, sound, light etc). It is driven by a series of pneumatic pistons which bend the facetted surface covering the building. This affects the facetted terrains that surface the building, altering the architecture, and changing the perception of the building. Whilst the project is experimental, it is easy to see how the application can be used physically, protecting the building and deflecting light aesthetically, changing how the shape of architectural surfaces and how a building appears but also its spatial presence.

While the role of the surface is changing radically today, it promises to be even more dramatically different in the future. With the application of artificial intelligence and virtual reality, the cultures of space and surface are set to change radically over the coming decade. Whilst true hapticity is still very much in its infancy, the sensitivity of touch and surface is developing all the time. The refinement between the human body and the surface of objects,

110 Explaining spatial culture

FIGURE 6.3 Surface patternation, The Broad, Los Angeles. Diller Scofidio + Renfro Photo by Joey Zanotti. [Generic (CC by 2.0)] https://flickr.com/photos/45958601@N02/47931952697/in/photolist-2niWQWo-VUhXvA-2g2zMBx-2gwHBHQ-rSzyar-WxoneS

architectures and spaces is altering the way humans interact with space. This work is transforming conventional forms of spatial cultures, making spaces highly responsive and reactive to occupation. Museums and exhibitions have transformed through the development of surface and touch. This is through developing interactive technologies as well as virtual technologies which allow the visitors to interact with the exhibits. However, much of the technology is still very much one way, where the human touch is directing the need. Although the haptic feedback gained from surfaces is still developing and improving, driving more circular information back to the user. Surfaces are significantly driving the way spaces are used and formulated. Many surfaces in the built environment protect and coat buildings, but they are increasingly becoming more interactive, decorative and communicative. Buildings have traditionally been used for large-scale advertising hoardings, and most cities have a central square where buildings act as illuminated surfaces (Piccadilly Circus, London, Times Square, New York etc.), but these are now becoming highly sophisticated holographic surfaces with three-dimensional images that "project" out into the streetscape, called 3D Anamorphic Billboards.[3]

Surfaces in space have long been used to trick and fool people with their deception. This has been used in architecture and design for millennia. The selection of materials for the construction of the built environment has traditionally relied on digging most of it out of the Earth. The hard surfaces of a building like stone, brick and marble are generally constructed from the minerals of the Earth. Some are cut and used as they are. Others are manufactured and formed from clays and stones derived from the Earth. Traditionally these have been formed and used quite truthfully. Certain properties and conditions are selected specifically for use and have constructed large parts of the built environment. Huge ancient cities have been constructed from large slabs of stone from the Earth piled up, creating elegant earthly constructions with beautiful riven surfaces, sourced from local, ubiquitous sources. But as many of these materials are expensive to mine, many of them have also been copied, where substitutes are found to reduce cost or create sheer fakery. The surfaces in the built environment are not always as they seem.

The material world is also remarkably diverse. The earthly materials are probably the easiest to understand and longest-lasting, but some of the most unsustainable. These ancient materials were rough cut from the ground providing strong and permanent shelter and developing strong cultural metaphors for space and human civilisation. Other common materials that have been used to surface elements of the urban environment are timbers. Wood is probably the most common material used for interior surfacing, architecture, building and construction purposes. If properly managed it is the most sustainable and low-carbon natural material. Timbers have been used in furniture, building construction and housing for centuries. But over time large swathes of natural forest were lost and not replaced for centuries. With large parts of the world still cutting down forests quicker than they are replacing them, there is still much work to do. Only in the last 30 years has a genuine effort been made to replace forests and make the material truly sustainable. Timber provides a natural surface, which is strong, absorbent and specifically cut very thin and applied to materials. Boarding materials made from timber products (plywood, medium-density fibreboard etc.) are ubiquitous in furniture and construction and are much more economic.

Other materials that are used for creating surfaces are ceramics, glass and metals. These materials produce a whole suite of innovations that include materials that emit their own light, have physical and shape memory, and are chemically infused to react directly with other materials. Ceramic for instance is the material that everyone is aware of through the crockery in the house. But ceramics also are an important surfacing material. They are highly hard-wearing long-lasting and extremely hygienic. All toilets and sanitary ware are constructed from them. Most ceramics have high thermal properties, but also can be made transparent and light admitting. Ceramics also include many cement applications which are used for walls and cladding. They are also important in surfacing applications as most ceramics are heat resistant. Glass is a wonderful material which brings transparency and

112 Explaining spatial culture

building surface applications. It can be cast almost into any shape and is fully recyclable. It is very hard and heat resistant and can be drawn into tiny threads that enable superfast communication. Glass also brings light, luminosity and electrical applications to the built environment. All solar power is collected through glass surfacing and panels.

It is important at this stage also to mention the discipline of material culture and the anthropological relationship to the body in the senses (Tilley 2013, 125–186). This is described as a form of reality grounded in the social context by objects, architecture and people. It also includes the creation, consumption and usage of objects as well as including other cultural reference points like behaviours, ideas and rituals. It is a broad discipline and includes references to the use of materials but is concerned with the relationship of materials concerning cultural, social and historical contexts. Attention to the role of material culture in human society has focused on emphasising the representation of an idea (or object) that is an integrated dimension of culture and that there are dimensions of social existence that cannot be fully understood without it. But there is a difference between how material and culture are commonly regarded, often being driven in directly opposing contexts of the physical and intellectual realms. Ingold (2018, 88) deermines that "culture both drives what people do in their environment and finishes the means by which they adapt to it." Instead of behaviours, "Material Culture" frames a relationship between "things" and a cultured human society as an integrated part of being human and living together with others. However, this should not be confused with materialism, which has a more historical and socially constructed backstory. Harman (2018, 135–137, 258) outlines materialism as a historical concept creating a division between what is material and what is not. His discussion focuses on the notion of "matter" and specifically the relationship to objects. He distances his concept of object-orientated-ontology from materialism. By rationalising the divisions of how culture is embodied in an environment we can begin to unpick how object cultures are embedded in and influenced by human society.

Experience

When considering the design of space and how it impacts human physiology and psychology, it is important to consider the experience of space. On a physical level, the spatial experience is explained by our senses. The exterior information of the site and environment comes into our bodies through our receptors, building a complex map of our environment. Some of this we choose to focus upon and some we ignore. But this allows us to gather an understanding of the *spirit of the place* (Genius Loci), *the site* or *the space* (and sometimes all three, but not usually simultaneously) that we are occupying either directly or indirectly. But our senses also fluctuate and give us pieces of information, snapshots and perspectives that help us understand where we are and what we are doing. By understanding our levels of need,[4] we can start to understand the instinctive basis upon which we form and develop experience and how central the range of needs is to the environment. Experience is built from both physical (external senses) and immaterial (internal senses) aspects. Perception, memory, intelligence, personality and emotion all contribute to the spatial experience that can build the spatial environment for the user. When we design environments we have to consider how the human body will react to any given environment. This of course is also individual, and all experiences of environments are nuanced specifically to the individual. Also, humans have an inbuilt sense of precognition to spaces that they might occupy. Anticipation and planning also help humans understand what their spatial experience might be. This builds a psychological expectation of space. If we apply this to the theatre and the sense of performance we get a deeper understanding of "stage fright". Understanding what an experience in space will be like (even if you have been there before) is part of the experience-building process.

One of the distinctive elements of the spatial environment is developing an "experience" of space. The ultimate experience is where every sense is tingling and telling you about different experiential aspects of the spatial experience impacting your body. However, whilst often fun and exhilarating this means that all the senses are being triggered at the same time (Figure 6.4). The best forms of experience are where this is gradual and structured. This could be

FIGURE 6.4 Citizen M Hotel, Victoria London
Author

114 Explaining spatial culture

through an intimate restaurant with high-quality food, an interactive museum that enables knowledge through a new form of learning, or a huge architectural atrium that sets out the spatial impact. This experience is not necessarily time-based and is often a series of connected experiential dioramas and moments experienced by the user.

Sight provides the initial context for the understanding of place using light. This builds an understanding of the scale and size of the space, the colour, the patterns and how the space is orientated and planned. Using hearing allows direction and balance to be created. Sound levels of movement and ambient music or digital devices alert us to the other human users of the space. Sound also helps to orientate us, building experiential profiles of the environment, detecting materials and the volumes of the spaces. Haptic sensors[5] help us to use touch to understand surfaces and the proximity of items, people and interior surfaces. The taste and smell systems tend to work in harmony and are essential in building nostalgia and heritage. As the smell sense is a powerful tool connected with memory, it is a background sense, but can deliver important messages evoking and building interior experiences. A smell can reconstitute memory and can often hold the key to unlocking old memories of places, ensuring that lost experiences remain deep within our subconscious. Taste is not as powerful as smell, but taste sense helps construct experience and is often attributed to the "now" experience of the digital age. Taste helps develop strong cultural tags involving food and drink and often is the conduit when understanding the cultural location and developing semiotic spatial experiences. Food is a powerful cultural marker that can build repetitions of experiences and helps to unlock other biological senses that enrich the sense of space, like balance, temperature, time, movement and volume.

It is the unseen senses that help glue the experience and spatial narrative together; Böhme (2017, 29) describes the phenomenon of spatial atmospheres as "vague, indeterminate, intangible". Human psychology of spatial experience allows an exploration of non-physical activities in space. When all levels of thought are applied (in spatial perception, memory, intelligence, personality and emotion) to physical activity (as it naturally happens), it creates a more rounded detail of the physical experience. In particular, memory, where the brain gathers, stores and retrieves information is vital to human experiences and boosts the context for physical actions. The unfolding action connects with other momentary experiences, building and retaining a composite 3-dimensional picture of what has occurred. This binds the spatial and cultural experiences into a catalogue of life experiences, building knowledge and wisdom that use the interior as a backdrop to the "lived experience".[6]

Cultural Trail

Visual cultures stem from the range of objects and images that refer to media designed for purposes of perception or developing our visual capability and knowledge. The area of exploration is broad and encompasses both academic and mainstream media applications. It is defined mainly through the critical nature of the visual image including static and moving, electronic and digital. It embraces different creative disciplines have different forms of visual culture and often communicates in different ways. Importantly visual culture also questions what the visual can mean, developing cognitive science, image and understanding. It is both part of the design of the environment and the location of culture in space. Connected to this is material culture which deals with the study and inquiry of objects, resources and spaces that reflect and define different societies and environments. By drawing from the practices of social sciences and humanities its interdisciplinary nature sheds light upon objects, their properties, materials, and the way the relationship with people and things affects our understanding of space.

Less developed, but equally important are aural (Sound), olfactory (Smell) and gustatory (Taste) cultures that are used to define typology and wider experiences of space. These senses help to stretch the phenomenon of space (as centred by Pallasmaa [2012], Steven Holl [2019], Peter Zumthor [2006] and Kenneth Frampton [2001]) using multi-dimensional sensory abilities. The human body can sense, react and understand space using many of the senses simultaneously. This allows an understanding of the space and the experience to be used to build a picture of the environment from different perspectives. This mobile sensing enables a snapshot of space but then moves into the concept of place which surrounds the body in motion contributing directly to the spatial cultural canon. The next chapter completed the understanding of spatial culture through a textural realm which explores the final four themes drawing the threads of space and culture together.

Notes

1 An important reference on the objects of the home is Forty (1995, 11–28).
2 An example of this is the hypo surface available at www.hyposurface.org and http://www.decoi-architects.org/2011/10/hyposurface/
3 An example of the 3D Anamorphic Billboards is Meta Quest https://www.youtube.com/watch?v=CKQoXx6pqAA.
4 A good place to start analysing the need within the interior related to experience is the Theory of Human Motivation (1943). Abraham Maslow outlines a theoretical mechanism that humans use to motivate their behaviours. This paper is a seminal work outlining a pyramid structure that creates human need and can be directly applied to the environment by the three components of self-fulfilment, psychological, and basic needs.
5 Hapticity is an important growing sense for the interior. Globally, with the development of smart screen technology, our sense of touch has been overhauled, making us more conditioned to how touch can make us feel and enrich our experience. The interior has been transformed with hyper-sensitive materials and touch-active technology ensuring this sense has become a fully fledged global

116 Explaining spatial culture

sense-building experience. A good reference for this is the work by Architect Juhani Pallasmaa (2012).
6 "Lived experience" is the concept that experience is gained from everyday life and the phenomena of living. Further reading should include Lefebvre (1991, Chapters 2, 3, 4).

7

UNDERSTANDING SPATIAL CULTURE

Colour, Light, Taste and Place

This final central chapter completes the examination of spatial culture through a textural realm which explores the final four themes (Colour, Light, Taste and Place). These themes are used to explain the nuances and subtleties of the urban, architectural and interior environment and how these impact the experience and representation of the cultures of space. These themes can be described as ethereal in nature but often critically influence the atmosphere and feeling of the space. By defining a textural realm, we build a deeper patternation of spatial volume allowing spaces to be understood more definitively, enriching the spatial experience. The themes are visceral in architectural and interior forms and help define the exteriority and interiority of space concerning aesthetics, texture and emotion. They explain space in different ways forming textuality, agility and mobility of space, by changing the temporal ways and formats (second, minute, daily, annually), depending on the relationships between natural and human contexts. They are also dependent on individual proclivity, both immediately and in a forecasting mode. Interestingly they are all interrelated textual themes, impacting each other through the selection, trends, scales and locations of the space. The textuality and personalisation of spaces differ depending on their integration and trans-scalar levels of exposure and intimacy. De Certeau (1988, 118–120) sets out a compelling proposition called "the narrative fabric". He draws from a medieval rectilinear mapping of space, in a series of "tours" and "maps" of urban and domestic spaces. Whilst much of this mapping is (traditionally) aerial, he describes a series of passageways through spaces as both symbolic and anthropological language, shifting the emphasis from an "ordinary" spatial culture to a scientific one. By documenting the movement and recognition of space in this way, an unfolding textural narration emerges which surrounds the human body and dispels traditional boundaries. This spatial journeying

DOI: 10.4324/9781003270393-8

118 Understanding spatial culture

encourages deep textural connections between "ordinary" structural navigation and the themes which simulate the senses (and memory) cohering experience with both traversing the spatial environment and establishing a recognisable cultural presence.

Colour

Colour is a fundamental component of how we experience the world around us. It is often seen as a statement; it directs and anchors trends and is a wonderfully joyous gift that most humans can enjoy. Remarkably, the human eye can recognise over 1 million colours, shades and tones. But the human eye "sees" colour as reflected light (or coloured light) bouncing off a surface. It receives this information, processes it and recognises the tone, shadow and colour of that light. We are taught from an early age what colour is and at school we learn about the range of main (Primary) colours and their relationships to each other, and how pigments (and light) colours are formed.

The visible spectrum there is also remarkably small compared to the entire electromagnetic range. St Clair (2016, 13–21) documents the mechanics of the eye and how each of the sections of the retina absorbs different forms of colour and light. She makes a point on deception arguing "the colour we perceive an object to be is precisely the colour it isn't: that is, the segment of the spectrum that is being reflected away". Our eye's role is to receive light into the back of the eye and for the light-sensitive cells (rods and cones) to absorb and respond to certain kinds of black and white and coloured light. The rods deal with shadow and low levels of light and are very sensitive. The cones which are placed in the centre of the retina absorb colour wavelengths. Humans can detect shadow, density, hue and huge tonal ranges. Humans use colour to align human activity and recognition. Each group of colours represent different messages and signals. These groups of colours are ingrained into our cultural identities. Many of these identities are signals from our human body or the environment that surrounds us. Whether it is the colours that we see or associate with the body, our immediate environment, or our planet, we use instinctive and historical contexts for the colour, to help make sense of and understand our world. As human civilisation developed, colours took on special meanings and cultural significance. Early civilisations used natural colours to signify, display and demark territories. Civilisations built cities from single materials giving a unified colour presence of the built environment. Colour is used to create identity and unity, often derived from the colours of the national flag. This national identity and cohesion help to collectively cohere nationalism and strength of cultural character. Community and societal groups use colour as a state of belonging and harmony. Throughout human civilisation, colour and its associated cultures (pigment and light) have been imperative to the broad representation of human society and its performative cultures (Figure 7.1).

Understanding spatial culture 119

FIGURE 7.1 TV Studio – Eurovision song contest Stockholm 2016
Photo by David Jones. [Generic (CC by 2.0)] https://flickr.com/photos/davidc
jones/33225534494/in/photolist-2n7n3gw-SC2xR1-Tju7iu-TECfUd-SEK6AD-TUr
J1Z-SC2AC3-SC2A6b-Tju85Q-Tju89N-TECh5E-Tju8FE-Tju8Ho-TUrLPK-SC2CcL-SE
K7Ua-TECfhm-SEJXtX-SEJXog-TQTouh-TECkLs-SEJYQz-TECiMh-TjtZcW-SEKbqi-
SEJZjv-SEKcya-TjtXS1-SEJXXH-SEJWJv-SEKbRZ-Tjub9A-Tju9py

When we begin looking into the cultures of colour, the early exponents and masters of the Bauhaus Design Schools in Germany (1919–1933) began to explore and reveal the importance of colour and its relationship to form. They actively introduced colour training to their students in the design of objects, through painting composition and harmonisation. By developing harmony of colour, they provided a rich commentary on how colour could be used in the formation of design. Three of the most interesting exponents of the use of colour of the Bauhaus School were Paul Klee (1973), Josef Albers (1963) and a relatively unknown master Gertrud Grunow (Rössler and Otto 2019). Klee developed his own colour theories based on the associations in nature. He specifically used the conventional theories on complementary colours to examine a non-authentic pairing of colours by moving around the colour wheel. His colour theory was called the "canon of colour totality" which described the changing dynamics of colour through movement. This movement was the physical movement of pigment on canvas but also the movement of light throughout the day. Paul Klee's students were encouraged to experiment with three primary colours and the pendulum movement across the colour circle. He continually experimented with the expressive power of colour, breaking the traditional rules. His colleague

120 Understanding spatial culture

Josef Albers set the mark for understanding the interactions of colour, significantly developing colour knowledge and its contribution to visual culture. His work examining colour juxtaposition deepened the appreciation of colour use and application. He specifically worked on demonstrating the quality of colour on both canvas and in space. His extensive colour exploration positioned the harmony of spaces (concerning colour) as a critical part of both colour development and the use of colour in society.

> Colors appear connected predominantly in space. Therefore, as constellations they can be seen in any direction in any speed. And as they remain, we can return to them repeatedly and in many ways.
>
> *(Albers 1963, 39)*

Grunow was a musician and theorist who explored the relationships between colour, sound and movement. In the Bauhaus course, this was called the theory of harmonisation and became a central pillar of the early Bauhaus theories and practice. She advocated the use of all the sensory organs in an equal and harmonious manner, using the body and movement in space to describe colour. She explored the various relationships between colour, tone, form and materiality, integrating the essential elements of artistic practice as taught at the Bauhaus into her teaching. She encouraged her students to gain greater access to body and soul, letting consciousness and intellect recede into the background, instructing them to imagine a colour as an inner light that contributed to the development of a colour culture, the body and space.

It is important to note that colour cannot exist without light simply because colours are other names for various mixtures of radiant and electromagnetic energy. Colour is also divided using pigmented colour and light colour. Both are formed from slightly different primary and secondary colours and the principle of "mixing" applies to both. These can be seen in modern printers which have three coloured cartridges and a black one and can produce all colours when mixed accurately. Light undergoes a similar process; three coloured lanterns and white light can illuminate a stage with any colour when mixed in certain quantities. Colour harmony is achieved when arranging colours into practical colour schemes that harmonise with each other. There are many colour systems which use a systematic approach to determine colour harmonies and develop guidelines for arranging colours based on an ordered and layered approach. Architects and designers establish a colour scheme when selecting colours which are interpreted and modified according to the situation. Most colour schemes do not follow these rules exactly and are often arranged through experience and by the "eye" and should both harmonise and vibrate to create impact. Architecture and design palettes are usually described as *monochromatic* (where a single hue is used in tints, tones and shades), *analogous* (colours are used that are adjacent on the colour wheel) and *complementary* (colours are used in contrast that are directly opposite on the colour wheel). Other schemes including *neutrals, split, tetrad* and *double complementary* allow colour systems to be deployed across the built environment, shaping, controlling and stimulating behaviours. This is where coloured environments can directly impact the way human culture is formed and represented.

Light

Light and lighting are core components of the built environment and spatial experience. The human eye requires a light source for the eye to be able to receive information for the brain to be able to react and respond to the outside world. Light regulates our circadian biological rhythms (Oliver 2002, 53) that help the body determine position, alertness and fatigue (see Anthes' [2020, 81–90] descriptions of the well-living lab in Chapter 2). These rhythms are affected directly by the amount of light that surrounds the body, determining our cultural routines that involve when we sleep, when we wake, how we work, when we go out, when we stay in etc. Culturally speaking, these rhythms form routines and patterns of our behaviour. These are more biologically driven than culturally driven, but do impact directly on how and when we use space.

Natural and artificial lighting are fundamental to the interactions and satisfaction within most environments and whilst Pallasmaa (2012, 12–13) argues that humans have an occular dependence within the spatial environment, many environments are now fully navigable and equipped with inbuilt sound, tactility and olfaction so that they can be moved through without the use of only sight. Most commercial building regulations (in the UK) stipulate that all door entrances, stairs, ramps and interaction points (switches, room controls) are set out in contrasting colours so that restricted vision does not inhibit interaction with the environment. The control and flexibility of lighting form a key aspect in most urban and architectural design settings, where artificial lighting is located for beauty, safety or drama. Lighting on buildings is an important part of the cityscape and contributes to the cultural identity of place. Whether this is the night view towards the elevated Hong Kong harbour front or an urban light festival (Figure 7.2), the illuminated urban environment is a powerful demonstration of how light can both beautify and secure the environment.

Natural light and specifically sunlight impact the way the built environment is spatially and culturally represented. Ambient and light quality varies in different parts of the globe. The intensity and reflectivity of sunlight in certain parts of the Earth create a different form of ambient daylight. Countries with high levels of sunlight require building external shades and reflectors (brise soleil) so the buildings do not become overheated. The orientation of urban environments is considered by the way the sun moves over the

122 Understanding spatial culture

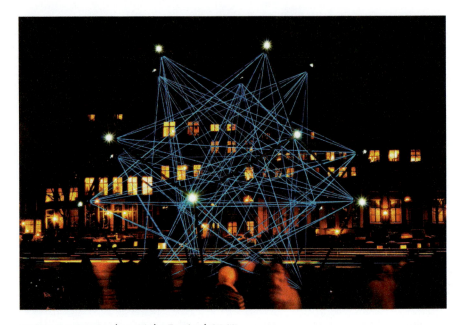

FIGURE 7.2 Amsterdam Light Festival 2015
Photo by Edwin van Buuringen. [Generic (CC by 2.0)] https://flickr.com/photos/edwinvanbuuringen/23570001530/in/photolist-BUNqhJ-dGHSJp-CMx66S-dGPjqh-2o43hx7-iKbLtj-iK9Rvi-dGHXxH-iK9QYM-BQPbBi-iKbVjf-dGPoHU-dGPnH1-2mRjArX-iSLuE7-iKbUNf-iUJf9f-iKbLpG-dGPk6w-2kR1XPe-iKbK5s-iKdSRh-qfGQNb-CDogg2-iKbn6X-2o43hwF-Cw66Dt-qdCMWS-iK9ZBP-Ch9poN-iKbmZp-CMwVGG-CMwYpA-C5cddM-CFa65i-CFa7Lz-Ch9rtE-pyJECp-iSGyKi-eMKLKE-2o3XrMX-C553xQ-pkZRRL-CB6iNy-2o3XrYU-Ct5yQk-iSJA9W-CzVo4M-gkAPtS-iKdPpN

horizon. Public squares and piazzas are designed to be shaded. Exterior activities are shaded from the sun. Societal cultures have formed to protect humans from both the heat and the light of the midday sun. These periods or siestas allow rest periods when the light and heat are intensive. However, this intensity also improves the quality of the light. This brightens colours and deepens the intensity of reflection. The rise and fall of the sun directly (sun path) impact the way the spaces of the urban environment are used. At night, artificial light illuminates most of the urban environment. Roads, streets, pathways and squares are well-lit for safety, helping to create and define the external spaces of the city. Light is used to illuminate major city landmarks, key buildings, riverbanks, bridges, and other urban "nodal" contexts.

The way the sun orientates over a city alters how natural light and shadow create urban textures and landscapes. Blending the use of natural light with artificial light changes the way internal spaces are used and perceived. Whilst sunlight is often shielded in the building, it is not desirable to completely block out sunlight, as this helps the body regulate the cycles of the day. Buildings are designed to have thinner architectural footprints to increase natural light and allow for better light control for the occupants. The interior designer brings interior cultures to life through the design and control of natural and artificial light. Light helps to guide visual tasks, shapes circulation and affects mood, determining behaviour and attitudes. Lighting contrasts the brightness and darkness of space, creating dramatic effects that emphasise spatial volume, circulation, emphasis, proportion and harmony, developing specific characteristics for space. Bright direct light is stimulating, and low levels of illumination can be quiet, soothing and meditative. Warm-coloured lights tend to be cheerful and cool-coloured lights restful. The appearance, definition, and character of objects and spaces are greatly affected by the kind of light that makes them visible. When light strikes an object, light may be reflected, absorbed, or allowed to pass through it. This will depend on the degree of texture, transparency or opacity in the material. There are many different types of lighting involved in interior spaces. These include deflectors, reflectors and shades, and the lighting sources like energy-reducing fluorescents, fibre optics, cathodes, neon and strip lights. The main groups of lighting are ambient, freestanding, track-mounted, portable, task, spot and specialist lighting. When these are applied to a spatial setting, they contribute to the cultural *spirit* (Genius Loci) of how space is perceived and understood.

Taste

Taste can be both classed as an individual and socially constructed cultural phenomenon. But care is needed that taste does not become confused with style, which is quite different. Taste is much older and has been drawn from centuries of divisions and separations within society. It does contemporise the nature of culture and suggests a temporal framework for culture to operate in, introducing cultural longevity as a potential societal boundary. As Bayley (2017, 3) critically points out, taste as a form of social discrimination was "hijacked and its meaning inflated by an influential elite [who] use the expression 'good taste' simply to validate their personal aesthetic preferences while demonstrating the vulgar presumptions of social and cultural superiority". He laments that "all human affairs are no more than a jungle of ethical and cultural relativity" but does make some powerful statements that taste is directly formed from human experiences of design architecture and the built environment. Whilst in many cases this still rings true, the cultures of interior tastes (both spatially and aesthetically) have changed incrementally and the appreciation and the care given to people's homes has considerably changed. He takes a particular swipe at the interior environment (ibid., 116–119) suggesting it is a vacuous place that not only creates specific individual tastes but drives the "helplessness and gullibility of

124 Understanding spatial culture

consumers" and infers "interior design is required only in houses where the owners have no discriminatory judgement of their own". Taste runs much deeper and is more attached to the historical cultural environment than style. It is particularly evident in western societies, where social class has shaped the differences in taste (and style) and is part of the cultural continuum which directly affects the design and aesthetics of space. But decisions of taste do not always encourage critical judgement as they can form wider attitudes and societal perspectives, with many people actively projecting their tastes without concern for social correctness or embarrassment. Kitsch is a modern phenomenon where elements of culture are selected and remodelled using flamboyant colours and decoration. It is a form of imitation and has a specific style of its own but is often used as a counterpoint to good taste. Culturally, taste (good and bad) is the basis for much social media activity, promoting "good" taste or tastes that people can relate or aspire to. The notion of taste "influencer" has been around since Prince Albert developed the idea of the Great Exhibition (1851) to improve public taste. The exhibition was popular and highly influential, both for the general public and wider society. It forged the relationships between culture, industry and design, all housed in the revolutionary Crystal Palace building in South London.

Taste (in its broadest sense) can also be seen to calibrate different groups of society. What might be deemed as taste in one's society may not be seen as taste in another. This is often deeply embedded in different communities where culturally led and societal structures play a significant part in community location or cohesion (possibly through religion, food, celebrations or other community activity) or more prosaically where social elevation is an important part of society. Taste can be through food preferences or aesthetic considerations where fashion, graphics or interior selections drive the current zeitgeist and visual modes. Significantly, as tastes change, they (and aesthetic trends) can move at different paces and can conflict with each other, giving rise to some strange visual juxtapositions in the spatial landscape. This could be through the placing of traditional furniture in a modern building or mixing of architectural styles where modest housing estate properties have been dressed with high front walls, large wrought iron gates and porches with Greek columns and porticoes over the front door. Whilst this aesthetic might be acceptable, it can generate mixed reactions and often creates new hybrid forms of visual cultures. Plunkett (2020, 109–128) comments on the mid-century, post-war desire to update interior tastes by stripping out Victorian ornamentation and to "remove mouldings, in the name of hygiene and easy maintenance. Crumbling cornices and old fireplaces, which collected dirt and were difficult to repair, were removed. Door mouldings were hidden behind sheets of hardboard, the rudimentary, easy-to-paint sheet material, the forerunner of MDF which would take the same role fifty years later". Whilst covering Victorian plasterwork and pine doors might constitute a change in aesthetics, it signalled simplification of styling and a modernist approach to the spatial environment.

By reviewing previous architectural and design styles it is possible to trace how tastes and aesthetics have altered. There are many recognisable aesthetic movements and these usually sequentially react against each other, creating new forms of aesthetics, design and styling. The reactions between movements demonstrate a fluidity of culture and the richness of the cultural landscape. For example, the life expectancy of an urban environment could be 200 years, a piece of architecture 70 years, an interior 8 years, and fashion only months. This speculates that the further away from the human body you move, the better longevity you could have. This suggests a form of order and spatial hierarchy that centralises the spaces around the body but also adds a level of fickleness to the selections of taste. However, the creative disciplines of architecture, design and fashion provide a continual narrative of aesthetic, historical and cultural influence. This includes a diverse range of examples, including the simple little black cocktail dress by Coco Chanel[1] in 1926; the arts and crafts "Glasgow Style" masterpiece, Hill House by Charles Rennie Mackintosh[2] in 1902 (Figure 7.3) or James Dyson's revolutionary invention, the DC01 Vacuum[3] in 1993. Zaha Hadid set new standards for innovative and sustainable sports venues in 2012 with the landmark Aquatic Centre for the London Olympics[4] in 2012. The stylish and

FIGURE 7.3 Hill House – Charles and Margaret Macdonald Mackintosh 1902. Drawing Room Detail
Photo by Tony Hisgett. [Generic (CC by 2.0)] https://flickr.com/photos/hisgett/37376575552/in/photolist-XYkEGi-XUThXY-XYkHgg-BTuess-YVnHQw-YAQuC3-YWQJv5-YXf2sq-XYkMYc-YVM2uy-YZYTMg-YZAFna-YVM6rm-YWQHJq-YZYW9F-YWQF9q-YBefe7-BTuhy7-BTummh-YVnRm3-BTujuJ-BTUiRQ-YZAHZK

126 Understanding spatial culture

colourful exhibition space at the London Design Museum by artist Morag Myerscough[5] provided the backdrop for the first permanent exhibition space in 2016, and Ilse Crawford's elegant interior of the Ravintola Savoy (2020)[6] showed great restraint, reworking Alvar Alto's classic Helsinki restaurant. Many successful designs establish themselves as classics or are regarded as important works that demonstrate a level of quality at the time of completion. Many get reworked or are used as the basis for new designs as human needs alter and society develops.

However, it is important to note that aesthetics and tastes usually return in cycles, not necessarily in the original guise, but in hybrid forms that continue to influence tastes and aesthetic culture. Urban and architectural environments influence and react more slowly to emerging taste due to their scale and solidity. Their designs will last much longer, influencing aesthetics over a longer period. The interior of buildings has an immediate impact on users experiencing the space. However, the interior is usually shrouded inside the architecture and therefore has traditionally not impacted the landscape of the city. However, with increased exposure via television in social media and the opening-up of architectural spaces into the wider cityscape, the interior has become more visible and influential. By adding its impact and crossover between internal and external spaces, it has become an important standard and arbiter of taste. Product design adapts and renews its products, services, and offers more quickly by directly responding to or leading emerging and changing human needs. It updates and positions furniture, objects and technology in new sociological positions, recognising and developing aesthetics and tastes. It oscillates between object-based design to more service, augmented and virtual environments, shaping and influencing spatial tastes and the relationships with the designed environment. If you apply the same principles to graphic design, you see the impact and influence of the communicative environment on society's tastes and values. This might be the use of breakfast cereal typography in the kitchen or the large-scale moving billboards on the street. The branding, messaging and typography are powerful influences on culture and visual literacy, highlighted through the power of graphic design in Venturi et al. (1977, 3–52). Fashion design has been the cornerstone of trend and taste for the last 400 years. Its process of shaping and dressing the human form has been one of the key drivers of aesthetics, styling and taste. Modern manufacturing enabled speedy and responsive manufacturing, but this has become out of taste as it became highly wasteful and damaging to the planet. Taste has shifted to ensure that the planet is protected in all human activity and endeavour. Taste is inherent to each human being in their own unique way. Hicks (1979, 76) wrote that

> Taste is a particular person's choice between alternatives. It is choosing a tie to go with a shirt to go with the suit to go with an occasion. It is the way you arrange oranges in a greengrocer's shop, the way you like your

room; the colour you choose for the outside of your motor car. It applies to food, to interiors, to manners, to everything where it is a question of choice between one alternative and another in connection with colour, style or behaviour.

The connection between taste and style is often connected to the ideas of social and creative rules and this can be applied through different spatial trends and movements. Two good examples are minimalism and maximalism. These two aesthetic and stylistic traits are directly opposed and represent different forms of stylised taste. Minimalism is a form of pervasive social and spatial trend which is driven primarily by an anti-consumerist ideology. This paired-back individual lifestyle choice encourages a simplified, pure taste that promotes an ethical approach to living. By reducing the number of objects and possessions, your behaviour and taste are purified, limiting your impact on the planet and creating a less chaotic and more productive lifestyle. However minimalistic style (and taste) is also seen as being cold and anti-human. A minimalistic house can lack a sense of homeliness and endearment. By limiting an emotional response to space, a minimalist house can be seen as lacking warmth and any sense of taste. Maximalism is increasing in popularity to enhance and express personal ideas, culture, behaviours and individual uniqueness. This bold and expressive form of taste empowers the use of light and colour specifically using pattern and texture as one of its signature traits. An example of this kind of taste is expressed through the interiors and styling of Anthony Duquette (Wilkinson 2009) where he used the phrase "More is More" to promote the maximalism ideology as a direct contradiction to Mies van der Rohe's modernist mantra, "Less is more".

Place

Given the ubiquity of place, it is a problem that no one quite knows what they are talking about when they mean place. As described in Chapter 5, there are differences between a place and a space. Both can be related to the inside or the outside. Both are also directly connected with human experience and can be planted in memory, but they are also quite different in their relationship with the textual account of the human body.

Lefebvre (1991, 229–239) differentiates between the qualities *of space* and the qualities embedded *in space*. By separating this qualitative relationship, he highlights different geneses for the "cultural models" of space and place. He describes the origins of *absolute space* (ibid., 234) by using places named by nomadic and seminomadic "pastoralists". These places had no space and were a place for action and movement, becoming reassigned as the moments of living changed. The nature of nomadic life meant that the populations were continually restless and moving nomadically or semi-

128 Understanding spatial culture

nomadically, creating places for living and working that were never permanent. Lefebvre (1991, 236) also suggests that absolute space (place) has no dimensions, orientations (left and right, up and down etc.) or high and low, suggesting, "it has *no place* because it embodies all places and has a strictly symbolic existence; "whatever space and time mean, place and occasion mean more. Full space in the image of man is place, and time in the image of man is occasion" (Van Eyck 1963, 20).

Place is both a simple and complicated term. It has a distinctive resonance with the individual and community. Whilst it is often not seen as a physical entity (Lefebvre [1991, 236] suggests it is only symbolic), it plays a critical part in the design of the spatial environment. It has been specifically located in this chapter as it has powerful textural considerations when aligned with the design of space. Place embodies a significant tool in the overall context of design and human understanding of space. It sits embedded in the lexicons of architecture urban design, interior design and the spatial arts. But it also has an important position outside this in the wider understanding of the human position and activity on Earth. It could be described as being part of a landscape, an external viewpoint, and has a long-standing historical context. Imagine a Renaissance painting that has been constructed to explore religious iconography. It will be set in a specific location, a specific place to demonstrate both the quality of the painting and the religious message. Place can have distinct geographical connections and can fluctuate between the inside and outside of any given building envelope. It can help bridge understanding across the spatial environment, allowing movement between different kinds of spatial environments and settings. In cultural terms, it is highly representative and has a strong cultural determination and identity. Whilst place develops much knowledge of the location, a *sense of place* deepens the connection and enriches the experiences of space. Place can embed an understanding of permanency; its location can also be fleeting temporal, almost momentary, just enough to be remembered (Figure 7.4). Agnew (1987, 1–11) reinforced place as a "meaningful location" through *Location, Locale* and *Sense of place*.

Our perceptions of volume, spatial language and textual syntax are revealed as we move through it. How space is presented to us and how it unfolds and changes as we pass through it, is often described as place-making. This place-making is described by Austin (2020, 44–48) as the "joint efforts among all stakeholders or actors in an environment, including its citizens, artists, businesses, visitors and local government, to produce convivial places to live which support multiple narratives" suggesting that place-making would "increase social cohesion, cultural, education and in its economic opportunities; foster well-being and active civic engagement; and make the location unique and desirable to visit as well as environmentally sustainable".

As we move through space, a place gives a sense of textual movement and *kinetics* or *non-static* existence. As the user stands still within an environment, the movement of vision (focusing and refocusing on objects or

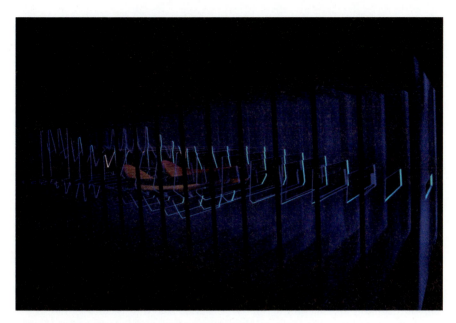

FIGURE 7.4 Spatial interpretation. Venice Biennale 2019
Photo by Aleksandr Zykov. [ShareAlike Generic (CC by 2.0)] https://flickr.com/p
hotos/84292292@N00/50830832451/in/photolist-2krKiyX-2krKG1b-2gyc7ai-
2gycKLw-2gycKBD-2gycj8b-2gyciWj-2gycixi-2gycJuZ-2gycJtr-2gycJmH-2gycJgC-
2gyci4c-2gychYN-2gycHQh-2gycHN3-2gycHGb-2gycHwM-2gycHun-2gychdp
-2gycGJK-2gycGFd-2gycffw-2gycEZ2-2gycECa-2gycBpw-2gycatT-2gyczi7-2
gyc5MD-2mtfovN-2mt6xgP-2hBVPEi-2mt6wCu-2hBUUca-2hBUTQD-2gycetr-2gy
cL1E-2gyciFK-2gycJLq-2gyciBg-2gycJyM-2gycJwY-2gycJpy-2gycicP-2gychPQ-
2gychLi-2gycHKc-2gycHCP-2gycHrg-2gycH11

space) will create changing relationships, both physical and psychological. Human senses permanently detect and relay spatial positioning. Space is static, but the *located* position of the viewer is continually altering and adjusting. Place is reflexive and directly related to the motions and textuality of the body. It is a varying construct, often a more abstract concept than space and usually in motion, fluid, constructing and deconstructing as the narrative passes through space. Place has a defined presence, encouraging a pause, a dwelling in and deeper consideration of the environment. It connects people and draws actions together. It is more reflective and binds other conditions like memory, figurative traces, and constructions of a spatial and *spiritual* narrative. It is a global phenomenon but is perceived quite differently when cultural, religious and spatial dynamics are applied. A place is quite different inside and outside the architecture and is defined by its people, history and use (Auge 2009, XIX).

If we take the example of Cinderella's Castle at Walt Disney World in Orlando, Cresswell (2015, 77) describes such tourist destinations as being

130 Understanding spatial culture

"Placeless" or "Pseudo-Places" as they have no real history or any strong sense of belonging. Culturally Walt Disney World is a phenomenon and arguably highly fluid, imaginary and textually inventive. Starbucks coffee is a globally recognised brand and the company has worked hard (placement, design, experience) to also be a ("glocally") recognised place, building its branding and global presence, but its global omnipresence and sameness mean that it lacks a connection to place, even though its ubiquity attempts at *locating* place. Tsing (2005, X) considers a global universality and how this connects through a "particularity" of place. Striking the right balance between understanding the cultural contexts for place and the setting of the location for human participants is quite challenging. Auge (2009, XVIII) introduces the idea of the "cultural trait". He elaborates by suggesting that this could either be a material (a physical object or an active process) or an immaterial (a ritual, deity or belief) invention. He positions the circulation and diffusion of these traits as one of the primary forces for change within world societies. He also highlights (ibid., XIX) an increasing difficulty to "distinguish [culturally] between the exterior and the interior, the elsewhere and the here". He suggests that "various domains of creation" align place as a hinterland between global and local definitions, setting out some of the divisions and diversities in the world. Auge (2009, 66–67) summarises by suggesting that humans may be tempted to contrast a symbolised space of place with a non-symbolised space of non-place, highlighting space as an abstract term; the nomination of place is usually connected to an event (which has taken place).

Place builds temporal and adaptable (but repeatable) relationships with people helping communities to transform. Place is particularly flexible as it can utilise spaces of the city and, specifically, the non-spaces of the city. Examine any market in any city and you will see how the places of the market are set out and used for selling, usually adapting flexibly to the confines of the streets. A place affects all levels and sizes of community and often builds emotional ties and identity affiliations with human groups, forming a bond and a strong sense of belonging. This helps develop a richer cultural diversity and intensifies the power of place (and space) to form new contexts for cohering people together.

By using exhibition design to describe places of narrative and encounter, Austin (2020, 99–105) describes different forms of movement through exhibition and display environments. There are four different linear "storyshapes" which help to describe movement through places set out in exhibition formats. The shapes demonstrate different movements and pause through and around exhibition formats and islands. The process of building story narratives of place helps to design and configure each of the processes as the general public move through the spaces. There are also descriptions of non-linear story shapes which describe a much more fragmented and individual approach to moving through the exhibition areas. She specifically describes non-chronological stories which begin to align with the way humans consider encounters. Human nature and cognitive brain function drive different forms of understanding and encounters. Edwards (1979, 40–42) describes perceptual understanding by using different sides to the left-mode and right-mode characteristics of the human brain. She outlines how the right-hand side of the brain sees spatial context and encounters, and specifically how it constructs a complete understanding of the environment.

FIGURE 7.5 Place – traditional Funfair environment
Photo by Nikolay Vorobyev on Unsplash. [Generic (CC by 2.0)] https://unsplash.com/photos/iM5Lm4qz77Q

132 Understanding spatial culture

Encounter as part of the culture of a place can be unexpected and uncomfortable. Some places that humans create are designed to agitate and be actively unsettling. Take a series of places set up and created around a mobile funfair or human circus (Figure 7.5). The premise is usually around the idea of an event, and the places that are created are temporary, traditional and highly cultural, forming places of entertainment. This entertainment process seeps into traditional and (often) spiritual contexts and is designed to be entertaining (and sometimes frightening). With most funfairs and circuses usually set up to be open at night, they are lit to be a place of attraction and congregation. Culturally, they are usually temporarily moving regularly across the country, attracting different audiences in different places. They provide entertainment but also present traditional and cultural values. The places they create are often unexpected. The culture of place is aligned with experiences and crossing different boundaries of spatial proximity where the encounter uses the different senses to create and experience "the spirit of the place" as defined in different contexts by Exner and Pressel (2009) or Norberg-Schulz (1980).

Cultural Trail

This chapter has used the textural realm as a way to describe several key components that are used when designing different forms of space. None of the four themes sits alone and all contribute to the development and textural presentation of space. The use of colour and light are often seen as additional contexts for space, often defining how space is received physically, emotionally and spiritually. They are cultural markers, used as international symbols for religion, death, good luck, gratitude and truce.[7] They are used to define space and signify place. They provide fundamental texture to the way space is presented and bring into focus the temporary way humans use space. They can be used dynamically and boldly or in a highly subtle and layered way. Importantly, when using pigmented colour, it is important to note that the way light bounces and reflects on it can change the way the colour is seen. This is specifically true in periods between natural and artificial light. The colour (and culture) can ultimately change depending on the time of day that the space is viewed. Supporting this, light dynamically alters the texture and sense of space. This can be through the timing of natural daylight reflected from buildings as well as sunlight piercing through windows into the contained interior spaces. Light directly influences the cultural dynamics of space.

The use of taste also helps to present spatial culture in an expressive and individual manner. The importance of taste has been re-calibrated by social media, repositioning it away from the formalised social structures. It directly impacts the way spatial cultures are represented and helps to contemporise the nature of culture, suggesting a possible individual textural framework for a new aesthetic culture to operate in. Place helps to draw together the other three themes in this chapter. It can be applied directly as a filter in a cultural

Understanding spatial culture **133**

setting, driving different textural and temporal locations and contexts. It has a broad and open interpretation and remains a critical part of the proximal environments that are created by humans in a spatial setting.

The following chapter explores the differences between the physical and digital spatial realms through the mapping presentation of culture (from the Spatial Probe) concluding the Cultural trail.

Notes

1 The Coco Chanel cocktail dress has been a Fashion Icon since the 1920s. More information is available here: https://www.marieclaire.co.uk/fashion/little-black-dress-524293 Accessed 19 Dec. 2022.
2 Hill House is currently under restoration. More information is available on the National Trust for Scotland website: https://www.nts.org.uk/visit/places/the-hill-house Accessed 19 Dec. 2022.
3 The DC01 was the first upright Dyson vacuum cleaner. More information here: https://www.lb.dyson.com/en-LB/community/aboutdyson.aspx Accessed 19 Dec. 2022.
4 Zaha Hadid Architects. More information on the London Aquatic Centre: https://www.zaha-hadid.com/architecture/london-aquatics-centre/ Accessed 19 Dec. 2022.
5 https://www.moragmyerscough.com/commissions Accessed 19 Dec. 2022.
6 https://www.studioilse.com/projects/ravintola-savoy/ Accessed 19 Dec. 2022.
7 Please see McCandless (2009, 76) for further references to national identity, colour and culture.

8

CULTURAL PLACEMENT MAPPING

Physical/digital cultures

This chapter explores the spatial culture link between physical and digital spaces and the relationship this has on the cultures of home, work and leisure. The chapter outlines new forms of physical and alternative spatial cultures through animation, virtual reality, artificial intelligence and holographic visualisation which reveals an increasing intimacy and personalisation of space through the presentation of urban, architectural and interior forms. The proliferation and ubiquity of digital and social media alter the perceptions and presence of spatial culture. The chapter extends the primacy of the cultural terrain through physical exploration of global domestic dwelling sizes which is supported by the analysis of the cultural placement mapping (from the spatial cultural probe) demonstrating some new research on how and where culture is placed in space.

Physical cultures

By exploring the cultures within and of space, it is possible to begin to understand the constructions and compositions of *space* and *place*. By using boundaries/thresholds and margins of space, it is possible to identify space(s) and develop the patterns and agility of location by defining cultural reference and the placement of objects. It is possible to *contain* and *control* cultural placement using specific boundaries or spatial thresholds that connect parts of spaces together. As spatial culture binds and integrates across and within the built environment, exploring identifiable and measurable examples helps frame the impact of cultural space. Take the size of the average space used by the populations in domestic dwellings in different parts of the world (Figure 8.1.). Whilst recognising the differences in geography, politics and spatial setting, the differences in physical space that people use and live

DOI: 10.4324/9781003270393-9

in can be identified. The meterage set out is *per capita* suggesting the amount of space that each person, in each country, occupies in their domestic setting. This data is averaged so, within each country, there will be wide variation, but this indicates how, and the conditions of where spatial culture is located. The general trend here is that the relationship between population and the amount of available space for habitation drives the amount of space that humans use for dwelling. Some of this is by choice, but it is mostly through other external factors that impact how and where people live. It is impossible to fully establish the impact of culture on this data, but it must be assumed that a geo-cultural perspective must impact the decisions of occupation and dwelling. The data does suggest wide differences between different populations in different countries and cultures. However, Hall (1990), Sommer (2008) and Rybczynski (1987) highlight the differences between individual cultural groups located within different countries. This is particularly prevalent as different cultural groups set up communities in other countries, altering how the population chooses to live. Often, the amount of space that people occupy in the man-made environment is an indication of prosperity. Urban and living spaces are directly related to wealth, with some of the poorest people living in informal settlement (slum and ghetto) environments with tiny amounts of space per individual. According to the United Nations (2022), almost 25% of the world's population now occupies these kinds of living environments. Massed living conditions like this can bind and separate communities, developing new forms of community culture and living environments. Many informal settlements develop over decades or longer (Dharari [see Figure 8.1] in Mumbai was established in 1884) and are set to remain as part of the cultures of many developing cities. They create and forge new types of physical spatial environments for the population, building their own economies, employment and industries that maximise the use of space between living and working. They often have their own cultural "rules", developing new forms of cultural placement. The cramped conditions often impact human health, however they are a crucible for developing new *rules* of social cultures and a rich diversity of cultural tropes (street fashion, music, performance, cultural art, street food, sport, graffiti) that find their way into the mainstream impacting the wider population.

Whatever the situation is for dwelling, usually affluent and stronger economic nations have more developed housing markets which help afford larger, more complex dwellings (and this is reflected in Figure 8.1). However, larger and more composite dwellings do not necessarily mean that the culture is better or more socially entrenched. Cultures located in space are complex and varied. To establish an integrated relationship between human culture and the built environment, it is important to explore the location and position of cultures in space. This positioning can be achieved through a process of mapping an environment and determining the locations of cultures and its setting. This process is complex as the entire environment, city

136 Cultural placement mapping

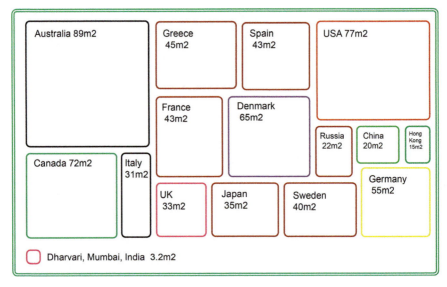

FIGURE 8.1 Residential floor space[1] per capita in m^2
Author

or street can represent a culture. A way to understand cultural location is through the location of cultural objects inside a domestic dwelling. This measurement is through a process of placement documentation, location analysis and object identification that examines the cultural setting and relationship to other cultural objects. Research and analysis into cultural placement mapping are set out below.

Cultural placement mapping

As described in the previous chapters, this book explores the contexts between culture and space. There are many examples of spaces being mapped and documented to understand and place human activity in space. In Miller (2008), 30 portraits reveal a highly interactive process between humans and the spaces they call home. This study documents incredible detail of the interior. It contextualises each of the individual histories by placing the individual inside the spaces that they have created. Many of the portraits include direct references to human experience and the objects that surround them. Personal, inherited and memory items that develop a real story connecting people and spaces together (Portrait 12, Portrait 23 and Portrait 25 are further good examples). In Gola (2022, 51–69) there is a rich description of the positioning of material culture inside a Palestinian *duyuf* (a form of reception room for guests). The text provides some real insight into culturally important room layouts and object identities. There are some important descriptions of the positioning of furniture and the hierarchical relationships when rooms are designed. There is a rich set of visual diagrams that document the placement of religious and cultural items and the positional relationships that are set out in space. There is a reference to colour, taste and how the room is used on arrival and departure. In Austin (2020, 87–97) there is evidence of emotional mapping of museum spaces (completed by the design company Duncan McCauley), which provide a visual document of how museum spaces communicate and interact with the visitor experience. This is a good example of how design can simultaneously document stories, objects, spaces and media visually.

These texts provide a triangulated and layered approach to the documentation of space. By using this as a stimulus, it is possible to consider the cultural placement and object mapping based on the spatial probe in Chapter 3. This primary research gives an analysis of the cultural diversity and similarity of domestic interior space, revealing glimpses of the spaces that people live in. This unique sample positions cultural placement within domestic environments across the world. In Chapter 3, the probe also asks for a series of objects that are placed within each of the selected rooms. There was a primary object which is documented in this table but also documents some supplementary objects (usually three additions) that were selected and documented in Table 8.1. The supplementary objects were requested as additional cultural markers (in the broadest sense) and seen in context (mapped) to the setting, enabling separated and potentially disparate objects to be culturally grouped into interior micro-cultural habitats (articulated or one room) around the positioning of the objects and inhabitants. Analysis of each space has enabled the definition of a **cultural impact area** within each space demonstrating the relevance, selection and purpose of the grouped objects in the space and the behaviours of the occupants. This chapter extends the results from the probe which are mapped in Table 8.1 in descriptive and diagrammatic and planular form (Figures 8.2, 8.3 and 8.4), revealing the placement and proximity of objects in a domestic setting. These objects have been grouped and selected (by the respondents) into eight different cultural categories (*Structural, Personal, Familial, Decorative, Community, Religious, Antiquity and Empathetic*) and document the placement and location of culturally relevant objects in domestic settings (mostly a single space). The outline conclusions are set out at the end of this chapter and in the final summary.

Digital cultures

As space influences how culture is presented in physical and architectural forms, we are prompted to ask questions about how this will be changed through our expanding digital world. The phenomena of space and our understanding of conscious reality allow an understanding of our cultural contacts from a position of *things* being real or as Heidegger (1962, 138–145) suggests

TABLE 8.1 Cultural mapping objects (detail from Table 3.1)

Cultural Mapping objects (detail from Table 3.1)

Country	Digital Diary	Digital object: cultural interior object/element that signifies a representation of interior culture. Results include the overall area of the room and the defined area of the Cultural Impact Area created by the location of the objects.	Cultural mapping and descriptors: original object (from Chapter 3) and mapped objects. - Structural, Personal, Familial, Decorative, Community, Religious, Antiquity, Empathetic.
Australia	Old Farmhouse in the Outback bush (1926). North of Adelaide. Used as a domestic home/farmstead for 100 years: kitchen	Interior with furniture. (Kitchen) Farmhouse family table (old unpainted timber table, scared, marked and raw). Traditional turned legs and boarded tabletop (**Structural** object) (Seats 8 with matching chairs) (Kitchen – **Approximate Area 32m^2 – Cultural Impact Area 11.23 m^2)**	Table and 3 domestic objects. 1 x **Personal** – glass biscuit jar 1 x **Familial** – photograph frame 1 x **Decorative** – fish crafted in shells Plan of location of objects in the kitchen (documented on paper).
Brazil	Family flat (4 Bed) in Vila Mafra, San Paulo. 1985. Interior Modern. Lounge/living space.	Main (double) doorway between two main living rooms. Frames, embossed and differentiated. Ornately carved doors (**Structural** object) (Replaced original doors from a previous dwelling). Opening French (Portuguese) doors. Open plan living. (Two Rooms – **Approximate Area 66m^2 – Cultural Impact Area 21.18 m^2)**	Carved doors and 3 cultural objects. 1x **Structural** – decorative stained-glass window (garden/growth reference). 1 x **Community** – banner of a local music group. 1 x **Antiquity** – traditional tribal headdress. Placed on a wall. Plan of location and descriptions of objects in open plan lounge (on a postcard from the probe).

Canada	Toronto Flat above a hardware store. (date unknown). Originally used for storage. 1 Bed *"Maisonette Style"* duplex flat now converted into 2 Bed with balcony over the street. Large kitchen/dining space.	Hybrid kitchen. Centrally placed in a big kitchen with an island. Modern glass-topped table (**Familial** object) with cast iron legs. Seats 6. High-backed chairs. Appears quite "temporary" and open loft-style room. Large pieces of furniture, in large rooms. Lots of space. (Kitchen – **Approximate Area 20m^2 – Cultural Impact Area 6.65 m^2**)	Glass-topped table and 3 cultural objects 1 x **Personal** – photograph frame with family gathering. 1x **Community** – ceramic decorative sports plate (Montreal Olympics?) 1 x **Community** – Sports fridge magnets of ice hockey teams (on a fridge). Plan of location of objects in the maisonette kitchen (on a postcard from the probe, digital image).
China	(a) City suburb flat. Duplex style. (1999) Part of huge "out of town" development Beijing NE. Wangjing Residential District. Living space. (b) Chinese longhouse (1850). Single story, barn-like in style. Traditional farm building converted for a domestic dwelling. Heng Chun Bridge, Shanghai.	Glass panel details on a wall between corridor and flat. Modern glazed vision panels/window-styled surfaces (**Structural** object). Coloured patterned glass. Brings coloured light into the space. Original panel authentic spaces. (Corridor **Approximate Area 22m^2 – Cultural Impact Area 6.54 m^2**). Traditional farmhouse converted into two houses. Large Chinese lantern (**Decorative** object) houses single-story with converted living spaces into the roof (converted windows). The interior appears quite traditional, decorated with modern appliances and traditional Chinese decoration. Large kitchen. (Living space – **Approximate Area 32m^2 – Cultural Impact Area 14.78m^2**)	Glass panels and personalised cultural objects. 1 X **Personal** – 3 x Buddhist statues. 1 X **Personal** – book 1 x **Decorative** – carved wooden light stand. Sketched plan (on parchment-type paper) of the location of objects in the duplex corridor. Chinese lantern and 3 cultural objects. 1 x **Personal** – painting landscape. 1 x **Antiquity** – scroll document (in frame). 1 x **Empathetic** – stone ern (ashes/remains?) Plan of location of objects in a large kitchen (on a postcard from the probe, digital image).

France	(a) French farmhouse and gite (1901) (Lombardy). Porch/veranda. (b) Large French town/city house (1920). Rennes City Centre	Domestic environment and holiday let spaces. Quite different in terms of quality and authenticity. External veranda chair (**Empathetic** object). (Lounge and veranda – **Approximate Area 45m^2 – Cultural Impact Area 15.85m^2**) Set over four floors with full-height windows. Decorative plasterwork, wrought iron staircase bannisters (**Structural** object) large open staircase Entrance hall. Wall and hung lighting feature richly decorated large paintings. Traditional ornamentation and furniture. (Open hallway/staircase – **Approximate Area 78m^2 – Cultural Impact Area 21.45m^2**)	Veranda chair and three cultural objects. 1 x **Structural** – carved totem column 1 x **Familial** – X-Box gaming unit and VR headset. 1 x **Antiquity** – Terracotta pot 75 cm with herb garden Lighting unit and 3 cultural items. 1 x **Decorative** – staircase Bannister detail 1 x **Religious** – female sculpture in the hallway of a house. 1 x **Empathetic** – ceramic hand prints of family. Plan of location of objects in a large open hallway (on a written note with images). (Note from the probe).
Hong Kong city (1/1)	Small two-bedroomed flat in a skyscraper (1965) bedroom	Small double bedroom with window. A foldable bed (**Structural** object) allows for additional storage and for the room to be used as a study when not used for sleeping. Ingenious design. All furniture is stackable. One wall used Full storage. Dark colour. (Bedroom – **Approximate Area 68m^2 – Cultural Impact Area 13.90m^2**)	Bed and two cultural objects. 1 x **Personal** – waving lucky cat 22cm (Traditional item) 1 x **Antiquity** – antique bowl. Keys, coins, small items. Plan of location of objects in a bedroom (on a card and photographed)
Italy (1/2)	Italian farmhouse (1864) – (Tuscany). Lounge space.	Old blanket trunk (**Decorative** object). Upper story lounge. The object matched the quality of the space and was bought with the property. Timber (chestnut), metal hinged and feet. Used as a seat and for object display. (Lounge – **Approximate Area 38m^2 – Cultural Impact Area 17.25m^2**)	Blanket trunk plus three items. 1 x **Personal** – sculpture of water buffalo. 1 x **Antiquity** – prayer bowl. 1 x **Empathetic** – patolli oil burner. Plan of location of objects in lounge space. (Postcard drawing.)

Japan (1/1)	Flat (1 Bed), apartment block (1969) – Asami-nami, Hiroshima. Living/lounge space.	Small flat in city. Straight-sided glass jug/sculpture (**Familial** object) in dining space. Glass objects, Japanese glass arranged with two other glass items (French and Bolivian glass). Green in colour and influences the colour of the whole room. Swirling marbled effect. (Living Space – **Approximate Area 42m^2 – Cultural Impact Area 21.45m^2**)	Glass jug and four cultural objects. 1 x **Structural** – an integrated light unit. 1 x **Personal** – model car yellow Toyota 2000 GT (1967). 1 x **Decorative** – folding screen for a window. Embossed paper 1 x **Antiquity** – ceramic vase, artificial flowers. Plan of location of objects in living space. (Drawing/Japanese Calligraphy).
Kenya, (1/1)	A 2 bedroom apartment in a large housing block. Living spaces. Nairobi, Africa	Large 2 bedroom apartment with Open Plan living spaces. Sofa-bed (**Community** object). The lounge/dining space opens to a balcony. A colourful and bold interior with strong use of black to define the edges of walls flooring etc. Hard materials with the use of soft textiles and furnishings. (Living Space – **Approximate Area 84m^2 – Cultural Impact Area 31.86m^2**)	Sofa bed and three cultural objects. 1 x **Personal** – bold tribal wall hanging. Woven tapestry based on the diverse colouring of the face. 1 x **Antiquity** – painted animal skull (on the wall). 1 x **Empathetic** – metal stool (Made from recycled aluminium). Plan of location of objects in lounge/living space (written note). Photographed and sent (from the probe).
Malaysia (1/2)	Urban/suburban house (2010) (3 bedrooms) Bandar Peru, Penang. Living space.	Suburban house – television/computer screen (**Familial** object) in main Living space. Room focal point. No fireplace. (Living Space – **Approximate Area 62m^2 – Cultural Impact Area 27.38m^2**)	Television screen and 3 cultural objects. 1 x **Familial** – picnic basket/food basket? Used for transporting food/days out. 1x **Community** – community metal plaque on the wall (Ecological action). 1 x **Religious** – photo frame with Family event. Plan of location of objects in living space (on a postcard from the probe, digital image).

South (1/1) Africa	Terrace House. Eikenbosch, Cape Town (1999). Lounge space.	Terrace house. Sloped hills suburban development. Range of African art. Large canvases (4). African Art. figurative/urban/rural Landscapes (**Decorative** object). Culturally powerful. Bold and colourful textiles. (Lounge/living space – **Approximate Area 90m^2 – Cultural Impact Area 43.84m^2).**	African Art and 3 cultural objects. 1 x **Personal** – woven/printed wall covering. Image of Village Community Hall and people gathering. Tribal Art. 1 x **Antiquity** – clay pots (water collection). 1 x **Empathetic** – woven scarfs (recycled and reused on the sofa). Diagrammatic plan of the location of objects in living space (on a probe postcard, from a digital image).
South Korea (1/2)	Slimline Korean house. Daegu. Two stories, 2 rooms on each level. The dwelling is only 4m wide. (1985 Approx.) Kitchen.	Ultra-small and compact kitchen. One wall contains kitchen storage, fridge and cooking surfaces. Food pickling jars (**Familial** object). Whole room is only 2 m x 1.2 m. High ceilings. White. Small colourful graphics on the wall. Good lighting. (Kitchen – **Approximate Area 3.5m^2 – Cultural Impact Area 1.78m^2)**	Food pickling jars and 3 other kitchen items 1 x **Personal** – decorative ceramic trivet for the display of the kimchee fermentation pot. 1 x **Decorative** – set of retro coasters with metallic inlay. 1 x **Antiquity** – gold banner for the marathon. Printed plan. Location of objects in living space (on postcard from probe, digital image).
Spain (2/2)	(a) Terraced villa (2001), 3 bedroom, lounge/balcony overlooking orange grove/farmland. Sagunto, Valencia. Lounge/living space. (b) Modern Spanish 3 bedroom house. Traditional layout in outskirts suburbs in Mostoles, Madrid. Living/dining space.	Villa in a Spanish town. Modern complex apartment. Air-conditioned, hard materials, poor lighting. All walls are painted white, stone floors and no fireplace. Beautiful view over farmland and orange grove. Beautiful coloured objects, designer furniture (**Structural** object). (Lounge and balcony – **Approximate Area 88m^2 – Cultural Impact Area 31.67m^2)** Modern interior with clean surfaces, new kitchen and European-style interior spaces. Plenty of light and reflective surfaces. Sculptural glass lighting (**Decorative** objects) surrounded by clean modern comfortable furniture. Folding doors into garden space. (Living/Dining space – **Approximate Area 68m^2 – Cultural Impact Area 44.78m^2)**	Designer furniture and 3 other cultural objects. 1 x **Structural** – glazed structure/window between lounge and balcony 1 x **Community** – set of handbells from a local church 1 x **Religious** – small religious shrine – ceramic. Plan of location of objects in lounge/balcony (on a written note with images, from the probe). Glass objects and 3 other cultural objects. 1 x **Familial** – gold cups for windsurfing /sailing/ archery. Specified plan location of objects in Living/dining space (written note with images (from the probe). 1 x **Decorative** – glass decorative plate on wall 1 x **Religious** – decorative plaque. Painting of landscape with Church

Cultural Mapping objects (detail from Table 3.1)

| UK (2/3) | (a) Small English terraced Victorian house (1899) Whalley Range, Manchester. Bedroom (b) Flat in town centre, Stourbridge, West Midlands (1901) Lounge space. | Small 2 bedroom terraced house. Fireplace in main living space. Carved wooden fireplace (**Antiquity** object) (1930) Arts and Craft Style with metal fittings and edges. Tiled Fireplace. (Living space – **Approximate Area 22m^2 – Cultural Impact Area 9.84m^2**) 2 bed Flat, Ground floor. Small garden. Range of comic toys (**Decorative** objects) (Personal collection on display in cabinet). Modern cabinet with built-in light for display purposes. (Lounge – **Approximate Area 17m^2 – Cultural Impact Area 6.78m^2**) | Fireplace and 3 other cultural objects (including a dog!) 1 x **Familial** – dog … living cultural object! 1 x **Decorative** – carved wooden figures on fireplace. 1 x **Community** – Environmental certificate Litter picking on beech. Decorative plaque. Specified plan with (moving) location of "objects" in living space (written note from the probe). Comic toys and 3 other cultural objects (including plants) 1 x **Structural** – large potted plant (cheese plant) (moves between garden and house depending on the season). 1 x **Personal** – small machine turned cigarette case – metal. 1 x **Empathetic** – Duke of Edinburgh silver Mentor Awards. Outline plan of the location of objects in the lounge (on a written note from probe). |

Cultural Mapping objects (detail from Table 3.1)

USA (2/3)	(a) Townhouse (1916) Auburn Hills, Detroit. 3 Beds. Lounge space. (b) Brownstone house – 2 Bed flat. (1920s) Brooklyn Heights, New York. Lounge space.	Interior high ceilings. Large ornate fireplace and surround. Artwork, ceramics and interior objects. The interior used to house a range of artistic and cultural items for hanging display. On walls, cabinets/shelves etc. Large coloured ceiling light feature (**Familial** object). Carpets/ rugs on hard wooden floors. (Lounge/entertainment space – **Approximate Area 68m^2 – Cultural Impact Area 18.98m^2)** Funky flat with high ceilings and large windows in a traditional New York building. Eight flats in one big house. Small 2 bed flat that has large windows and supersized American pop graphics (**Decorative** objects) throughout. Furniture all lowered to be at floor level. Thick textiles and wooden floors. (Lounge/ kitchen – **Approximate Area 56m^2 – Cultural Impact Area 31.56m^2)**	Ceiling feature and 3 other cultural objects (includes plant). 1 x **Personal** – graduation certificate 1 x **Decorative** – colourful woven Arabic (style) rug. 1 x **Antiquity** – coin collection in wooden case. Sketched plan (on graph paper). Photographed and digitalised. Supersized American graphics and 3 other cultural objects (includes a plant). 1 x **Personal** – crystal port decanter (with glasses) 1 x **Familial** – carved family crest displayed near the fireplace. 1 x **Decorative** – 2 x distressed metal signs (airline brand and oil company) Drawn plan of location of objects in the lounge/ kitchen.
20 from 33 Total returned 33 (60 Sent)		Rooms selected – Average Size – **50m^2**. Average Cultural Impact Area **19.94m^2**	• Structural: 11 • Personal: 14 • Familial: 11 • Decorative: 15 • Community: 7 • Religious: 4 • Antiquity: 11 • Empathetic: 7 Total objects documented: 80

Cultural placement mapping 145

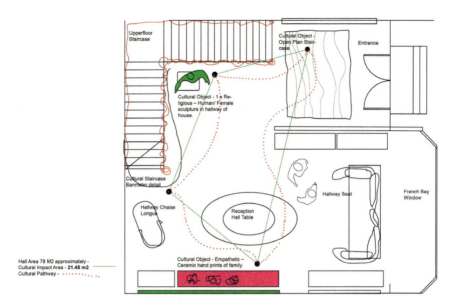

FIGURE 8.2 Floor plan of French town/city centre house (Constructed 1920). Rennes City Centre. Hallway
Author

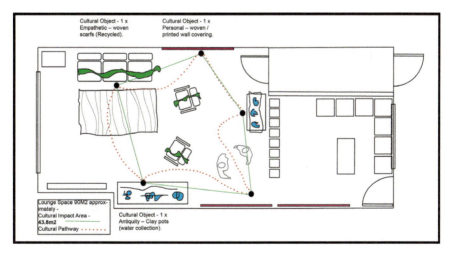

FIGURE 8.3 Floor plan of suburban Terrance House. Eikenbosch, Cape Town. (Constructed c.1999). Lounge space
Author

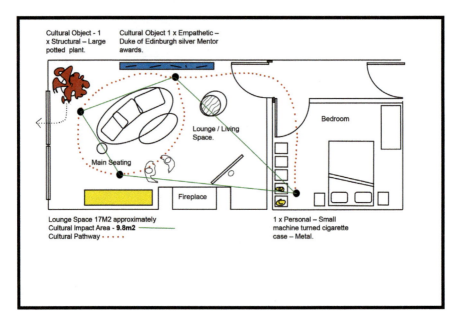

FIGURE 8.4 Plan of flat in the town centre, Stourbridge, West Midlands, UK (c. 1901). Lounge space

Author

that "being-in-the-world" is not placed from a position of the inside or the outside, but having harmony with the world through a closer understanding of a detailed "life-world" (Inwood 1997, 32). This philosophical stance describes the relationship between humans and the phenomena of living. In an attempt to understand the reality of an environment, Inwood (1997, 33) outlines a detailed account of a table in a setting. He recounts how Heidegger describes the specifics of *the* table, embracing both the objective and subjective aspects of use. He combined them allowing a visualised account of the interior setting capturing how humans embrace the physical and non-physical aspects of an object. This is an aspect of spatial culture that is developing through the use of digitalised spaces. Most of the existing and emerging digital cultures utilise both existing and imaginary environments which blend reality and non-reality together to forge a new augmented understanding of space. Most recognise digital spaces as a distinct cultural group (as opposed to physical), but with their increasing complexity and interactivity it becomes increasingly difficult to differentiate between real, augmented and artificial digital space. This becomes increasingly more complex when we add the spatial fluidity of interactive animation, virtual reality, artificial intelligence, holographic visualisation and the emerging metaverse. This is generating a new form of hybridity and understanding of space, developing new located cultural identities. Each of these emerging digital platforms transforms our understanding of our human position in space. Digital advances move from construction software and games (like Google SketchUp or Minecraft) to constructed virtual reality environments (metaverse) where a networked platform allows humans to enter various avatar forms. Initially, this began as a form of extended gaming platform but has been transformed into an environment that runs in parallel to reality. Not only can avatars interact with each other, but they can buy clothing (using crypto-currencies) and "live" in an alternate spatial world. This is a new form of digitised spatial culture that directly mirrors and maps existing life and cultural identities. The "metaverse" is continually "on" and is made up of dozens of interconnected and uncontrolled virtual worlds where new places and positions are continually being added. Culturally the metaverse appears as an extended virtual reality environment, but it is becoming increasingly aligned with real environments with brands buying up virtual land "plots" for commercial development (Tidy 2022). However, as the metaverse develops, these emerging virtual spaces will have changing levels of location, detail and personalisation. As the metaverse becomes more enhanced, it will form new complex relationships between people and space. Commentators (Joshi 2022) are suggesting that the metaverse could create a polarisation of political, cultural and spatial diversity. So, to fully embrace a new digitised world, the existing physical world must develop more connected and seamless hybrid methods to connect and blend these two spatial cultural realms, forming a new incremental and purposeful reality of space and culture in the future.

Narratological culture

The origins of a spatial culture are rooted in the different experiences of the urban and built environment, which flex between physical and imagined experiences. Typically, this develops from the use of space *and* place and forms the basis for human location and habitation. Both are intrinsically different but connected as a spatial manifestation which is housed within the different constructed environments of the city (from Figure 1.2, Chapter 1). Specifically, human understanding of space flexes between the physical aspects of the environment that surrounds us, natural spaces, the city, its urban development, architecture, the constructed interior, furniture and objects, to *place*, the non-physical ideas of locations like memory, sound, atmosphere and ambience. These are binary attractions and encourage a primacy of spatial experience, establishing a balance between the solidity of a spatial location and a flexible practice for individuals to pause, engage and remember the different elements of the experience. Critically, this individuality of experience facilitates how people occupy, move, stop, pause, transition, explore and experience the different elements of the design. The spatial experience is designed to be distinctive and purposeful, and the spatial culture becomes defined from different forms of space *and* place, encouraging the binding of spatial action and environmental narrative. All

148 Cultural placement mapping

the diverse forms of spatial experience explore different categories of narrative. An architectural narrative is often concerned with the abstraction of an aesthetic ideal or a functional construction of the building. The interior develops this and often suggests a more user-centred and wider exploratory approach to the connections between the body and the senses which define the spatial typology and help with the assembly of the interior aesthetic.

The *cultural placement mapping* exercise creates a series of localised narratives within each of the identified internal settings. The use of the interior and objects in this structured exercise was selected as a way to map objects with cultural significance within space. The domestic settings capture an inherently personal perspective, where individuals select and present their own objects as part of their home. These objects shaped and defined a shifting interior and according to Harman (2018, 154–155 when citing Husserl) the "qualities of every object are shifting every instant due to the changes in sunlight, as well as a shifting distance and angle as we approach the object, not to mention our minuscule changes in mood as we go about perceiving it". This altered perception helps objectify an agile interior environment, presenting object culture as a flexing entity which is presented in different forms and types. With the individual participants categorising each of the objects, it is possible that two identical objects can be represented in different cultural forms and conversely diverse objects can contribute to a single culture.

Many of the items selected enrich a cultural narrative of human behaviours, where the object suggests behaviour that is both representative and instructional. The objects underpin and inform new knowledge and develop existing beliefs found in human society. The objects selected are generally representative of the creative arts, with "artworks" that demonstrate customs, behaviours and habits found in human society. The objects represent individual choices, displays and selections of cultural objects within an interior space. Each of the defined objects has been selected and recorded by the occupant and mapped to the location inside their domestic spaces. From the probe (in Chapter 3), the participants were asked to digitally return a selection of data, drawn visuals and information about their spaces. This included the selection and documentation of some of their cultural objects and their positioning in their own spaces. Of particular interest is the relationship to the space (where it is positioned and grouped) and specifically to each other (distance and organisation). Whilst each object is unique, the positioning within space allows for identification, positioning and cultural analysis within the home. Further spatial analysis is created through the definition of region of cultural impact that has been analysed from the probe data. This establishes an area within each space where the cultural objects directly impact the interior and the user's behaviour. These areas are a significant indicator of influence on the space. The results are varied but are directly relatable to the overall meterage outlined by each of the individuals in their spaces and provide a new commentary and narrative to the relationship between culture, its impact, and the use of space. In Figures 8.2, 8.3 and 8.4 the area of cultural impact has been marked with a cultural pathway that indicates roots between objects within the spaces. The boundaries of these areas do not restrict the impact of cultural objects on space (the sensing and viewing objects can occur at some distance), the areas provide a focus of influence and impact and allow for a deeper analysis of the orientation of culture within space.

Based on the identification of the objects and their positioning it is possible to identify some cultural traits and potential anomalies. The first observation would be the range and diversity of the objects in the study. There are many examples of visual cultures that have been used to decorate and dress interior spaces. These visual cultures range from paintings, sculptures, artworks and textiles. There appears to be a rich balance between two-dimensional and three-dimensional objects and most have a visual quality, in the sense that they are choreographed into the interior as aesthetic visual decoration or cultural markers. They have been selected based on a range of cultural *values*. These values and markers are often representative emblems of individual cultural groups and communities. A significant indicator of these objects is how the objects were categorised by the person into the eight cultural descriptors (Structural, 5; Personal, 14; Familial, 6; Decorative, 9; Community, 6; Religious, 4; Antiquity, 10; Empathetic, 6; total 60 objects). These themes were selected by the occupants and demonstrated a considered balance across each of the spaces selected, demonstrating a rich diversity and evenness to the process and methodology.

This helps to define the encounter within the space providing both a cultural *process* in which the interior can be experienced, but also encouraging a *reading of space* promoting ideas of spatial discovery and exploration. The cultural objects were displayed (and potentially curated) or demonstrated a form of human experience. This was shown as objects associated with travel, articles of artistic activity or forms of homeliness. Some of the items selected were inherently part of the structure of the building (Structural), like staircase bannisters, ceiling details and windows and it was difficult to fully understand their cultural position, other than a timeline connected with the architecture. The larger pieces of furniture and ceramics (Decorative and Antiquity) provided more of a human context, developing the ideas of origin, material culture and texture. The objects and materials considered the notions of population and organisation of space. The community pieces like plaques and banners also indicated an important location of community culture within the domestic setting. These emblems also included triumphal cups and trophies for sports (Familial) but also for environmental work like beach cleaning. The familial items also indicated the power of culture to draw family events together, grouping people and their activities

150 Cultural placement mapping

(demonstrated digitally with the gaming box and VR headset). These provided some context for the space and the idea that the family unit occupied (where appropriate) each of these houses. There are several food-related items like the Korean kimchi fermentation jars (and a trivet), a crystal port decanter, and a family picnic basket. These had a range of themes attached to them. The documentation of the kitchen (South Korean and Canada) demonstrates the cultural importance of food (attached to Personal/Antiquity). The personal objects are some of the most revealing, where the inhabitants documented some part of their items (cigarette case), collections (model car), charms (lucky waving cat) or selected art (water buffalo sculpture). Each one of these items is culturally individual, in that each one can tell a different kind of story and is personally related, a gift, community-related or has been selected as part of a cultural memory. There are also several religious items including talismans, decorated totem, a prayer bowl and handbells which positioned spirituality and faith as important cultural markers. The empathetic theme drove an interesting range of objects. These were mostly personal but all of them were designed to improve the quality of the space (and life). This was either through using scent in the air, protection of the planet through recycled objects or intensely personal family items that have a strong empathetic reference. There were also a couple of items that were unusual, adding interest and demonstrating the breadth of human cultural reference. The "mobile" cheese plant (that moved in and out of the interior) brings in the relationship between humans and nature and the inside and outside continuum. Documenting a dog as a cultural item is perhaps altering the angle of the (object-based) cultural narrative process, but carries an important link to the identity of creatures within the context of the space. The final specialist item of note is the large American super-graphics. Important because it embeds a relationship with branding and the promotional cultures of advertising design. All of the items were either documented in a simple list like fashion and returned or they had a complete narrative behind them (a good example of this would be the Japanese model car which has presented with a full back story).

Cultural Trail

This chapter has outlined the cultural relationship between the physical and the digital aspects of space. This dynamic is a distinctly emerging formulation. A cultural trail through this book attempts to document this relationship between real physical space and an imagined one as documented above. The cultures emerging between the physical and the digital worlds are continually colliding and will become the basis for cultural action and identity in the future. Currently, physical and non-physical spaces are separated spatially but are informed by each other's cultural and spatial traits. For example, there is recognition that a digital environment emulates the physical environment as a place that humans understand and can occupy. There are examples where the physical environment also relates to the digital environment by creating escapist and imaginary worlds that have altered scale and reference. A distinct spatial and cultural hybridity of these two worlds is still to be fully achieved. But as the digital world embraces a deeper reality and becomes more aligned and mapped to the physical world an alignment of the values embedded within the spatial states is required. This will not just be a reconsideration of actual financial value like between banknotes and digital crypto-currencies, but an exploration of the differences between the physical and digital worlds that explores the value of physical and digital cultures, their alignment, meaning and long-term impact.

Whilst the focus of this chapter has been mainly on the physical object, the recording of these objects in their individual spaces was done physically but represented digitally. This crossover encourages the hybridity of spatial cultures forcing a different understanding of the cultural value of space. Whilst the experience of many digital environments is extraordinary, it is still connected or supported by levels of physicality and physical experience. These boundaries are being diffused through levels of hybridity in augmented reality spaces which draw together the physical and digital. This blending of environments brings value to both situations. Introducing digital imagery into existing physical environments begins to reveal levels of hybridity where people can live physically and still be immersed through digital objects and applications in their environment. Utilising a digital environment by bringing real objects and settings into the virtual environment opens new connected environments that would remove boundaries and allow improved cultural alignment and spatial transcendency. Lehman (2017, 35–36) describes this blended approach with interactive environments, "boundaries become ambiguous as sensing spaces weave in and out of one another. Occupants can transcend space – as where they are can simultaneously become where they are going as well as where they've been".

However, the perception and acceptance of digital environments are changing. As they have become more mainstream and embedded as part of normal life, they are affecting human behaviours and activity, especially as they become more tangible and inserted as part of human existence, especially through increasingly immersive environments and experiences. This hybrid spatialised culture is growing in impact and placement and as the fully immersive metaversian digital universe[2] takes hold, our understanding and reference within the known real world could begin to dynamically shift, furthering the need for a reconsideration of what we mean by a spatial culture. Further analysis of this chapter is outlined in the following summary chapter.

Notes

1 The information for this image has been interpreted and adapted from https://shrinkthatfootprint.com/how-big-is-a-house/ and Wikipedia, Dhavari https://en.wikipedia.org/wiki/Dharavi#:~:text=With%20a%20population%20density%20of,populated%20areas%20in%20the%20world.
2 A good introduction to the cultures of Metaverse can be found here: https://sensoriumxr.com/articles/how-to-enter-the-metaverse

9

SUMMARY – A CULTURAL ANALYSIS

This chapter summarises the information taken from the Cultural Trail sections of earlier chapters and the conclusions from the spatial probe data. It completes the findings that underpin the central chapters (5, 6, 7) and extends the descriptions from Chapter 8, embedding the impact of the Spatial Culture Ecosystem described in Chapter 4. There are further descriptions of the structures and responses of the urban, architectural and interior environments and their impact on inclusion, social justice, poverty, age, race and gender. There is an analysis of how design can drive the development of new urban and domestic environments through the placement and emergence of responsive spatial cultures. It advances the narrative forward into the future, connecting reflective and agile spatial cultures that are responsible, transformative, emotive and relevant to society.

A designed and situated spatial environment responds to the needs and desires of the inhabitants either through a design process or their adaption and change through use. However, space and place are responsive and reflexive, often designed as holistic entities or emerging from a series of selected settings or elements. These shape the experience and atmosphere, developing the temporal engagement with the occupants, reforming and altering the space and its component assemblies as life unfolds. Whether it is designed or formulated through time, the space will change and becomes inclusive of the people and the activity and inhabitants. Venturi et al. (1977, 73–76) undertook an extensive review of the architectural dynamics of Las Vegas. They analysed all the main architectural and visual components of the city to understand how the city was formed, and assembled what could be learned. They comment:

> Las Vegas space is neither contained and enclosed like medieval space, nor classically balanced and proportioned like Renaissance space, nor

DOI: 10.4324/9781003270393-10

154 Summary – a cultural analysis

> swept up in the rhythmically ordered movement like baroque space, nor does it flow like a modern space around freestanding urban space makers. It is something else again ... not chaos but a new spatial order relating the automobile on highway communication in an architecture which abandons pure form in favour of a mixed media.

Dovey (2010, 16) suggests that spatial assemblages are created by the connections and relationships that exist between roads, buildings, trees, objects and people. She suggests that this is dynamic and always in flux. She uses the street as an example of the transiency of space: "It is the relations buildings-sidewalk-roadway, the flows of traffic, people and goods: the interconnections of public to private space". Therefore, *assemblage* theory can be applied directly to an "aggregated, mixed, composed" spatial position where building experience and narrative sensations combine to form an inclusive experience. Roberts (2020, 52–55) stretches the spatial continuum by restating the impact of *spatial bricolage*, which places the onus on the individual (or bricoleur) to collate the unseen outputs of space ("experience, knowledge, skills, insights, emotional rewards, sense of well-being and accomplishment") into a sense of spatial poetics. He cites Levi-Strauss (1966) "[he] speaks not only with things ... But also through the medium of things" to strengthen that "space and self are dialectically woven from the world as it is experienced, conceived and practiced". Buchanan (2020, 4–28) uses the notions of *strata* (or pieces) to describe the *constructions* (*drawing together*) and *assemblies* (*arrangement*) of territories and space. These assemblies are constituted from the inherent population. Because space and place are so multidimensional and reflective of the population, they position strong equality, diversity and social inclusion, developing specific social constructs and community justice. This is reflected in the components of the situated culture strands in the Spatial Culture Ecosystem (Chapter 4).

Through the pandemic, the positions of the city and the protections our architecture, interior spaces and homes offered us were sharply refocused. This reminded us of the primary role of the built environment where the buildings protected the population from external threats. A reimagined interior shifted from aspirational, influential and comforting, to one of protecting and immunising the population from each other in a short period. This period made the population become introspective, forcing a re-examination of the domestic spaces we occupy. The spatial probe was planned to start in the summer of 2020 coinciding with the global lockdown. It reveals an honest and realistic view of the spaces we occupy and benefits from the invited subjects being confined to their homes. The detailed data and imagery reveal an often surprising, but informative glimpse into the world of domestic interior spaces and their contents. It discloses a dialogic similarity to domestic spaces that are occupied across the world. The patterns and typologies appear similar, but it is the individual, the objects, the furniture, the textiles and the surface decorations that define the cultural threads running through these spaces. Through the captured data, it is possible to develop associations within each of these spaces. The *Cultural Impact Areas* within the plan drawings (seen in the case study examples in Figures 8.2, 8.3, 8.4), develop an understanding of the relationship between each of the selected cultural objects and holistically extend the interior space by plotting the position and location of each of the object/artefacts selected. The data reveals that the selected objects are arranged on opposing walls, giving the impression that the cultural objects are used to dress the interior and surround the occupants. This suggests that these cultural exhibits are significant in forming the interior aesthetic, but also in magnifying a display context, framing spatial individuality and developing an emergent narrative of the interior context. It is also important to magnify that the selections and contributions via the spatial probe must be viewed in an individual and global context. The invited participants have a broad cultural and geographical mix, with a diverse range of individuals, gender, race and age. Figure 9.1 sets out the visual analysis of the objects set out in the spatial probe.

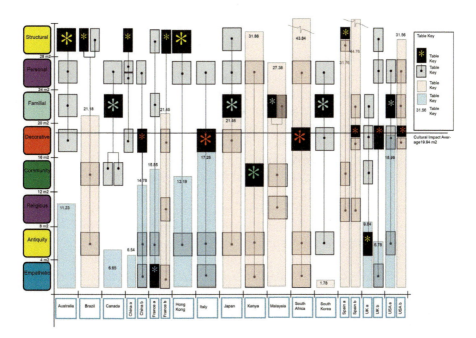

FIGURE 9.1 Analysis of the Cultural Probe Data
This includes a full listing of the primary and secondary cultural objects and the cultural impact areas created by the location and placement of the selected objects in the selected "rooms" (supported by Case Study examples in Figures 8.2, 8.3, 8.4).

156 Summary – a cultural analysis

This analysis captures the 80 objects selected as part of the spatial probe into the eight categories of Structural, Personal, Familial, Decorative, Community, Religious, Antiquity and Empathetic (coloured squares – left-hand side). In the main table, each of the primary objects is represented by a black square with a coloured asterisk (all object typologies are available in Table 8.1, Chapter 8). The secondary objects are shown as a grey square that is connected to the primary and other secondary objects and located longitudinally down to the country of origin at the base of the table. (Note that five countries have two entries a/b). The cultural mapping analysis is represented by elevated graph columns from the base of the table either as a blue (below m^2 average) or a peach colour (above m^2 average). Each column is represented by a square meterage number. The mid-graph black line crossing the table represents an average square meterage (based on the probe data) of 19.94 m^2 (Please also refer to the Table key in Figure 9.1).

Figure 9.1 reveals several findings allowing analysis of data from the probe. The first critical analysis is examining the objects, how they are categorised and where they are positioned. The primary objects (black squares) are mainly placed in the top half of the table (18/20) and categorised as Structural, Personal, Familial, Decorative and Community. This was not reflected in the secondary objects where the highest categories were Personal (14) and Decorative (15) followed by Community (11), Religious (11) and Antiquity (11). The lowest categorisation was for Religious (4). This suggests that there is a cultural shift between primary (the objects that were either selected first or had a higher level of hierarchy or importance) and secondary objects (selected next with a lower prioritisation). Where people categorise cultural objects that have structure and solidity (possibly relating to the sanctity and protection of the architecture and "home") as a primary selection, they position the hierarchy of culture over the more personally selected items. Primary items related to family and decoration were also high scoring and were (significantly) connected in several spaces, demonstrating a powerful connection between the home, family, and the surrounding environment. Other noticeable connections with repeating score lines were Antiquity, which had repetitive links with Decorative and Empathy. This suggests ancient and historical objects build empathetic relationships with the decorative dressing of inside spaces. The Religious category was strengthened with connections to Community and Empathy categories, indicating a cultural support process through faith. Most of the probes picked a primary and three secondary cultural objects for this exercise, although a pair (Hong Kong (3) and Japan (5)) selected different ranges and a couple that are represented by multiple objects in single categories (Canada [2x community], China a [2x personal], Spain b, USA b [2x decorative]).

Cultural impact analysis

The cultural impact area mapping data revealed some interesting contradictions. The area is measured on the plans arranged between a tiny South

Korean kitchen area of 1.78m^2 up to a massive 44.76m^2 for Spain b living area. Whilst these areas are quite speculative and would be adjusted as the interior and the objects moved around, it does give a measure of how culture is placed and its impact/influence inside an interior setting. One of the most revealing contradictions is the difference between the average meterage of residential floor space (see Figure 8.1) and what is revealed in the table (in Figure 9.1) regarding the area of cultural impact. The positioning of cultural objects is up to the individual and open to personalised interpretation. However, there are some marked differences between these, suggesting some of the countries with larger than average residential floor meterage (Australia, USA and Canada) position cultural objects in a much tighter group (hence the smaller meterage in Figure 9.1) relative to their floor area. Conversely, some of the countries with much smaller average residential meterage actively spread their cultural objects out (Spain, Japan, Hong Kong) relative to their floor area. Additionally, with this kind of randomised survey, it would be expected that the results would be closer to the average mark, in this case, 19.98m^2. Only four of the selected areas are within 2m^2 of the average mark. Many of the results are outside of the normal percentiles, suggesting that the cultural impact created by these areas is either more intense (smaller meterage) or less intense (larger meterage). There is also no specific pattern related to continental groups of countries, where the largest cultural impact areas are spread across Africa, Europe and the USA. Whilst these speculative results are quite compelling, further research (possible use of single-country probes would create deeper cultural analysis) and data analysis will be required to underpin these cultural conclusions on a country-by-county basis.

Cultural Trail summaries

Through analysis of the key components of the Cultural Trail at the end of each chapter, it is possible to summarise some of the emerging ideas that can be considered when designing space. These trends can be considered to unlock and fully integrate human culture within space.

Here are some key elements and connections formed through the Cultural Trail.

- The opening aspect of the trail is the introduction of an architectural phenomenon known as *Genius Loci* (Norberg-Schulz 1980, 3–18) which is used to describe the sensation of experience within any of the context of the built environment. The experience of the built environment is an important consideration (although often secondary) in developing human cultural reference. This *spirit* reveals itself in many of the phenomena of space and can be specifically aligned with the themes in Chapters 5, 6 and 7 that are grouped in the figurative, sensorial and

158 Summary – a cultural analysis

textural realms (atmosphere, character, experience, place; comfort, object, space, surface; colour, light, taste, place).

- The second connection developed across the Cultural Trail explores the territories of location and specifically between the rural and urban contexts, highlighting the differences and shifting settings between the community and individuals (Cultural Dynamics, Chapter 1). By understanding the patterns of urban growth and the historical movements between the locations, it is possible to locate human development through the migrations and relocations of culture. The trail highlights the importance of an individual approach and cultural determination by cultural groups forming integrated narratives for the urban landscape. Importantly, it also suggests the way culture changes metaphysically and generationally, altering its impact and pervasiveness. It introduces the idea of cultural boundary and terrain and how this is set out, documenting a constructed narrative that develops experience for the individual and the collective.

- This pivotable section of the trail highlights the importance of the individual and a more detailed personalised approach to understanding the cultures of space. Through identification, individual cultures collate to form and shape community-wide knowledge, beliefs and collective understanding. The trail highlights how an individual approach to culture can affect and impact the wider society and human development. The trail captures and summarises the work in the chapter and sets out the parameters of the international spatial probe, providing context and data for the remaining chapters. The probe collected a unique perspective on the domestic environment and the way culture was situated within each one of these spaces; it also references an important anthropological context for the built environment, leading to the development of the outlined Spatial Culture Ecosystem.

- The trail summarises the introduction of the Spatial Culture Ecosystem which captures the relationships that form between culture and environment. By using design thinking as a focus, the ecosystem was developed specifically to explore the located relationships that form and influence human development. Whilst this is quite complex, the trail outlines this fundamental relationship to connect the development of human society and the design of space. The trail also explores how the ecosystem emboldens the *design, emergence* and *agility* of space to reflect and capture human cultural reference. The ecosystem is designed to be read systematically and comparatively to understand the complex relationships at play. The trail references the further three chapters that are all based around the three figurative, sensorial and textural realms.

- The trail continues through the next three central chapters which present a series of related themes that present and unpick the detail within the spatial culture ecosystem and reveal how culture is presented through space. The chapter summaries capture each of the leading themes within each of the chapters. Chapter 5 which has a figurative theme explores how spatial culture is determined through the four figurative themes connected to space. This is presented to bridge between the physical and ethereal contexts. It reveals a crossover between space as a cultural entity (Atmosphere, and Character) and a vessel for culture to exist (Enclosure, Space). This links to Chapter 6 which explores the sensory nature of space, highlighting the importance of visual culture and specifically grounding the idea of spatial experience as a cultural form. The trail also includes references to material culture and how this bridges into the human and anthropological canon, introduced in Chapter 5 and the sensorial reference in Chapter 7.Chapter 7 presents an understanding of the textural realm in relation to culture, highlighting the differences between both the culture *of* space and *within* space. It specifically draws on components of culture like the taste and place, contemporising the nature of culture and outlining a temporal framework (and possible cultural longevity) as a reference for culture to operate in.

- The trail is then concluded through a process of exploring cultural mapping using the physical data from the spatial probe and digital environments. By concluding the trail in this way, the book draws together the relationship between physical and digital spaces. The inclusion of digital spaces allows the discussion of emerging spatial cultures to stretch the potency and relevancy of the spatial canon. The trail concludes by setting out some comparative reflections on new hybrid environments that develop the boundaries of spatial culture and the experiences of space.

Cultural futures

The references to humans as "spatial organisms" situate a human spatial condition which develops an internal proximity of space both within the body and above the skin, making an immediate connection with the environment whilst helping to improve our understanding of a wider societal position. The collective idea that human beings enjoy being in and "fusing" (Pallasmaa 2012, 12–13) with space is fundamental and pervasive to the human condition. This bonding with the environment (individually or collectively) enhances societal well-being and connection for our bodies, our minds, and our communities. The spatial environment enables a constructed paradigm for us to document and advance our cultural beliefs, ideas, customs, and patterns of behaviours, which help to elevate human civilisation and promote its long-term survival. This survival must embody a deep reflection of our impact on others, our spatial needs, and develop rich new spatial cultures that responsibly position our activities to maintain, repair and rebuild our relationships with our planet. The way humans

160 Summary – a cultural analysis

interact with the natural world through their spatial activities and behaviours must become an immediate priority. Spatial cultures must embrace a revolutionary future where the renewal of existing space and the design of new space becomes intrinsically tuned to the biology and ecosystems of the Earth. The design and use of space are fundamental to this future.

Through the descriptions of space and place, an emerging landscape exposes both fragility and sturdiness of the human condition. A consistent theme across the chapters is the spatial harness that forms between the exterior and interior environments. Specifically, around the terrain, borders and thresholds that separate and bind the two. Many of these kinds of spaces can be seen in cityscapes as spaces between territories or defined spaces, transitional or moving-through-spaces that exist simply to link other spaces together. These can be seen externally as transport hubs, roads, streets, passageways, alleyways or subways; or in architectural spaces as entrances, reception spaces, circulation spaces, corridors, staircases or lift lobbies. These liminal and in-between spaces (a focus here on space between the insideness and outsideness of buildings) are not immediately recognisable as a unused spaces that have become widely accepted as places for occupation or commercialisation that extend the spatial phenomenon. This developing spatial culture boosts the cityscape by recognising the hidden, forgotten and unused space and blending the position of urban spaces, architecture and the interior into new forms of spatial hybridity. By accelerating a position between Richard Neutra's (1954) bio-realism theory (Figure 4.2) and modern biophilic applications,[1] new extended forms of integrated "Bio" environments can be designed and assembled. This actively improves the condition and well-being of space, bridging the natural, scientific, creative and cultural relationships with the earth.

The fusing between humans and space helps to underpin and enhances societal well-being and the connections between our bodies, our relationships and our communities. The spatial environment enables a constructed paradigm for us to document and advance our cultural beliefs, ideas, customs, and patterns of behaviours, which help to elevate human civilisation, promoting long-term survival. Whilst much human culture is derived from historical knowledge, the future of occupied space is determined by the embedded signs, traces and residues of human culture that are located within, or are embodied by, the spaces that people occupy. These traces are distinctive and form the building blocks for new cultures and transferable spatial knowledge. This experiential and dialogic process is constructed through cultural and spatial capital as part of the journeys that we take through space, providing familiar (and unfamiliar) perspectives and creating (sensual) touchpoints that help connect the human body to space. Spatial cultures are the expected, the familiar, the surprising and the reassuring experiences we interpret from designed spaces. Austin (2020, 2) suggests that we 'read' and interpret worldly spatio-temporal situations with our whole bodies, not just our eyes. The design of narrative environments therefore, involves a deliberate and coordinated three-part sequence of movement: the progression of *content*, through *space* and over *time*, in order to tell the story and communicate a message or messages to a particular audiences.

One way to develop new physical spaces is through an augmentation between physical and digital spaces. This will become increasingly prevalent as human needs alter using the environment to further support and amplify human advancement through a blending of mediums. As digital space is infinite, the physical and cultural conditions of space will adjust, allowing augmented space to become more widely accepted. This will balance physical spaces that embrace virtual objects and digital walkthrough experiences with real-time haptics and interactions; and virtual spaces that transmit real-time physical interactions and corporeal pop-ups that fully blend the augmented experience. This will bridge and maximise the spatial potential that underpins the needs of a changing society. These new spatial realms will need further definition and acceptance (as defined in the last chapter) but have the potential to fundamentally alter the human relationship with space. As new digital environments emerge and new virtual communities become more pervasive, new forms of immersive and interactive behaviours will emerge, digitally coating the urban environment and changing the processes, experiences and cultures of everyday life.

Finally, by exploring and interpreting a new meta-modern ideology, the design of space can be reconsidered as a series of new composites and opposing narratives that swing between different polarities of the designed cultural landscape. Whilst meta-modernism (Anderson 2021; Danilova and Bakshutova 2021; Vermeulen and van den Akker 2010) has been forming over the last decade, it offers a structure and ideology for the design of new spatial cultures to be considered. The book outlines a series of structured narratives that use paired polarities (inside/outside; space/place; physical/digital; rural/urban; repair/replace/renewal) that align with this thinking, underpinning new processes, structures and horizons for the design of the built environment. Treat this conclusion as a reflexive platform for further discussion, research and investigation into the formidable relationship between human cultures and the environments that surround them. They are an embodiment of ourselves, our creativity, our society and our diversity. We must ensure that this narrative continues to connect our long-term aspirations for our design futures. Richard Neutra initiated this thinking 70 years ago:

> Design is the cardinal means by which human beings have long tried to modify their natural environment, piecemeal and wholesale. The

physical surroundings had to be made more habitable and more in keeping with rising aspirations. Each design becomes an ancestor to a great number of other designs and engenders a new crop of aspirations.

(Neutra 1954, 5)

Note

1 Biophilic references: Nair et al. (2022). Other references include Heath (2021) and Coulthard (2020).

IMAGE CREDITS

Figure 0.1 Beamish Living Museum – General Store. Author
Figure 1.1 Durham Cathedral (2022). Author
Figure 1.2 Cultural dynamics of space-located culture – Levels 0–4. Author
Figure 1.3 A regenerative cultural circle illustration (based on Circuits of Culture Image, Du Gay 1998). Author
Figure 1.4 George Gilbert Scott – Grand Midland Hotel, St Pancras, London 1873. Author
Figure 1.5 IKEA furniture store. Kouhoku, Japan. 2006. Photo by midorisyu on flickr. [Generic (CC by 2.0)]. https://flickr.com/photos/midorisyu/276720 3904/in/photolist-5dwDj9-nm9Wu-5dwDcW-5dwCY1-5dsiwB-5dsiqr-5dwC VY-nm9VMnm9Vo-nm9Uy-4L6ZYQ-KpKgh-pKeWnH-pK1Krm-qpsAz9-Kp Pua-rTHWqs-2yTGz8-2yY5UW-nm9V1-77cvry-a9mr2ca9mpiv-a9pbHw-a 9pcES-a9mqfazgiv3-8BTU8t-8BTU4P-8BWYC3-qcEur-9MWLbPqcC8d-9zB cou-idtfgi-idtvVd-9zyczP-9zBcML-qcDud-HWUEG-9zyd1v-qcDqr-HWYm X-5Esxwf-qcErsqcEgr-9zycGD-qcE9E-qcEe3-9zBct7
Figure 1.6 Prada store, Tokyo. Herzog and de Meuron 2000. Photo by Forgemind ArchiMedia on flickr. [Generic (CC by 2.0)] https://flickr.com/photos/ eager/20246638006/in/photolist-a9pTj8-a9pJkZ-wR8j6CvWyY6R-wAQ6fs-wR8sJj-a9pToK-wAP5gq-wSHz83–6bp1Sc-2smHPJ-6bp1Q4-wTqVgk-Cj2H4-wTXJ2F-caGzPQ-vWxdj4-Cj2EA-wAN7d5-wSGuXG-vWyzn4-Cj2FQwAWYYM-Cj2ET-wTrnYi-wAPPEE-wSFeqb-wR7cTj-wAPnpq-wAP tUC-vWyJ54-vWprn5-wR7xa5-wTXenB-wAWhJt-vWzXnK-wTr75K-wR7AZE-wSGt6A-wAPx2uvWpLhj-wTqXm2-wAVeP2-Cj2Fm-641jbY-63W5pT-2nSa 2eF-wSHAFd-wSGatmwAWfAv

DOI: 10.4324/9781003270393-11

164 Image credits

Figure 2.1 Ancient chalk drawing, Uffington, England. By USGS – World Wind (go), Public Domain https://commons.wikimedia.org/w/index.php?curid=4302322

Figure 2.2 Island of Manhatton – City of New York (1850). Original from Library of Congress. Digitally enhanced by rawpixel. [Generic (CC by 2.0)] https://flickr.com/photos/vintage_illustration/50622870888/in/photolist-5u4owD-5u4pbp-5u8Nod-2k8nrQL-2iskFXy-efT5Ds-2k8rLpa-d997Zw-d8rFhY-7gf3Vp-28dvWVT-2k8rLqh-a95Di3-f9w3R-2k8reLR-2TVQhH-5m9UfM-a92RgP-5mebs7-7CMH7r-5m9Ucr

Figure 2.3 Houses of Bournville, Birmingham, UK. Photo by Elliot Brown. [Generic (CC by 2.0)] https://flickr.com/photos/ell-r-brown/7781336944/in/photolist-cRBonN-6x7fxJ-7SmN7L-6x7kbb-9y5BKF-erZAaC-5Rj2JL-6x7eAN-6x33eT-HTjN92-9y8ANY-6x7gzo-9y5CXe-6x39FX-7Sm62j-eubEAT-bnbtRW-6x7nqC-D7BaTX-6x3bcn-6x7mEf-2nmWdXi-xQuDB3-CMLKth-kqH8Ag-kqGohn-7SiwDH-6x365z-asjg2m-6x33Ln-euaWVn-eueQCh-asjgXN-eubDfn-9y8Cid-eueUqo-9y5Dsn-9y5FZR-asgPBM-9y5EsX-7Sm6k1-eubyEr-9y5EXn-asjtiL-6x3dgV-7Sm76w-6x3dL2-f938rS-eubJit-hpoCSU

Table 3.1 Exemplar pilot probe data

Figure 3.1 Contents of the (physical) cultural probe pilot – Japanese. Author

Figure 3.2 Domestic apartment (Japanese participant 2020) – Anonymous

Figure 4.1 Spatial Culture Ecosystem. Author

Figure 4.2 Bio-realism – Richard Neutra Design Philosophy that blended spatial atmospheres. Photo by Daniel Kim. [Generic (CC by 2.0)] https://flickr.com/photos/119658633@N07/34377421235/in/photolist-UnPgDe-T9dDv4-TMQ5Uf-pT3PAb-yVBt6a-xZPf7z-e49KW7-vSnF5-x8ik5b-zCLLVL-xbAeNs-2k4Yi9f-V2US5Y-qJCNmW-2k4Yi9k-8QyWVd-jXxk3t-2jXKCVh-jXwSYp-T6qAPC-TMQLTU-Ujas2o-T9dLQz-T9dnYH-T9d23V-8Pfmq6-kJaPq-PJM98Q-Nimgcb-saceRL-yCehaL-rdkzfm-vSnkc-2jXKCTy-xcyy1b-tGqhW-7go

KUn-rSLsxS-ySLDus-21vKWb-xnVUu7-e6GQw8-xHo39B-tGqee-pGv3qD-xWTavH-yZCvNE-yBaWuf-ySLW5w-2jXKCRj

Figure: 4.3 Spatial cultural territories. Author

Figure 4.4 Theme Vals Spa by Peter Zumthor (1996). Setting a powerful cultural indicator of space using atmosphere. [Generic (CC by 2.0)] https://flickr.com/photos/anonphotography/6379409381/in/photolist-KKm6Vr-pZyUVZ-aHJbuT-aHJaWr-8BUL8C-aHJ99V

Figure 4.5 Spatial proximities (based on proxemic spheres, Hall, 1990). Author

Figure 5.1 The Eames House. Case Study House No. 8, Los Angeles. Photo by Paolo Gamba. [Generic (CC by 2.0)] https://flickr.com/photos/abukij/21076589233/in/photolis
t-y7t2Fx-yLJNU7-z23k5A-dcDr5L-yLKnx1-y7sTfV-xuFkN-nDgcDf-4yv5sV-4yv5oz-dcDo3p-qFSLfq-7mg8ct-7mk2y9-Xd8hyY-z4kCJB-22Bm3Ao-CZhcV7-CztevC-3TVGH-3TVH3-9tJFHS-3TVHk-K75j2A-z4kwTD-a

23RwS-xuMmN-cT1hrw-HQAxgf-HZkjKH-UyAqbf-6FKZh-cT1hLj-23Szoin-cT167C-9HxQQq-djDyEq-dmB2V8-UyAqad-cT15dj-cT1biE-dmBd7b-cT1AAY-eiLUEG-dmB4BT-dXrw6Y-dmB8BL-dXrw3q-dmB2HR-cT1aY7

Figure 5.2 The Rabbit Hole Restaurant Durham. Credit Author.

Figure 5.3 Tobermory Harbour, Isle of Mull, Scotland – Example of spatial character "of Place". Photo by low cloud on flickr. [Generic (CC by 2.0)] https://flickr.com/photos/25709664@N00/274154942/in/photolist-qe7Hm-39Fszg-2bLrVgX-CMRsSa-2bLsfgv-CoY4z6-adjEaL-agsuoN-CoQXfN-PoVgt D-9i4K8v-2aJKu6X-2aJKMjV-agpEcM-agsnVC-W5rz-CMRyvK-cLTJz9-CoRfgb-8zyk8-28nc9f4-agsztu-QxtAsY-Dj34wY-29DtFxs-29mxKre-27 Z4oP7-2aJR9Rx-27YWnWQ-29DskjU-2aEvKB9-2aEw4VU-2aJTf9T-7YFUL Y-RzeZfq-LYTNZZ-RWrTrc-LYSRBp-S4Kwoh-2aEv1PW-27Z295b-2y h8EE-RxJvcW-fSnQfQ-GDW2gs-2aJP5vT-29mq23R-6ZKynA-2a JSNyz-NBbvzm

Figure 5.4 Glastonbury Festival – Character of place. Photo by Rachel D. [Generic (CC by 2.0)] https://flickr.com/photos/fussyonion/35573133015/in/p hotolist-WctB6z-CBiA8H-8Scyi-vziqWF-4YWzdi-vwCyHC-urVz62-6Zet8R-9WJDpJ-W4G7EV-8mi5We-f3meW1-2T4ix-cgZSBd-8mj1vr-6Zit6h-8miUba-8miTin-8mj5DP-8miMM4-8Sd6k-8mmZn1-8miFMM-8mmKJ1-8mn7pw-8mmNF1-f3mcvN-f3mafo-vzipJv-8mkYG1-uvhfLC-f3mf6C-f36ZnK-f374b4-f373Cz-f3mgeL-8mnedE-8mngDW-f374FR-f373Kn-f3maBm-f373dt-f373Tt-f3mgmj-f372mZ-f3mfDs-f3m8XQ-vwLHE5-f3741z-f36VAZ

Figure 5.5 Pierre Cardin's Bubble Palace (1975) By Frans-Banja Mulder, CC BY 3.0, https://commons.wikimedia.org/w/index.php?curid=46718076

Figure 5.6 Brutalist Architecture – Newcastle City Hall 1968. Author

Figure 5.7 Science Museum, London. Author

Figure 6.1 Farnsworth House. Mies van der Rohe 1951. [Generic (CC by 2.0)] https://flickr.com/photos/julielion/52344533384/in/photolist-2nKvq7U-2jR7dCU-ghkuhG-5stsdg-ghkPKw-2jR2Lrp-2hF7fMt-2jR7dD5-2jR2Lre-2hF7gjq-2hF4vAE-7SKviF-5Gd7zN-2jR6juV-2nKw4fN-2kKU6Gu-bMb88T-bMb8n6-2MRUs7-2MRW71-9Gbugw-4HnWXA-2MRSCL-9G8zBn-2M S5iW-2MS56h-2MRUFL-2MMtDX-9Gbu2S-2MMBDk-9Gbuko-9GbtWm-2MMH3p-2MMvUX-2MMGCV-2MRUcb-2MMvEr-2MRTdY-2MMxM8-2MRVWU-2MMG3e-2MMxfc-2MS6j7-2MRSoY-2MRVGN-2MMFMZ-2MMFnr-2MRRyW-2MRWjG-2MMGQi

Figure 6.2 Object collections from a domestic dwelling. Author

Figure 6.3 Surface patternation, The Broad, Los Angeles. Diller Scofidio + Renfro. Photo by Joey Zanotti. [Generic (CC by 2.0)] https://flickr.com/p hotos/45958601@N02/47931952697/in/photolist-2niWQWo-VUhXvA-2g2zMBx-2gwHBHQ-rSzyar-WxoneS

Figure 6.4 Citizen M Hotel, Victoria London. Author

Figure 7.1 TV Studio – Eurovision song contest Stockholm 2016. Photo by David Jones. [Generic (CC by 2.0)] https://flickr.com/photos/davidcjones/33225534494/in/photolist-2n7n3gw-SC2xR1-Tju7iu-TECfUd-SE

166 Image credits

K6AD-TUrJ1Z-SC2AC3-SC2A6b-Tju85Q-Tju89N-TECh5E-Tju8FE-Tju8Ho-
TUrLPK-SC2CcL-SEK7Ua-TECfhm-SEJXtX-SEJXog-TQTouh-TECkLs-SEJYQz-
TECiMh-TjtZcW-SEKbqi-SEJZjv-SEKcya-TjtXS1-SEJXXH-SEJWJv-SEKbRZ-
Tjub9A-Tju9py

Figure 7.2 Amsterdam Light Festival 2015. Photo by Edwin van Buuringen.
[Generic (CC by 2.0)] https://flickr.com/photos/edwinvanbuuringen/2357000
1530/in/photolist-BUNqhJ-dGHSJp-CMx66S-dGPjqh-2o43hx7-iKbLtj-iK9R
vi-dGHXxH-iK9QYM-BQPbBi-iKbVjf-dGPoHU-dGPnH1-2mRjArX-iSLuE7-iK
bUNf-iUJf9f-iKbLpG-dGPk6w-2kR1XPe-iKbK5s-iKdSRh-qfGQNb-CDogg2-
iKbn6X-2o43hwF-Cw66Dt-qdCMWS-iK9ZBP-Ch9poN-iKbmZp-CMwVGG-
CMwYpA-C5cddM-CFa65i-CFa7Lz-Ch9rtE-pyJECp-iSGyKi-eMKLKE-2o3XrMX-
C553xQ-pkZRRL-CB6iNy-2o3XrYU-Ct5yQk-iSJA9W-CzVo4M-gkAPtS-iKdPpN

Figure 7.3 Hill House – Charles and Margaret Macdonald Mackintosh 1902.
Drawing Room Detail. Photo by Tony Hisgett. [Generic (CC by 2.0)] https://
flickr.com/photos/hisgett/37376575552/in/photolist-XYkEGi-XUThXY-X
YkHgg-BTuess-YVnHQw-YAQuC3-YWQJv5-YXf2sq-XYkMYc-YVM2uy-Y
ZYTMg-YZAFna-YVM6rm-YWQHJq-YZYW9F-YWQF9q-YBefe7-BTuhy7-
BTummh-YVnRm3-BTUjuJ-BTUiRQ-YZAHZK

Figure 7.4 Venice Biennale installation 2019. Photo by Aleksandr Zykov.
[ShareAlike Generic (CC by 2.0)] https://flickr.com/photos/84292292@N00/
50830832451/in/photolist-2krKiyX-2krKG1b-2gyc7ai-2gycKLw-2gycKBD-2
gycj8b-2gyciWj-2gycixi-2gycJuZ-2gycJtr-2gycJmH-2gycJgC-2gyci4c-2gychYN-
2gycHQh-2gycHN3-2gycHGb-2gycHwM-2gycHun-2gychdp-2gycGJK-2
gycGFd-2gycffw-2gycEZ2-2gycECa-2gycBpw-2gycatT-2gyczi7-2gyc5MD-2m
tfovN-2mt6xgP-2hBVPEi-2mt6wCu-2hBUUca-2hBUTQD-2gycetr-2gycL1E-2
gyciFK-2gycJLq-2gyciBg-2gycJyM-2gycJwY-2gycJpy-2gycicP-2gychPQ-
2gychLi-2gycHKc-2gycHCP-2gycHrg-2gycH11

Figure 7.5 Place – traditional Funfair environment. Photo by Nikolay Vorobyev
on Unsplash. [Generic (CC by 2.0)] https://unsplash.com/photos/iM5Lm4qz77Q

Figure 8.1 Residential floor space per capita in m2 Author

Table 8.1 Cultural mapping objects (detail from Table 3.1).

Figure 8.2 Floor plan of French town/city centre house (Constructed 1920).
Rennes City Centre. Hallway. French B Plan. Author

Figure 8.3 Floor plan of suburban Terrace House. Eikenbosch, Cape Town.
(Constructed c.1999). Lounge space. South Africa plan. Author

Figure 8.4 Plan of flat in town centre, Stourbridge, West Midlands, UK (c.
1901). Lounge space. UK Stourbridge Plan. Author.

Figure 9.1 Analysis of the Cultural Probe Data. This includes a full listing of
all of the primary and secondary cultural objects and the cultural impact
areas created by the location and placement of the selected objects in the
selected rooms. Author.

BIBLIOGRAPHY

Abercrombie, S. (1990) *A Philosophy of Interior Design*. New York: Westview.

Adams, R. (2020) *Interior Design: A Global Profession*. London: Routledge.

Adamson, G., Kelley, V. (2013) *Surface Tensions: Surface, Finish and the Meaning of Objects*. (Studies in Design and Material Culture). Manchester: Manchester University Press.

Agnew, J. (1987) *Place and Politics: The Geographical Mediation of State and Society*. Boston: Allen and Unwin. 1–11.

Albers, J. (1963) *Interaction of Colour*. London: Yale University Press.

Alexander, C., Ishikawa, S., Silverstein, M. (1977) *A Pattern Language*. Oxford: Oxford University Press.

Alexander, H. (1906) *The Model Village and its Cottages: Bournville*. London: B. T. Batsford. https://archive.org/details/cu31924015178548/page/n39/mode/2up.

Anderson, L. R. (2021) *Metamodernity: Meaning and Hope in a Complex World*. Copenhagen: Nordic Bildung.

Anthes, E. (2020) *The Great Indoors: The Surprising Science of How Buildings Shape Our Behavior, Health, and Happiness*. New York: Picador.

Appleton, J. (1975) *Experience of Landscape*. London: Wiley.

Ashenburg, K. (2007) *The Dirt on Clean*. Toronto: Random House.

Attenborough, D. (2020) *A Life on our Planet*. London: Penguin/Random House.

Auge, M. (2009) *Non-places: Introduction to an Anthropology of Super-modernity*. Paris: Verso Book.

Austin, T. (2020) *Narrative Environments and Experience Design: Space as a Medium of Communication*. London: Routledge.

Azzarito, A. (2020) *The Elements of a Home: Curious Histories Behind Everyday Household Objects, from Pillows to Forks*. New York: Chronicle Books.

Bachelard, G. (2014) *The Poetics of Space*. London: Penguin.

Bailey, S. (2021) The Magnificent Fiasco of Mies Van der Rohe's Farnsworth House. *The Spectator Magazine*. 10th April.

Bayley, S. (2017) *Taste: The Secret Meaning of Things*. London: Circa Press.

168 Bibliography

Beanland, C. (2020) *Unbuilt*. London: Batsford.

Bell, P. A., et al. (2001) *Environmental Psychology*, 6th edition. New York: Harcourt Brace.

Benedikt, M. (2002) Environmental Stoicism and Place Machismo. *Harvard Design Magazine* 16: 1–8.

Böhme, G. (2017) *The Aesthetics of Atmosphere*. Ambiances, Atmospheres and Sensory Experiences of Spaces. London: Routledge.

Bourdieu, P. (1977) *Outline of a Theory of Practice*. Cambridge: Cambridge University Press.

Bradbury, D. (2021) *The Secret Life of the Modern House*. London: Octopus Publishing.

Brooker, G. (2016) *Adaptions: Strategies for Interior Architecture and Design*. London: Bloomsbury Visual Arts.

Brooker, G. (2013) *Key Interiors since 1900*. London: Laurence King.

Brooker, G. and Weinthal, L. (eds.) (2013) *The Handbook of Interior Architecture*. London: Bloomsbury.

Bruner, J. (1991) The Narrative Construction of Reality. *Critical Enquiry*. 18(1): 9 (Autumn).

Buchanan, I. (2020) *Assemblage Theory and Method: An Introduction and Guide*. London: Bloomsbury.

Cadbury, D. (2011) *Chocolate Wars: From Cadbury to Kraft – 200 Years of Sweet Success and Bitter Rivalry*. London: Harper Collins.

Casson, H.(ed.) (1968) *Inscape*. London: Architectural Press.

Canter, D. (1975) *Environmental Interaction*. London: Surrey University Press.

Coulthard, S. (2020) *Biophilia: You + Nature + Home*. London: Kyle Books.

Cox, B. (2014) *Human Universe*. London: William Collins.

Crawford, I., Thompson, M. (2005) *Home is where the Heart is?*London: Quadrille.

Cresswell, T. (2015) *Place: An Introduction*. West Sussex: John Wiley /Blackwell.

Danilova, E., Bakshutova, D. (2021) Metamodernism: The Phenomenon of Memory as Part of an Architectural Concept. In: *Advances in Social Science, Education and Humanities Research*, Vol. 600. Proceedings of the 3rd International Conference on Architecture: Heritage, Traditions and Innovations (AHTI 2021).

De Botton, A. (2014) *The Architecture of Happiness*. London: Penguin.

De Certeau, M. (1988) *The Practice of Life*. Trans. Steven F. Rendell. Los Angeles: University of California Press.

De Wolfe, E. (2020) *The House in Good Taste: The Original Guide to Interior Decoration and Organising your Home*. New York: Clydesdale.

Dosen, A. S., Ostwald, M. J. (2013) Prospect and Refuge Theory: Constructing a Critical Definition for Architecture and Design. *The International Journal of Design in Society* 6(1): 9–23.

Dovey, K. (2010) *Becoming Places: Urbanism/Architecture/Identity/Power*. New York: Routledge.

Du Gay, P. (1996) *Questions of Cultural Identity*. London: Sage.

Du Gay, P. (1998) *Production of Culture/Cultures of Production*. London: Sage/The Open University.

Eames, C. and Eames, R. (1977) *The Power of Ten*. [Film] IBM. Eames Studio. CA. USA. Accessed 8 Dec. 2022. https://www.youtube.com/watch?v=55Gpm1Q0abk

Edwards, B. (1979) *Drawing on the Right Side of the Brain*. London: Souvenir Press.

Edwards, C. (2011) *Interior Design – A Critical Introduction*. London: Berg.

Exner, U., Pressel, D. (2009) *Spatial Design*. Berlin: Birkhauser.

Bibliography 169

Fast, J. (2002) *Body Language*. New York: M. Evans and Co.

Forty, A. (1995) *Objects of Desire*. London: Thames and Hudson.

Foucault, M. (2001) *The Order of Things: An Archaeology of the Human Sciences*. London: Routledge Classics.

Frampton, K. (2001) *Studies in Tectonic Culture: The Poetics of Construction in Nineteenth and Twentieth Century Architecture*. New York: The MIT Press.

Fry, T. (2017) *RE-Making Cities: An Introduction to Urban Metrofitting*. London: Routledge. 23–24.

Gandy, M. (2005) Cyborg Urbanization: Complexity and the Monstrosity in the Contemporary City. In: *International Journal of Urban and Regional Research* 29(1): 26–49.

Gaver, W., Dunne, T. and Pacenti, E. (1999) Design: Cultural Probes. *Interactions*, January.

Geertz, C. (2017) *The Interpretation of Culture*. New York: Basic Books.

Gemzoe, L., Gehl, J. (1996) *Public Spaces Public Life*. Copenhagen: Danish Architectural Press.

Gideon, S. (1959) *Space, Time and Architecture*. Cambridge: Harvard University Press.

Gillian, N. (2019) *Future Office – Next Generation Workplace Design*. London: RIBA.

Glancey, J. (2006) I don't do nice. *The Guardian* Online. https://www.theguardian.com/artanddesign/2006/oct/09/architecture.communities. Accessed 1 Dec. 2022.

Gola, A. (2022) Material Culture of the Palestinian Duyuf. In: Schneiderman, D., Lasc, A. and Tehve, K. (2022) *Appropriated Interiors*. 51–69. New York: Routledge.

Griffiths, S., von Lunen, A. (ed.) (2016) *Spatial Cultures: Towards a New Social Morphology of Cities Past and Present* (Design and the Built Environment). Oxford: Routledge.

Grove, J. (2017) *Interior Design: A Professional Guide*. London: RIBA.

Hadid, Z. (2009) *Zara Hadid: The Complete Works*. New York: Rizzoli.

Hall, E. (1990) *The Hidden Dimension*. London: Anchor Books. (Originally published in 1966).

Hall, S., du Gay, P. (1996) *Questions of Cultural Identity*. London: Sage.

Hanington, B., Martin, B. (2019) *Universal Methods of Design*. New York: Rockport.

Harman G. (2018) *Object–Orientated–Ontology: A New Theory of Everything*. London: Penguin.

Heath, O. (2021) *Design a Healthy Home: 100 Ways to Transform Your Space for Physical and Mental Wellbeing*. London: DK Publishers.

Heatherwick, T. (2015) *Making*. London: Thames and Hudson.

Heidegger, M. (1962) *Being and Time*, trans. John Macquarrie and Edward Robinson. New York: Harper & Row.

Henderson, K., Lock, K., Ellis, H. (2019) *The Art of Building a Garden City*. London: RIBA Publishing.

Hess, A (1999) *The Architecture of John Lautner*. London: Thames and Hudson.

Hicks, D. (1979) *Living with Design*. London: Weinfeld and Nicolson.

Highmore, B. (ed.) (2009) *The Design Culture Reader*. London: Routledge.

Highmore, B. (2014) *The Great Indoors: At Home in the Modern British House*. London: Profile.

Hillier, B., Hanson, J. (1997) *Social Logic of Space*. Cambridge: Cambridge University Press.

Hnilica, S (2020) The Metaphor of the City has a Thinking Machine: A Complicated Relationship and its Backstory. 68–83. In: Figueiredo, S. M., Krishnamurthy, S., Schroeder, T. (eds) (2020) *Architecture in the Smart City*. London: Routledge.

170 Bibliography

Holl, S. (2019) *Compression*. New York: Princeton Press.
Howard, E (2010) *To-Morrow: A Peaceful Path to Real Reform*. Cambridge: Cambridge Library Collection – British and Irish History, 19th Century. (Original Publication 1898.)
Husserl, E. (1970) *The Crisis of European Sciences and Transcendental Phenomenology*. Northwestern University Press.
Hustwit, G. (dir.) (2011) *Urbanised*. Film. Available: ITunes. https://www.hustwit.com/urbanized.
Huxley, A (2007) *Brave New World*. London: Vintage Classic. (Original Publication 1931)
Ince, C. (2015) *The World of Charles and Ray Eames*. London: Thames and Hudson.
Ingelhart, F. R. (2018) *Cultural Evolution: People's Motivations are Changing, and Reshaping the World*. London: Cambridge University Press.
Ingold, T. (2018) *Anthropology – Why It Matters*. London: Polity.
Ingold, T. (2000) *The Perception of the Environment: Essays in Livelihood: Dwelling and Skill*. London: Routledge.
Inwood, M. (1997) *Heidegger – A Very Short Introduction*. Oxford: Oxford University Press.
Jodidio, P. (2022) *Niemeyer*. Berlin: Taschen.
Joshi, A. (2022) The Metaverse: A Universe without Culture. *The Stanford Review*. 22 June. https://stanfordreview.org/the-metaverse-a-universe-without-culture/#:~:text=Facebook's%20recent%20rebranding%20as%20Meta,that%20allows%20for%20interpersonal%20interaction. Accessed 4 Nov. 2022.
Julier, G. (2013) *The Culture of Design*. London: Sage.
Kaplan, R., Kaplan, S. (1977) *Humanscape: Environments for People*. New York: Ulrichs Books.
Klee, P. (1973) *Pedagogical Sketchbook*. Introduction by Sibyl Moholy-Nagy. Berlin: Faber and Faber.
Kopec, D. (2006) *Environmental Psychology for Design*. New York: Fairchild Books.
Lawson, B. (2001) *The Language of Space*. Oxford: Architectural Press.
Lefebvre, H. (1991) *The Production of Space*, translated by Donald Nicholson-Smith. Oxford: Blackwell.
Lehman, M. L. (2017) *Adaptive Sensory Environments*. London: Routledge.
Levi-Strauss, C. (1966) *The Savage Mind*. London: Weidenfeld and Nicholson.
Lewis, R. D. (2006) *When Cultures Collide: Leading Across Cultures*. Nicolas Brealey. Third edition.
Libeskind, D. (2001) *The Spaces of Encounter*. London: Thames and Hudson.
Libeskind, D. (2018) *The Edge of Order*. New York: Clarkson Potter Publications.
Low, M. (2018) *The Sociology of Space: Materiality, Social Structure and Action*. London: Palgrave Macmillian.
Low, S. (2017) *Spatializing Culture: The Ethnography of Space and Place*. London: Routledge.
Low, S., Lawrence-Zuniga, D. (eds.) (2003) *The Anthropology of Space and Place: Locating Culture*. London: Wiley-Blackwell.
Lynch, K. (1964) *The Image of the City*. Harvard-MIT Joint Center for Urban Studies Series. New York: MIT Press.
Lyndon, D. (1994) *Chambers for a Memory Palace*. New York: MIT Press.
McLeod, S. (2021) *Museums and Design for Creative Lives*. London: Routledge.
McCandless, D. (2009) *Information is Beautiful*. London: Collins.

Mallgrave, H. F. (2018) *From Object to Experience. The New Culture of Architectural Design*. London: Bloomsbury.

Maslow, A. H. (1943) A Theory of Human Motivation. *Psychological Review*, 50(4): 370–396. https://doi.org/10.1037/h0054346.

Merwood-Salisbury, J., Coxhead, V. (2018) Exterior Interiors: The Urban Living Room and Beyond. In: Schneiderman, D., Campos, A. *Interiors Beyond Architecture*. London: Routledge.

Mesher, L. (2010) *Retail Design* London: AVA Books.

Miller, D. (2008) *The Comfort of Things*. London: Polity.

Moore, R. (2017) The Bilbao Effect: How Frank Gehry's Guggenheim Started a Global Craze. *The Guardian*. https://www.theguardian.com/artanddesign/2017/oct/01/bilbao-effect-frank-gehry-guggenheim-global-craze. Accessed 1 Dec. 2022.

Mulholland, N. (2008) The Cultural Economy. *Renewal: A Journal of Labour Politics* 16(2): 35–44.

Munn, D. N. (1996) Excluded Spaces: The Figure in the Australian Aboriginal Landscape. In: Low, S., Lawrence-Zuniga, D. (eds.) *The Anthropology of Space and Place: Locating Culture*. London: Wiley-Blackwell, 92–109.

Nair, P., Minhas, P., Nakano, K. (2022) *Biophilic Design: Learning Spaces Inspired by Nature*. Independently published.

Neutra, R. (1954) *Survival Through Design*. New York: Oxford University Press.

Norberg-Schulz, C. (1980) *Genius Loci: Towards a Phenomenology of Architecture*. New York: Rizzoli.

Norberg-Schulz, C. (1985) *Concept of Dwelling: On the Way to Figurative Architecture*. New York: Rizzoli.

Oliver, K. (2002) *Psychology in Practice: Environment*. London: Hodder and Stoughton.

Pallasmaa, J. (2012) *Eyes of the Skin: Architecture of the Senses*. New York: Wiley.

Papanek, V. (2019) *Design for the Real World*. London: Granada.

Pawlyn, M. (2016) *Biomimicry in Architecture*. London: RIBA Publishing.

Perec, G. (1997) *Species of Space and Other Pieces*. London: Penguin. 5–39.

Petersen, S. (2021) The Vicious Porosity of Walls and People. Part One. 35–47. In: Stender, M., Bech-Danielson, C., Landsverk Hagen, A. (eds.) (2021) *Architectural Anthropology: Exploring Lived Space*. London: Routledge.

Phibbs, J. (2017) *Placemaking, the Art of Capability Brown*. Swindon: Historic England.

Plunkett, D (2020) *Taste: A Cultural History of the Home Interior*. London: RIBA.

Plunz, R. (2017) *City Riffs: Urbanism, Ecology, Place*. New York, Columbia University.

Rae, A. (2017) *The Land Cover Atlas of the United Kingdom*. Available at: https://figshare.shef.ac.uk/articles/journal_contribution/A_Land_Cover_Atlas_of_the_United_Kingdom_Document_/5266495.

Rice, L. (2020) After Covid-19: Urban Design as Spatial Medicine. *Urban Design International*. https://doi.org/10.1057/s41289-020-00142-6 Accessed 3 Dec. 2022.

Ritter, A. (2007) *Smart Materials, For Architecture, Interior Architecture and Design*. Berlin: Birkhauser.

Roberts, L. (2020) *Spatial Anthropology (Place, Memory, Effect)*. London: Rowman and Littlefield.

Rossi, A. (1984) *Architecture of the City*. New York: MIT Press.

Rössler, P., Otto, E. (2019) *Frauen am Bauhaus: Wegweisende Künstlerinnen der Moderne*. Munich: Knesebeck.

Rowntree, D. (1964) *Interior Design*. London: Penguin.

172 Bibliography

Rybczynski, W. (1986) *Home: A Short History of an Idea*. London: Penguin.

Schinkel, W., Noordegraaf-Eelens, L. (2011) *In Medias Res: Peter Sloterdijk's Spherological Poetics of Being*. Amsterdam: Amsterdam University Press.

Schneiderman, D., Dzis, L. (2022) Appropriation or Appreciation: A New COVID Street View. 102–113. In: Schneiderman, D., Lasc, A. and Tehve, K. (2022) *Appropriated Interiors*. New York: Routledge.

Schön, D. A. (1985) *The Design Studio: An Exploration of Its Traditions and Potentials*. London: RIBA Publications.

Sennett, R. (2016) Interiors and Interiority. Lecture, Harvard Graduate School of Design (GSD), April 26. You Tube: https://www.youtube.com/watch?v=hVPjQhfJfKo. Accessed 9 Oct. 2022.

Silleck, B. (dir.) (1996) *A Cosmic Voyage*. [Film] Available at You Tube: https://www.youtube.com/watch?v=tQGz76_1feY. Accessed 26 Aug. 2022.

Sloterdijk, P. (2011) *Bubbles – Microspheres: Spheres Vol. I*: Translated from German by Wieland Hoban. Los Angeles: Semiotext(e).

Sloterdijk, P. (2014) *Globes – Macrospherology: Spheres Vol. 2*: Translated from German by Wieland Hoban. Los Angeles: Semiotext(e).

Sloterdijk, P. (2016) *Foams – Plural Spherology: Spheres Vol. 3*: Translated from German by Wieland Hoban. Los Angeles: Semiotext(e).

Smith, T. (2019) A Brief History of Beijing's 798 Art District. The Culture Trip. Online Article. https://theculturetrip.com/asia/china/articles/a-brief-history-of-the-798-art-district-in-beijing/. Accessed 1 Dec. 2022.

Sommer, R. (1974) *Tight Spaces: Hard Architecture and How to Humanize it*. New York: New York: Spectrum Books.

Sommer, R. (2008) *Personal Space: Updated, The Behavioral Basis of Design*. New York: Bosko Books.

Sorrells, K. (2015) *Intercultural Communication: Globalization and Social Justice*. New York: Sage.

St Clair, K. (2016) *The Secret Lives of Colour*. London: John Murray Publishing.

Stewart, J. (1972) *The Theory of Cultural Change. The Methodology of Multilinear Evolution*. Illinois: University of Illinois Press.

Stewart, K. (2011) Atmospheric Attunement. *Environment and Planning D: Society* 29(3).

Stone, S. (2020) *UnDoing Buildings. Adaptive Reuse and Cultural Memory*. London: Routledge.

Sudjic, D. (2016) *The Language of Cities*. London: Penguin.

Tabb, P. J. (2020) *Biophilic Urbanism*. London: Routledge.

Taylor, M (2007) Hertzian Space. In: *Thinking Inside the Box: A Reader in Interiors for the 21st Century*. London: Middlesex University.

Tidy, J. (2022) Billions Spent in Metaverse Land Grab. BBC online News Technology. https://www.bbc.co.uk/news/technology-63488059. Accessed 4 Nov. 2022.

Tilley, C. (eds.) et al. (2013) *Handbook of Material Culture*. London: Sage.

Tsing, A. L. (2005) *Friction: An Ethnography of Global Connection*. Princeton, NJ: Princeton University.

Tuan, Y. (2001) *Space and Place: The Perspective of Experience*. Minnesota: University of Minnesota

United Nations (2022) Sustainable Development Goals, Number 11. Make Cities and Human Settlements Inclusive, Safe, Resilient and Sustainable. https://unstats.un.org/sdgs/report/2019/goal-11/. Accessed 6 Nov. 2022.

Van Eyck, A (1963) Beyond Visibility. In *For Us*20. http://www.artefacts.co.za/main/Buildings/style_det.php?styleid=1105 Accessed 31 Oct. 2022. Reference also in Lawson, B. (2001) *The Language of Space*. Oxford: Architectural Press.

Venturi, R., Scott Brown, D., Izenour, S. (1977) *Learning from Las Vegas*. Massachusetts: MIT Press.

Vermeulen, T., van den Akker, R. (2010) Notes on Metamodernism. *Journal of Aesthetics & Culture* 2 (1): 5677. doi:10.3402/jac.v2i0.5677.

Weinthal, L. (2007) Towards a New Interior. In: Hollis, E. et al. (eds.) *Thinking Inside the Box, A Reader in Interiors for the 21st Century*. London: Middlesex University Press.

Whitehead, J. (2017) *Creating Interior Atmosphere*. London: Bloomsbury Visual Arts.

Wilkinson, H. (2009) *More is More: Tony Duquette*. New York: Abrams.

Wilson, O. E. (1984) *Biophilia*. Cambridge: Harvard University Press.

Wiscombe, T. (2014) Discreetness or Towards a Flat Ontology of Architecture. *Project* 3: 34–43.

Zahavi, D. (2018) *Phenomenology – The Basics*. Oxford: Routledge.

Zevi, B. (1993). *Architecture as Space. How to Look at Architecture*. Rome: Da Capo Press Inc.

Zumthor, P. (2006) *Atmospheres: Architectural Environments, Surrounding Objects*. Berlin: Birkhäuser GmbH.

INDEX

Abercrombie, S. 64
absolute space 127
"active conditioner" 43
Adamson, G. 108
aesthetics 10
agile 11; *agile space* 2
Agnew, J. 128
Albers, J. 120
Alexander, C. 92
Alto, A. 126
ambience 84
Amsterdam 121
analogous 120
animation 134
Anthes, E. 44
Anthropology 67; anthropological
    research 50; relationship 112
Appleton, J. 97
architecture 1, 72, 156
artificial intelligence 134, 146
Arts and Crafts 90
Ashenburg, K. 91
assemblage theory 154
assemblies 154
Atmosphere 81; atmospheres 77
Auge, M. 130
augmentation 161
aural 115
Austin, T. 129, 137, 160
Azzarito, A. 105

Bachelard, G. 71
Bauhaus 119

Bayley, S. 124
Beamish Living Museum 2
Behaviour 13, 15
being-in-the-world 146
binary attractions 147
bio-realism 72, 160
biological 35
biomimicry 88
biophilic 160
"biosocial" 81
Böhme, G. 114
borders 74
boundary 20, boundaries 74, 134
Bournville 40
Bradbury, D. 72
Brave New World 98
Brazilla 43
bricolage 14
Brooker, G. 64, 81
Brown Lancelot 'Capability'
    (1716–1783) 16
Bruner, J. 81
brutalism 38; Brutalist Architecture 93
"bubble" of personal space 78
Buchanan, I. 154

Cadbury 40
Canter, D. 79
Casson, H. 43, 102
Castlefield Sky Park 90
celebratory buildings 39
Chandigarh 43
Character 81

Index 175

circadian 121
Citizen M Hotel, Victoria London 113
civic quarters 38
civilisation(s) 3, 16
claustrophobia 45
Coco Chanel 125
Colour 61, 117; colour totality 119
Comfort 100
communities of activity 85
Complimentary 121
concept of dwelling 4
constructed meaning 9
constructed virtual reality
   environments 147
constructions 154
contain 134
control 134
counterculture 12
Crawford, I. 126
Creswell, T. 96, 130
Crystal Palace 124
Cultural: agility 22; analysis 153;
   attachment 7; attitudes 24; beliefs 8;
   categories 137; considerations 24;
   container 98; context 23; descriptors
   149; diversity 23; domesticities 4;
   dynamics of space 20; ecology 15, 25;
   encounter 47; exchange 12; fluidity 12;
   futures 159; histories 5; identities 18,
   42; ideology 1; impact 149; Impact
   analysis 156; impact area 137;
   individualism 27; knowledge 13, 95;
   mapping 50; mapping analysis 155;
   Mapping Objects 137; markers 137;
   materialism 15; mix 20; modelling 4;
   narrative 12; nodes 39; *norms* 8; origins
   16; pathway 149; perspective 9;
   phenomenology 33; placement 134;
   Placement Mapping 134; positioning
   95; regionality 77; science research 34;
   sensitivity 102; storytelling 4;
   sustainability 20; territories 74,
   transmitter 98, tropes 135, *values* 149
Cultural Trail 10, 13, 33, 48, 65, 80, 98,
   114, 132, 150; Cultural Trail
   summaries 157
cultural traits 15; "cultural trait" 130
cultural transference 44
"cultural zones" 22
"Culture wars" 6
cultures 1; *cultura* 34
cybernetic hybrids 98

De Certeau, M. 117
definitions and identities 2

design 1
design culture 25
design of interiors 42; design of space 43
designed 11, *designed space* 2
Designed proximity 77
designed, emergent, agile 51; designed,
   emergent, agile 59
digital cultures 134, 137
Diller Scofidio + Renfro 109
Distance 44
domestic dwelling 23
Dovey, K. 154
Duquette, A. 127
Durham Cathedral 19
dwelling 26
Dyson, J. 125

Eames, C. 81; Eames House, The 82
ecological habitats 10
Edwards, B. 131
Edwards, C. 78
embodying culture 42
emergent 11; emergent narrative 155;
   emergent space 2
emigration 9
emotional mapping 137; "emotional
   sensibilities" 83
enclosure 12, 45
Enclosure 81
encounter 48
Endogenous 87
environmental psychologists 31
ethnography 11, 25, 67
evolutionary complex 15
Exner, U.132
Exogenous 87
Experience 100
experience-building process 113
experimental spaces 44
exteriority 71

Fallingwater 72
Farnsworth house 103
Fast, J. 45
Figurative 81, 88; realm 10
floor plans 145
food experience 84
"force field" 83
Frampton, K. 115
Fry, T. 78
Funfair 132
Furniture 61

garden city movement 39
"gathering" 96

176 Index

Gaver B. 50
Gehl Jane 17
genealogy 4; genealogies 4
Genius Loci 33, 98, 113, 123
geo-cultural perspective 135
geoglyphs 35
Glastonbury Festival 87
globalisation 34
Gola, A. 136
Grand Midland Hotel- St Pancras 28
Great Exhibition (1851) 124
Grunow, G. 119
gustatory 115

habitation 50
habitus 15
Hadid, Z. 1, 125
Hall, E. 45, 79, 102, 135
Hanington, B. 51
haptic 100
hard and soft sciences 71
"hard architecture" 64
Harman, G. 112, 148
Harmonisation 119
Harmony 120
Heidegger, M. 135
hertzian space 89
Herzog and de Meuron 29
Hicks, D. 107, 126
Highmore, B, 101
Hill House 126
Hillier, B. 108
Hnilica, S. 98
Holl, S. 115
holographic visualisation 134, 146
"home" 25, 69; design 101
Hong Kong 36, 121
Howard, E. 39
Human civilizations 25
human condition 1, 9
human experience 2, 84
human settlement 20
human-orientated spaces 31
Huxley, A. 98
hybridity 146

Identities and experience 18
identity of culture 2
IKEA furniture store 29
Imagined (place) 7
immersive 12
immigration 9
immunization 20
in-between spaces 8, 160
indexical process 79

industrialisation 9
infection 47
"information age" 44
Ingold, T. 64, 67, 81
inhabited 1
"inscape" 17, 43
inside 43
interactive animation 146
Interior: aesthetic 148; condition 71;
    cultures 7; *expression* 26
interiority 17, 71, 90
international style 103
intimacy 17
Inwood, M. 146

Jacobs, J. 17
juxtaposition 8

Kennedy, J.F. 83
"kinetics" 32, 65
kitsch 124
Klee, P. 119

Las Vegas 154
Lautner, J. 72
Lawson, B. 72
layers 83
Le Corbusier 43, 74
Le Modulor 74
Lefebvre, M. 64, 69, 91, 107, 127
Letchworth 40
Levi-Strass, C. 154
Libeskind, D. 47, 100
life-world 146
light 117; Lighting 62
liminal 160
"lived experience" 114
Lloyd Wright, F. 72
located: culture 8; cultural reference 22
"looped" structures 25
Low S. 44, 83
luxury 101, 105
Lyndon, D. 65

Mackintosh, C,R 125; Mackintosh, C and
    M, 126
"make-over" 29
Malgrave H. 64
mapping 18; mapping of space 117
margins of space 134
material culture 112; world 110
materiality 8
Maximalism 127
McCandless, D. 133
medicine 20

Index 177

mega-styling 38
membranes 108
memories 77
Meta-modernism 161; movement 19; meta-modernistic 12; ideology 161
Metaverse 146
Miller D. 50, 106, 136,
mimesis of the body 75
Minimalism 127
mise-en-scene 64
mobile spatial field 69, 79
mobility 15, and place 4
Modernist interior spaces 23
"moments" 91
monochromatic 24, 120
monuments 39
"mood" 84, moods 77
motion 101
Munn, D. 69
Myerscough, M. 126

narrative 117
narratological culture 147, narratological cultural landscape 38
National Trust 91
nationalism 118
natural light 121
nesting 45
Neutra R. 36, 43, 72, 160
New York city 37
Niemeyer, O. 43
"non-static" 65: *existence* 32
Norberg-Schulz, C. 81, 132
normative design domains 51
nostalgia 114

object 15, *100*: Objects 62
object-based experience 12
olfactory 115
optical 100
outside 43

paired polarities 161
Palestinian *duyuf* 136
Pallasmaa J. 64, 74, 104, 121
pandemic 47, 50
"pastoralists" 127
patternation of zones 83
patterns 32
perception 17, 34, 113
performance 69
Personal space 28, 29, 46
personal taste 28
personal traces 71
personalisation 134

"personalised: bubble" 18; space 46
Petersen, S. 94
phenomenological 44; phenomenology 33; phenomenon of identity 18
Physical: (space) 7; cultures 134
Pierre Cardin's Bubble Palace 89
Place 11, 18, 20, 30, 61, 117, 134,
place destination 24
"placeless" 130
placemaking 65
placement of culture 10, 11
playfulness 51
Plunkett, D. 124
polychronic 24
Pompidou Centre 109
popular opinion 29
Prada store, Tokyo 30
preliminary probe findings 60
privacy 71
private place 28
prospect-refuge theory 97
protective shells 108
proximity 2, 14, 45; proximal 70; proximities 160;
psychological 35; expectation of space 113; needs 102

quakers 42

Rabbit Hole, The 84
reading of space 64, 149
reflectivity 121
regional identity 20
relationships 10
renaissance 90, 128
reprogrammable space 64
residential floor space 135
ripple "effect" 7
Roberts, L 154
Rybczynski, W. 51, 135

Scandinavian design 102
Schon, D. 51
Science Museum, London 95
Sennett, R. 71, 89
Sense: of humanity 102, *of place* 128
senses 83, 101
"sensescape" 18
sensitive skins 108
sensorial narratives of space 64; relationships 106
sensory 100, 120; sensory realm 10
situated culture 69
Sloterdijk, P. 65, 69
social coding 18

178 Index

social constructivist approach 47
social hierarchy 18
social theory 31
socialisation 71
societal cultures 122
socio-political landscape 78
solitude 71
Sommer, R. 46, 135
Space 11, 20, 30, 60, *81*, 134
space: conceived 91; embodiment 75; "fielded" 69; "inscribed" 69; lived 91; perceived 91; physiological intricacies 95; production 91
Spatial: analysis 47; cultures 1, 4, 14, 134; *bricolage* 30, 154; continuum 86; constructions 47
Spatial cultural probe 51, spatial design probe 11, 50, spatial design probe analysis 155
spatial culture 117
Spatial Culture Ecosystem 11, 68, 153
spatial: dwelling 30; encounters 11; landscape 36; *layers* 97; mood 83; narrative 94; realm 12; syntax 108; *turn* 44; typologies 91; volume patternation 117
Spatial narrative investigations 50
"spatial organism(s)" 81, 159
spatial proximities 79
spatio-cultural context 14,
spatio-temporal situations 161
spherology 20
"spirit" 19
St Clair, K. 118
Stewart, K. 83
stillness 101
"storyshapes" 130
streetscape 17
structured narratives 161
suburban 38
Surface 100
symbolic meaning 64, 88

tablescapes 108
tabular rasa 36

taste 10, 117
Taylor, M. 89
territories 74
textual 117, realm 10
textuality 117
The Broad, Los Angeles 109
Theme Vals Spa 76
thinking machine 98
third-space working 80
thresholds 83, 134
topology 38
traces 75
trans-disciplinary design 1
trans-scalar 12, 117
transition 101
"transparency" 24, 123
tribal herding 99
Tsing, A, L. 130
TV Studio 119
typologies 2

ubiquity 134
United Nations 135
unity 16
urbanization 9
urban: "*blur*" 6, 77; "cityscape" 6; design 1; realms 6; systems 39; threads 11

values 10
van der Rohe, M. 103, 127
Van Eyck, A. 128
Venice Biennale 128
Venturi, R, 126, 153
viewpoints 23
virtual reality 134, 146

Walt Disney World 129
Washington DC Bridge-park 90
Well-living lab 44, 121
Whitehead, J. 64, 76
Wilson, Edward, O. 16
womb 69, 88

Zeitgeist 124
Zumthor, P. 76, 83, 115